Hoards from the Neolithic to the Metal Ages

Technical and codified practices

Session of the XIth Annual Meeting of the
European Association of Archaeologists

Edited by

Caroline Hamon
Benedicte Quilliec

BAR International Series 1758
2008

Published in 2016 by
BAR Publishing, Oxford

BAR International Series 1758

Hoards from the Neolithic to the Metal Ages

ISBN 978 1 4073 0197 6

© The editors and contributors severally and the Publisher 2008

The authors' moral rights under the 1988 UK Copyright,
Designs and Patents Act are hereby expressly asserted.

All rights reserved. No part of this work may be copied, reproduced, stored,
sold, distributed, scanned, saved in any form of digital format or transmitted
in any form digitally, without the written permission of the Publisher.

BAR Publishing is the trading name of British Archaeological Reports (Oxford) Ltd.
British Archaeological Reports was first incorporated in 1974 to publish the BAR
Series, International and British. In 1992 Hadrian Books Ltd became part of the BAR
group. This volume was originally published by Archaeopress in conjunction with
British Archaeological Reports (Oxford) Ltd / Hadrian Books Ltd, the Series principal
publisher, in 2008. This present volume is published by BAR Publishing, 2016.

Printed in England

BAR titles are available from:

            BAR Publishing
            122 Banbury Rd, Oxford, OX2 7BP, UK
EMAIL   info@barpublishing.com
PHONE   +44 (0)1865 310431
FAX   +44 (0)1865 316916
            www.barpublishing.com

TABLE OF CONTENTS

Caroline HAMON & Bénédicte QUILLIEC   1-4
Hoards from the Neolithic to the Metal Ages: Technical and Codified Practices - Introduction

David FONTIJN   5-17
'Traders' hoards'. Reviewing the Relationship between Trade and Permanent Deposition : the Case of the dDutch Voorhout Hoard

Caroline HAMON   19-28
The Symbolic Value of Grindingstones Hoards: Technical Properties of Neolithic Examples

Karsten WENTINK & Annelou van GIJN   29-43
Neolithic Depositions in the Northern Netherlands

Cécile Veber   45-51
Interpretation Elements of Hoards from the Late Bronze Age in Lorraine and Saar through Technical Studies (forming process and metal composition)

Alicia PEREA   53-58
Iberian Psycho. Deliberate Destruction in Bronze Age Gold Hoards of the Iberian Peninsula

Maréva GABILLOT & Céline LAGARDE   59-65
Voluntary Destructions of Objects in Middle and Late Bronze Age Hoards in France

Bénédicte QUILLIEC   67-78
Use, Wear and Damage: Treatment of Bronze Swords before Deposition

Shaun MOYLER   79-90
Doing away with Dichotomies? Comparative Use-Wear Analysis of Early Bronze Age Axes from Scotland

Ewen IHUEL   91-101
Hoards and Flint Blades in Western France at the End of the Neolithic

Steven MATTHEWS   103-120
Other than Bronze: Substances and Incorporation in Danish Bronze Age Hoards

HOARDS FROM THE NEOLITHIC TO THE METAL AGES: TECHNICAL AND CODIFIED PRACTICES

-

INTRODUCTION

Caroline HAMON, Bénédicte QUILLIEC

As an introduction to this publication, we would like to thank the organisers of the XIth congress of the European Association of Archeologists in Cork (Ireland) to have accepted in 2005 this topic of session and are mostly grateful towards the participants who contributed both by their presentations and the discussions which followed, to make this day a scientifically stimulating meeting. Our wish to debate around a new aspect of hoard's understanding throughout the pre and protohistory was reached, according to the new pespectives of reflexion that emanated from this meeting.

Hoards and hoarding throughout pre and protohistory

Throughout Europe, from the Atlantic to the Black Sea, deposition of objects in earth or water was a frequent practice during Prehistory. Hoards can be considered as a real archeological structure, as a real pratice. The hypotheses and interpretations of deposits as meaningful acts and gestures may confer its appropriate state of 'hoard' to an archeological structure. Besides, the distribution, location and density of hoards may be sufficient to determine the status of a concentration of objects.

While some of these hoards can easily be interpreted as funeral offerings, the signification of others is still discussed today. The signification of hoarding (tools, weapons or ornaments) generally depends on the context of their discovery: settlements, humid areas, border areas. On a broad chronological and cultural scale, from the Neolithic to the Early Iron Age, hoards show recurrent characteristics despite their diverse expressions. Examining the contexts of these deposits, such practices appear as deliberate and as codified as funerary behaviour, with a votive or symbolic meaning. The quantity of hoards, their location and their composition (selection and number of objects) certainly correspond to specific rules and social or cultural needs.

Interpretations are numerous: reserve of raw material, foundation ritual, religious, social or territorial markers of identity, sacred offerings to divinities or secular people. Nonetheless, these hypotheses are comparable from one period to another. The deposit of isolated objects and the deposit of associated objects of similar or different functions ('complex' hoards) take on various expressions, apparently specific to each context. The coherence of these archaeological assemblages lies in the codification of the arrangement of objects, which follows significant rituals. Thus, how can we interpret the repetition of deposit of objects of different nature? On the contrary, what value should be attributed to similar deposits in totally distinct contexts?

The technical point of view

The study of objects suggests that precise, codified acts have been carried out. The technical signification of this practice (materials used, techniques of manufacture, superficial state of the objects) had to be discussed, following detailed examination of the modes of manufacture, use, re-use and recycling of objects.

Thus, the deliberate or non-deliberate breakage and even destruction of objects (lithic, metal and ceramic) are widespread. The act of deposit may express the need to extract an object from its 'traditional' life cycle, in order to preserve it or, on the contrary, to damage it partly or entirely. The precise study of the objects themselves (just shaped out, with use-wear, completely or partially destroyed) may help us re-define the signification of this practice.

In this session, we wished specialists of different periods and fields, to confront and discuss their observations. How are the technical signification and the expression of a specific ritual linked in the deposit gesture? What correlation can be made between the state of the objects and their deposit? Criteria must be defined in order to identify neglected and abandoned objects (domestic refuse, waste from workshop) and to help interpret symbolic spaces, either territorial (borderline, 'doorway') or social (settlements). How can archaeological contexts be used to differentiate these acts of deposit and how are they expressed in specific cultural or geographical contexts? Which archaeological clues can inform about the technical practices of hoards?

For a redifinition of the hoard phenomenon ?

New technological and functional approaches and methods of study lead to a more intrinsic analysis of the objects of deposition rather than the simple observation of the manifestations of this practice. Statistical methods based on the calculation of the weight, the quantity or the density of the objects are used (cf. M. Gabillot-C. Lagarde, K. Wentink, this volume). Technical and traceological approaches enlight the state of the objects, their use, their life and the condition of their 'death' (cf. C. Hamon, E. Ihuel, S. Moyler, B. Quilliec, A. Perea, C. Veber). Spatial analysis integrates informations about the location, distribution, frequency, presence or absence of hoards and their link with other archeological structures (cf. D. Fontijn, K. Wentink, this volume).

Hoards can be considered as codified and ritual practices as they share reproductable features. Any practice can be defined by one purpose and its opposite (cf. D. Fontijn, this volume). Therefore, hoard signification can wear intentional versus fortuitous character, profane versus ritual meaning. But these dichotomous conceptions often don't resist to the concepts which rule prehistoric societies (cf. K. Wentink).
As proposed by S. Matthews, a 'compositional approach' may be tone of the key of the understanding of the hoard phenomenon (cf. S. Matthews this volume). Hoard may designate either one single object or a group of objects of same or different nature. Must we assimilate one single object as a hoard (cf. B. Quilliec, this volume)? May the presence or lack of one type of object be meaningful (cf. S. Matthews, this volume)? The frequency, scarcity and propagation of these objects may be as meaningful as their state at the moment of the deposition. Whether they are rough-out or craft rejections, brand new or worn, entire, fragmented, partially destroyed or recycled, the objects may give information about the practice of hoarding itself. The diversity or homogeneity of the objects deposited must also be taken into a count, as much as the relation between them (cf. S. Matthews, this volume).

Defining a hoard value can also consist in evaluating the value of the deposited objects. But how defining such a value? The value of an object can be generated by its scarcity, its raw material, its weigh, its merchandizing or symbolic value. The scarcity of an object may be difficult to evaluate when the raw material is highly recycled as for metal (cf. B. Quilliec, this volume). On the other side, how a very spread material can keep its symbolic value, following the Grand Pressigny flint example (cf. E. Ihuel, this volume), and this whatever the context of discovery is (hoard, workshop, tomb)?

The concept of adding value of an object introduced by D. Fontijn during the discussion may be useful to clarify the sense of these observations. This idea lead to define the hoard from the life of the deposited objects, from their biography (cf. S. Moyler, this volume). This includes a complete approach of the 'chaîne opératoire' of acquisition, production and in case breaking of these objects (cf. C. Hamon, S. Moyler, B. Quilliec, this volume). This implies to considerate the life of an object between its production and its deposit, and also between its breaking or damaging and its hoarding. The traces worn by an object can help identify the main features of an object life (cf. S. Moyler, this volume).

What saying about brand new objects deposited, as blades or cores (cf. E. Ihuel, this volume)? Which status must be given to organic deposits (cf. Matthews, this volume). As shown by K. Wentik, the value of an object can also come from the invest put in its acquisition and origin. In these cases, the idea of a long distant supplies (cf. K. Wentik, this volume) or of surplus production has been proposed (cf. E. Ihuel, this volume). On the contrary, a traceological approach can help define the intensity of the use (cf. S. Moyler and C. Hamon, this volume).

One single object can also wear different values throughout its life, depending in particular on its context of use. The value of an object can also be deduced from its belonging to a group of objects linked by their function or their production context (cf. C. Véber, this volume). This correponds in the definition of the links between the objects before their deposit, in order to precise if this association is herited from the object life or if it is completely articificial.

At last, the value of an object can even be given by its destruction (cf. M.Gabillot-C. Lagarde, this volume). Why destroying objects of high merchandizing value without any recycling (cf. A. Perea, this volume)? The value of an object goes over the one of its raw material. Know-how and technical invest are also necessary for the elaboration of an object. For these reasons, the value of an object cannot be define only by its function (prestigious objects).
Finally, the sacrifice, recycling, or storage of objects can explain a hoard. Can we affirm that hoards take part in the economic systems or on the contrary that they extract and remove produce from it (cf. D. Fontijn, this volume)?

Two parameters seem essential for the comprehension of the hoard phenomenon: time and space. Time notion is crucial to evaluate the length of an object life, the intensity of its use and the notion of cycle. One main question lays also in the temporary or permanent aspect of the hoarding. Besides, we should ask ourselves upon the constitution of these hoards : are they constituted in one or several times, and in that case, on which range of time (cf. C. Veber, this volume)? The main interpretations of these practices generally include a territorial aspect. Whether hoards are hidden or visible, which signification can be given to this notion? Do hoards express any kind of owning of a land, as a kind of fundation ritual (cf. C. Hamon, this volume)? Do they materialize some way of circulation, some place of exchange, some borders (cf. D. Fontijn, K. Wentink, this volume)?

All these considerations converge on the social aspects underlining hoards constitution. Who are the men behind these practices? The intervention of a craftsman know-how at all the stages of the constitution of a hoard, in particular for metallic objects, may inform about the status of the bronzemaker as a specialist or craftsman (cf. B. Quilliec, this volume). Hoards may be linked with the community: a person (powerful character), a family (aristocratic), a guild (craftmen) or a religeous order may be involved in its constitution (cf. S. Moyler, this volume). The comparison with funerary deposits can be of great help to define the nature and symbolic meaning of hoarded objects in link with their social status and treatment in individual tombs (cf. S. Matthews, K. Wentink, this volume).

As a matter of fact, the frequency and longevity of hoards in Neolithic and Metal Ages communities seems to correspond to a real need, whatever it is of social, economical or religious meaning. The complexity of the notion of hoard is illustrated and discussed through the eleven papers gathered in this work in order to reconsider hoards' technical features. These aspects are reexamined considering the technical systems they depend on, throughout the Neolithic and the Bronze Age.

'TRADERS' HOARDS'. REVIEWING THE RELATIONSHIP BETWEEN TRADE AND PERMANENT DEPOSITION: THE CASE OF THE DUTCH VOORHOUT HOARD

David FONTIJN

Abstract:
This contribution studies the relation between bronze trade and the permanent deposition of trade stock by means of a detailed case study of what seems to be an outstanding, almost paradigmatic example of buried trader's stock: the Voorhout hoard. This hoard consists of a collection of eighteen bronze axes and a chisel that were deposited in a former dune area near the Dutch coast and the Rhine mouth during the Bronze Age (c. 16th-15th century B.C.). Traditionally interpreted as temporarily buried trade stock, this article argues that its interpretation is more complicated. The hoard appears to consist of a mixed collection of useable artifacts and scrap from various regions (Wales, England, France) that were outside their traditional distribution area. Opposing established views, the hoard is likely to represent a deliberately permanent deposition of material acquired by overseas trade. It will be argued that such a deposition may nevertheless have been linked to a more general short-term commodity exchange of scrap material from abroad that was intended to be locally reworked and remelted.

Samenvatting:
Deze bijdrage bestudeert de relatie tussen bronshandel en permanente depositie van handelswaar gedurende de bronstijd door middel van een gedetailleerde studie van het depot van Voorhout. Deze vondst wordt algemeen gezien als een excellent, bijna paradigmatisch, voorbeeld van een 'handelsdepot'. Het gaat om 18 bronzen bijlen en 1 beitel, vermoedelijk daterend uit de 16e of 15e eeuw voor Chr., die tesamen in voormalig duingebied langs de Westnederlandse kust en de monding van de Oude Rijn zijn gevonden. Bij nadere beschouwing blijkt de interpretatie van dit 'handelsdepot' gecompliceerder te zijn dan gedacht. Het bevat zowel bruikbare objecten als materiaal dat eerder als 'schroot' te klassificeren is. Ook blijken de objecten een diverse herkomst te hebben (Noord-Wales, Engeland, Frankrijk). Er wordt aannemelijk gemaakt dat deze collectie doelbewust is gedeponeerd met de intentie om haar niet meer te bergen. Zo'n handeling wordt in verband gebracht met processen waarbij grote partijen verhandeld brons voor inheemse verwerking acceptabel worden gemaakt door er een selectie van 'ritueel' te deponeren.

Introduction

In 1907, sand extraction in a former dune area near Voorhout, a village near the western coast of the Netherlands, led to the discovery of a highly remarkable set of prehistoric artefacts. In a square pit (50 by 50 cm), a Bronze Age hoard of eighteen bronze axes and one lugged chisel was found (fig. 1 and 2; table 1). Throughout the 20th century, the hoard figured in many publications on the Northwest-European Bronze Age, and its artefacts were re-examined many times (in particular by Butler 1959; 1963; 1990; 1997; Butler & Steegstra 1997/1998; O'Connor 1980; Northover unpublished). The hoard has always been seen as an outstanding, almost paradigmatic, example of buried traders' stock. The reason lies in its homogeneous content: it consists mainly of palstave axes, most of which of the same type. Since the 1950s, it has been clear that all of its content must have been imported from abroad, mainly from Britain. 'With no doubt', Butler argued, they represent 'the stock of a bronze smith or trader' (Butler 1959: 131, translation mine). This precious stock, then, must have been temporarily hidden in the ground for some reason or another, but was never retrieved (Holwerda 1908; Van den Broeke 1991: 242). Thus, the hoard was seen as a neat illustration of the 'cosmopolitan' bronze trade that was by then generally considered to be a hallmark of the Bronze Age making it a significant period in European history. This view of the Bronze Age still stands, and so does the interpretation of the Voorhout hoard as an example of buried trade stock, imported from afar. This becomes apparent, for example, from the discussion of the Voorhout find in the extensive, recently published synthesis on Dutch prehistory (Louwe Kooijmans *et al.* 2005). In a discussion on the types of hoards encountered in the Netherlands, hoards are categorized as 'ritual' deposits from wet places, or more profane ones like traders' or founders' hoards. Although the author of this chapter is rather cautious, the interpretation of the Voorhout hoard is seen as one of the more straightforward ones: 'sometimes there appears to be little doubt about the nature of a deposit. Large, homogeneous hoards like that comprising eighteen bronze palstaves and a chisel which was found at Voorhout may have been the stock of smiths or traders' (Van den Broeke 2005: 662). The present article aims to show that things are more complicated than that. Closer inspection of both content and context of the hoard points out that the Voorhout find is not the unproblematic typical example of a 'traders' hoard' that it is supposed to be. Rather, it will be argued that Voorhout probably reflects a mixed collection of useable artefacts and scrap from various regions that were outside their traditional distribution area. Moreover, opposing established views, the point will be made that these objects are much more likely to represent a deliberately permanent deposition of bronze acquired by overseas trade. The implicit assumption that such 'rational' trade is irreconcilable with 'ritual' and 'irrational' permanent deposition makes the Voorhout find a remarkable interpretative problem. It will be argued, however, that this problem may be of our own making and that 'profane trade' and 'ritual' deposition may have been much more closely linked than usually assumed.

Content

Since its first publication by Holwerda (1908), the hoard's content established its reputation as a typical trade or merchant's hoard as defined by Childe (1930: 44), so it seems obvious to start our discussion there. The hoard consists of eighteen bronze axes and one bronze lugged chisel. Fourteen of the axes are palstaves and two are stopridge axes. There is one flanged axe and one axe hard to define as either a flanged axe or a palstave. On the basis of typochronology of the axes, the hoard should be dated to Butler's 'Ilsmoor horizon' (1963: 59-62), which is now seen as falling in the British 'Acton Park'phase, c. mid. 16th to 15th century B.C.. The Voorhout hoard probably dates relatively late in that period (Butler 1990: 84; Fontijn 2002, fig. 1.4; Lanting & Van der Plicht 2001/2002; Schmidt & Burgess 1981: 115-125). The content of the hoard can be characterized as follows, mainly based on the recent publications of the hoard by Butler (Butler 1990: 78-84: entire hoard; Butler 1995/1996, 194-5; 222-3; 227-8: flanged axes and stopridge axes) and by Butler and Steegstra (Butler 1997/1998: 180-5: palstaves; see figure 1 and 2 and table 1 of the present publication for details).

A. Six primary shield palstaves type 'Acton Park' (as defined by Burgess & Schmidt 1981: 117-25), characteristic for North Wales. They have a broad blade with shield-shaped indentation beneath the stopridge.

B. Two other palstaves (h. 1908/10.2 and h. 1908/10.10; resp. dbnos 537 and 1675 on fig. 1) have the same shield-shaped indentation but are a somewhat smaller variety. This also applies to a third example, h. 1908/10.4 (dbno 1679), which is also a type Acton Park palstave but smaller than usual and with leaf-shaped flanges. Butler argues that the latter has more affinities with axes from South England or North-West French than with those from North Wales (1990: 78).

C. Four primary shield palstaves type Acton Park with the same shield-shaped indentation below the stopridge but now with a vertical rib inside the shield.

D. Another Acton Park palstave with shield-shaped indentation below the stopridge and vertical rib inside the shield, but with a narrower body and cutting edge like Schmidt and Burgess' type Colchester.

E. Two stopridge axes of the Northwest French type 'Plaisir'. Both have high thin cast flanges and an expanded blade.

F. A parallel-sided long and high-flanged axe of 'Atlantic' type also with numerous parallels in Northwest France (Brittany) (Briard 1965), but very rare in Britain. Northover's analysis shows that its metal is of an unknown source.

G. An incomplete very thin axe, flanged axe or palstave, of highly unusual form. It has low cast flanges and faint traces of an incipient stopridge.

H. A lugged chisel of British/Irish type. Its metal composition seems to confirm that it has a North

inv. no	dbno.	type	remarks on affiliations	remarks on use-wear and damage
A: primary shield palstave				
h.1908/10.7	542	Acton Park	comparable to 'North Welsh' types	
h.1908/10.4	539	Acton Park	"	
h.1908/10.12	1677	Acton Park	"	asymmetrically resharpened edge
h.1908/10.11	1676	Acton Park	"	worn edge
h.1908/10.5	540	Acton Park	"	broken cutting edge
h.1908/10.9	544	Acton Park	"	worn edge
B: primary shield palstave				
h.1908/10.14	1679	Acton Park	prob. South-English or NW French?	
h.1908/10.2	537	Acton Park	less typical AP	
h.1908/10.10	1675	Acton Park	"	resharpened cutting edge
C: primary shield palstave, vertical rib in shield				
h.1908/10.13	1678	Acton Park	'North Welsh'	
h.1908/10.15	1680	Acton Park	"	asymmetrically resharpened edge
h.1908/10.3	538	Acton Park	"	resharpened edge
h.1908/10.16	1681	Acton Park	"	edge and butt end broken
D: idem but less typical				
h.1908/10.1	536	Acton Park	aff. with type 'Colchester	damaged cutting edge
E: stopridge axes				
h.1908/10.6	541	Plaisir	North-West French	damaged cutting edge
h.1908/10.8	543	Plaisir	"	
F: high-flanged axe				
h.1908/10.17	1682	'Atlantic', parallel-sided	North-West French	butt end broken off in antiquity
G and H: other				
h.1908/10.18	1683	palstave/flanged axe?	unknown	broken in antiquity
h.1908/10.19	1684	lugged chisel	'North Welsh metal'	sharpened edge

Table 1. Information on the objects of the Voorhout. 'Inv. no' refers to the code by which the object is identified in the collection of the National Museum of Antiquities (Rijksmuseum van Oudheden). 'Dbno.' refers to Butler's database, as published in Butler 1995/1996 and Butler/Steegstra 1997/1998. Remarks on affiliations and condition: based on these publications and Butler 1990, and on my own observations.

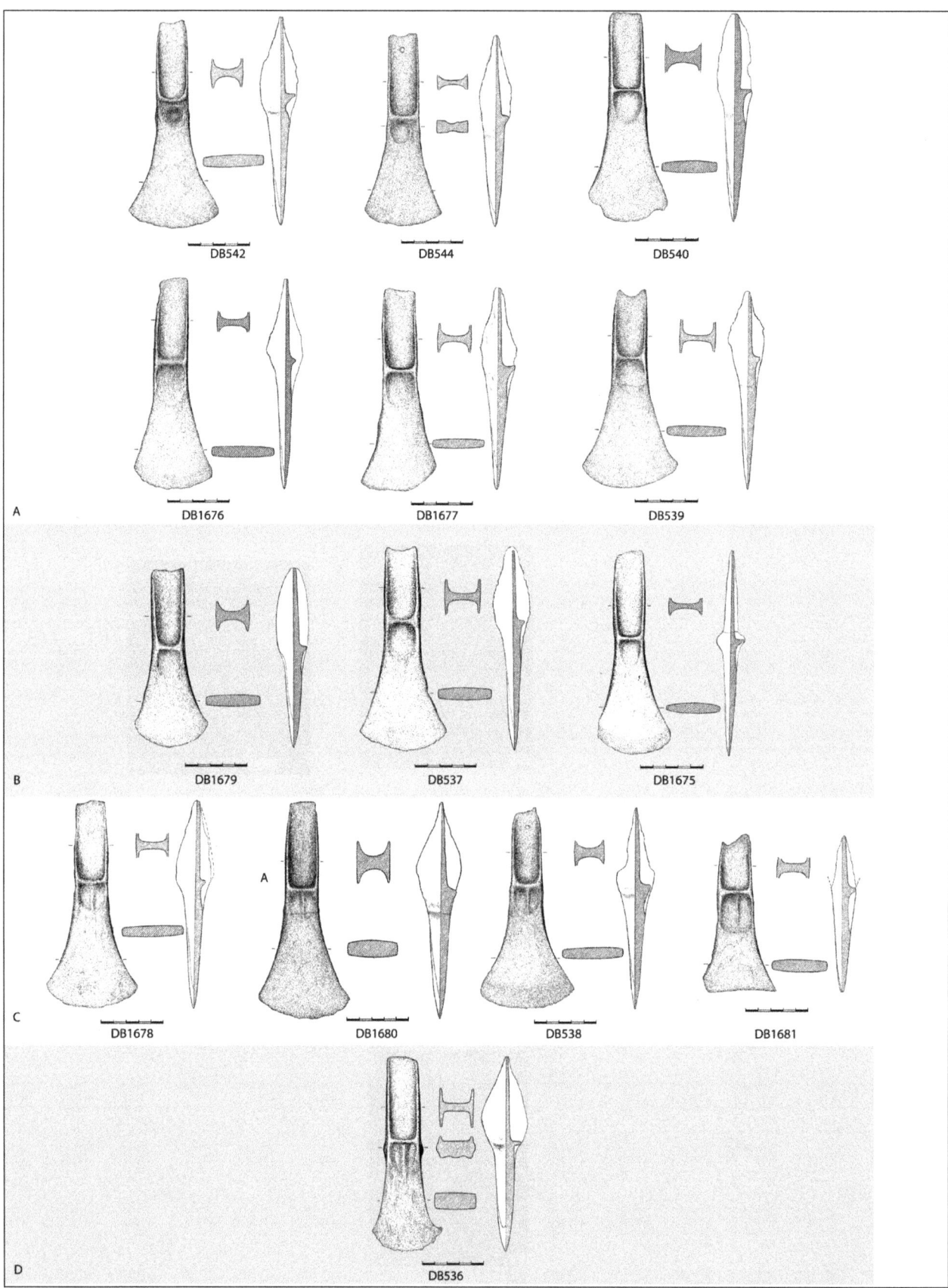

Fig. 1. Content of the Voorhout hoard I. Acton Park(-like) palstaves. A to D are described in the text. 'DB 1680' refers to Butler's database. Copyright axe drawings: Groningen Institute of Archaeology (formerly BAI), University of Groningen.

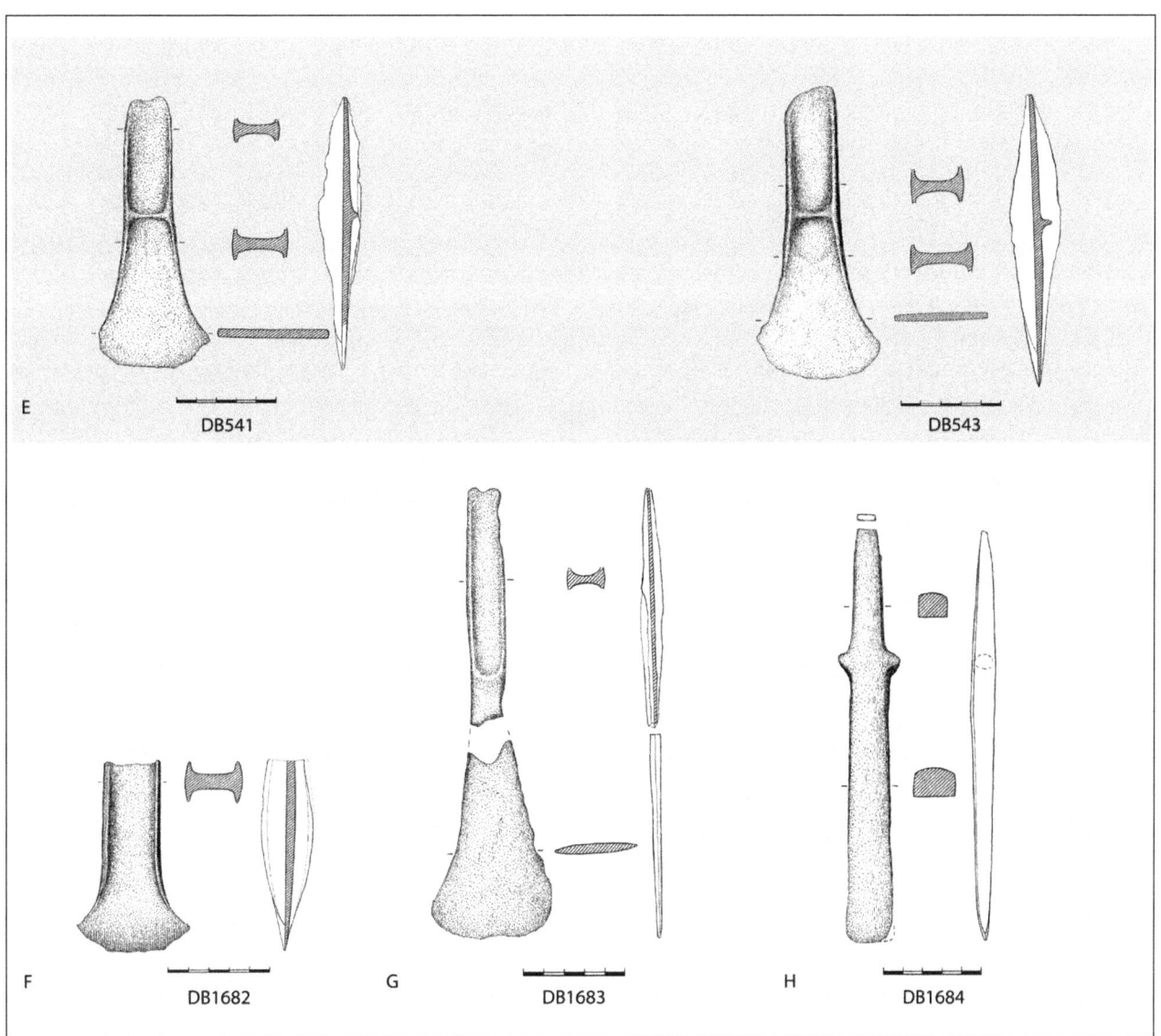

Fig. 2. Content of the Voorhout hoard II: other objects. E to H are described in the text. 'DB1684' refers to Butler's database. Copyright object drawings: Groningen Institute of Archaeology (formerly BAI), University of Groningen

Welsh provenance just like the Acton Park palstaves (Northover cited in Butler 1990: 78).

Already in his 1963 publication, Butler suggested that the primary shield palstaves that make up the greatest part of the hoard, all came from the same region in Britain. A North Welsh provenance for these palstave and the chisel later seems to have been corroborated by Northover's analysis of their metal composition. Although the results are still unpublished, thirteen out of fourteen objects appeared to be of Northover's 'M Metal' (Northover cited in Butler 1990: 78). From the early 20th century onwards, archaeologists have been mapping Bronze Age metalwork trade routes on the basis of distribution maps of hoard finds. Particularly those believed to be merchant's, traders' or 'commercial' hoards, were pivotal in these studies. Traders' hoards are usually defined as consisting of almost entirely new or half-finished articles generally of the same type (Childe 1930: 44). As buried caches of stock, it was thought that they gave a more or less one-to-one impression of the material traded in the long-distance Bronze Age metalwork trade. In an influential study, Sprockhoff (1941) was able to identify major European trade routes in the Middle Bronze Age on the basis of traders' hoards consisting entirely of palstaves. And this is where the Voorhout hoard comes in, for the axe-hoards discussed by Sprockhoff consisted of palstaves of a type affiliated to the North Welsh palstaves from the Voorhout hoard. Well-known examples are the Polish Pyrzyce (formerly Pyritz) hoard, with twenty axes only slightly larger than Voorhout, or the Habsheim hoard in the Alsace. In his book on Bronze Age connections across the North Sea, Butler (1963) showed that Voorhout was another example of such a large palstave traders' hoard, and he argued that all these hoards reflect widespread trading activities of itinerant smiths/traders in one particular phase (Butler 1963: 59-62).

Since the 1980s, the theory that 'traders' hoards' like Polish Pyrzyce reflect widespread trading activities of British itinerant smiths has been nuanced. The palstaves in large hoards like Pyrzyce or Habsheim in the Alsace are now more likely to consist of locally-produced palstaves with – admittedly - affiliations to true North Welsh Acton Park axes (Butler & Steegstra 1997/1998: 185). Voorhout, however, really seems to contain British imports, and this point together with the 'port of trade-like' location of the site near the Rhine mouth and the North Sea coast, may explain why it is seen as a characteristic traders' hoard up until today. There are, however, a number of observations that need closer attention.

First, emphasis has always been on the North Welsh Acton Park palstaves. This is logical as this is the most largest artefact category in the hoard. However, the hoard is not the en bloc imported set of items many authors believe it to be (e.g. Butler 1990, 84). One 'Acton Park' palstave (h.1908/10.14) is more likely to be a South English or North-West French axe than one of a North Welsh type. The remarkable thin broken palstave or flanged axe h.1908/10.18 (fig. 2: dbno. 1683) even seems to lack parallels in both Britain and the near-continent. It is particularly striking, however, to note that the hoard also contains two stopridge axes of type Plaisir as well as a high-flanged Atlantic axe. Both are very rare in Britain but known in large numbers from North-West France (Butler 1990: 78). The metal composition of the high-flanged axe also does not seem to fit into one of the metal types Northover recognized for the British Isles (Northover 1982). The Voorhout hoard, then, rather seems to represent a more complex collection of exchanged artefacts, involving several exchange partners (Welsh, English and coastal French/Belgian?).

Second, it is rarely realized that most objects in the hoard are worn, severely damaged or even scrap. This is true for the North Welsh Acton Park palstaves of both the type with and without vertical rib inside the 'shield', but also for the French stopridge axes. The high-flanged French axe has patinated breaks, so it must already have been broken when it entered the ground. It also applies to the unparalleled very thin palstave/flanged axe h.1908/10.18 (fig. 2: dbno. 1683) which misses its middle part and for the Welsh palstave h.1908/10.16 (fig.1: dbno. 1681). Several of the Acton Park palstaves have clearly resharpened or asymmetrical cutting edges, implying that they have been (intensively) used (e.g. h.1908/10.10; h.1908/10.12; fig. 1: dbnos 1675 and 1677). In no way does the hoard represent the set of freshly-made, or half-finished castings awaiting future use that 'true' 'traders' hoards' are thought to consist of (Childe 1930: 44). The artefacts in both the Habsheim and Pyrzyce palstave hoards which Voorhout is usually compared to were indeed deposited in such a pristine condition. Rather, the Voorhout hoard represents a deposition of used artefacts in conditions ranging from worn but still useable to straightforward scrap.

Third, a traders' hoard is seen as a collection of items awaiting further distribution. With this in mind, it is then striking to realize that most of the artefacts in such a supposed 'traders' hoard' are totally unknown in the Netherlands outside this hoard, even though now hundreds of palstave finds are known (Butler & Steegstra 1997/1998). This applies to the Acton Park palstaves of both varieties. It is only for the smaller, more graceful axes dbnos 537 and 1675 (fig. 1) that a possible parallel can be mentioned, also from the coastal dune area: a stray find from Den Haag-Savornin Lohmanplein (Butler 1990: 78). In the southern Netherlands there are some more axes of type Plaisir known, as well as one find of a similar high-flanged axe from another site in the dunes (Hillegom/Lisse, in the vicinity of Voorhout; Butler 1995/1996: 195). However, the greater part of the hoard, the North Welsh Acton Park palstaves, are completely alien to the Low Countries. This also makes it different from hoards like the one from Pyrzyce, as the axes in this Polish hoard are not alien to the region: comparable palstaves seem to have been found in North Poland (Butler & Steegstra 1997/1998:184). The conclusion that Voorhout consists of objects far beyond their normal region of distribution was only recently made. It made Butler suggest the scenario of a vessel from Britain 'cruising along the Northwest French coast, blown off its course in a storm and ending up on the Dutch coast' (Butler & Steegstra 1997/1998: 185).

Context

A further complicating factor in the interpretation of the Voorhout hoard as a clear example of buried trade stock, is the context of the find. When the hoard was found, it soon raised local antiquarian interest, and shortly after its discovery, J.H. Holwerda, director of the National Museum of Antiquities in Leiden visited the site. In a very early example of interdisciplinary research, Holwerda was accompanied by a geologist, J. Lorié who investigated the geological context of the find. Quite soon after their on-the-spot investigation, both published their findings in two separate articles in the same volume of the annual museum bulletin, the Oudheidkundige Mededelingen van het Rijksmuseum van Oudheden te Leiden (Holwerda 1908; Lorié 1908). Holwerda clearly states that the objects were found in a square pit of 50 by 50 cm (implying that the axes were not hafted when deposited). This pit was dug into a peat layer. Although the precise location can no longer be reconstructed, this must have been a boggy hollow as they are known to have formed in between dunes in this region. Obviously, a boggy layer is not a logical place to hide precious trade stock in, as it is extremely hard to retrieve material that has sunk down in a bog.

Already by the early 20th century, there was a long-standing debate on the interpretation of Bronze Age hoards, whether they should be interpreted as profane or ritual depositions. Holwerda explicitly refers to hoards from peat bogs in Denmark, which by that time were usually interpreted as 'ritual' deposits in view of the fact that such hoards were practically irretrievable and therefore cannot represent temporarily hidden caches (Holwerda 1908; Verlaeckt 1995: chapter 3). Nevertheless, the peat context of the find did not influence Holwerda's conviction that the Voorhout hoard represents a (profane) cache of valuables. What is much more remarkable that Holwerda's and Lorié's attention for a study of the hoard's context did not pay off until very recently: the numerous publications and discussions of the Voorhout hoard that followed since the 1950s did not mention the contextual evidence once! It is only in his 1990 publication that Butler returns to this observation, but only to argue that the corroded condition of the finds indicates that they were not purely in the peat, and that it is unclear in which peat layer the hoard was found (Butler 1990: 78). However, in a later publication of the hoard, Butler and Steegstra again bring up the issue of the peat context of the find, but it now takes centre stage in the discussion and is for the first time recognized as an interpretative problem, yet one they leave unsolved. 'It is not easy to suggest an explanation for the presence of the Voorhout hoard in a boggy deposit in the coastal dune area'(Butler & Steegstra 1997/1998: 184).

The Voorhout hoard as an epistemological dilemma

Reviewing the interpretation history of the Voorhout hoard since its first publication in 1908, it might be considered a rather peculiar one. The first remarkable observation may be essentially the theory that the Voorhout hoard represents buried traders' stock. Since its first in-depth publication in the 1950s, all publications have been subscribing to this theory, up until now. Remarkably enough, however, this interpretation was actually never sustained by arguments based on the evidence itself. What was well-argued was the theory that the primary palstaves were British imports, a clear example of items shipped across the sea. A great part of all bronze objects in the Low Countries are imports however, so the question needs to be asked why this particular find has always been so straightforwardly linked to trading activities. I suspect that this may be because the Voorhout hoard as a collection of (similar) axes evokes a notion of serial production and mass commodity exchange we ourselves feel some familiarity with. Also, its 'port-of-trade-like' location may have added to this feeling. At any rate: we never find a clear argument why Voorhout continues to figure as an almost paradigmatic example of traders' stock up until today, an interpretation which is reached with 'little doubt' even in the recently published synthesis of Dutch prehistory (Van den Broeke 2005). It is almost as if this 'traders' hoard' interpretation is something that goes without saying. This is particularly remarkable as we have now seen that there has always been a number of arguments that makes the traders' hoard interpretation increasingly problematic, and it must be said that only Butler himself seems to have been realizing this in his most recent studies of the hoard (Butler 1990; Butler & Steegstra 1997/1998). The hoard is not a set of one-typed items from Wales ready for future use, but a heterogenous collection of scrap and worn objects from a variety of sources on both sides of the Channel and North Sea. As such, it is in no way comparable to the classic 'traders' hoards elsewhere in Europe as Habsheim or Pyrzyce that keep on being mentioned as parallels. On top of that, it is now clear that the majority of the Voorhout items are not known in the Low Countries outside the hoard. Perhaps the most important objection is the one that has been explicitly recorded from the outset by Holwerda, but ignored in any interpretation until very recently: the peat context of the find. If this hoard consists of trade goods, why then was this material buried in a boggy hollow in the dunes? It is as if an interpretation of Voorhout as a permanent deposition of material was seen as so irrational when compared with the pragmatic, self-evident, traders' hoard-interpretation that it was not even discussed in the first place.

The interpretation history of the Voorhout hoard exemplifies some of the problems of the way in which archaeologists have made sense of hoards and depositions in general. In Sacrificial landscapes I made an analysis of all interpretative literature on European Bronze Age hoards that were accessible, from the mid-19th century until recent times (Fontijn 2002: chapter 2). An important conclusion was that a distinction between 'profane' and 'ritual' explicitly or implicity governed all approaches. The way in which a hoard was categorized as 'profane' or 'ritual', however, was not done on an equal basis. Practical behaviour is presupposed and self-explanatory, whereas ritual is something that requires efforts above what is needed in functional terms. As recently argued by Brück (Brück 1999), such an approach echoes a Post-Enlightenment view on what is rational (pragmatic, economic) and irrational ('ritual) action. We may ask ourselves whether such views, including the 'ritual-profane' dichotomy that stems from it, are of any help in making sense of depositions. We have seen that the interpretation history of the Voorhout hoard is a case in point: its repeated identification as a temporary stock of hidden valuables (pragmatic, rational trade) is reached with 'little doubt' (Butler 1959; Van den Broeke 2005: 6: 62), whereas this view was never sustained by arguments. Some of the 'odd' or 'irrational' observations were usually left out of the discussion. The dilemma Voorhout confronts us with is not an empirical but mainly an epistemological one.

Approaching hoards

In order to overcome the epistemological problems related to using clear-cut rationalist dichotomies like the one between profane and ritual practices, I developed an approach that is based on patterns in the evidence itself (Fontijn 2002). The reason for this is the initial observation that many of the metalwork finds appear to be found in certain contexts only, avoiding others. This seems to reflect a process of selective deposition. Basing myself on a representative set of evidence from one region, the southern Netherlands and Northern Belgium, some 1300 finds were investigated. In what contexts did they enter the ground, what was the life-path of the objects in question? Are patterns in deposition and life-path discernable that are not the result of selective preservation and missing evidence? The approach, its theoretical and empirical background, its possibilities and limitations have been described at length elsewhere (Fontijn 2002), for the present discussion I will only repeat a few conclusions that are relevant here. Throughout the entire Bronze Age, evidence was found for practices in which bronzes were deliberately deposited in the landscape apparently without any intention for future retrieval. Items were thus 'removed' from society. It is quite clear that this happened only rarely, but not arbitrarily. A striking, long-term pattern is that such depositions seems preferably to have taken place in 'natural' environments, particularly in watery places. Most of the objects seem to have had a specific sort of life-path, many must have been the subject of long-distance circulation and/or were intensively used. From this it was deduced that the objects apparently became meaningful as a result of a certain life-path, or 'cultural biography' in the sense of Kopytoff (Butler 1986). The burial of this object in a specific type of environment, then, seems to have been the appropriate end of such a biography. Deposition did not take place arbitrarily, but was highly structured. Particular objects ended up in particular types of places and not others (Fontijn 2002). This 'selective deposition' implies that objects accrued distinctive and circumscribed meanings. Certain types of objects were never associated in hoards, and certain types of objects were only deposited in certain types of wet places (e.g. swords in rivers; Fontijn 2002: chapter 10). From such a selective attitude, it can be inferred that in deposition the objects were not regarded as 'things' or mutually exchangeable commodities but as 'valuables' (ibid., chapter 2 and 3).

The Voorhout hoard is found in a coastal region west of the one that was central in the study just cited. Culturally and in terms of subsistence economy, we are dealing with communities that were closely related to the ones from both the southern and the northern Netherlands (Arnoldussen & Fontijn 2006; Fokkens 2005). There are some differences, however, that need to be emphasized. With regard to bronze finds, the coastal region is relatively rich, if we take the low intensity of research into account, especially in the coastal dune area in which the Voorhout hoard was found (Butler 1990 ; Van Heeringen *et al.* 1998). The provenance of a number of these bronzes suggest that the coastal region was linked up in a somewhat different network of exchange from both the southern and the northern Netherlands. Although a more detailed investigation is badly needed, a scenario for this region as actively participating in coastal seafaring seems likely. It is likely that such voyages brought the items found in the Voorhout hoard to the Dutch coast. In general, the coastal region seems to follow depositional patterns of selective deposition as they have been laid bare in the southern and northern Netherlands and Belgium (Essink & Hielkema 1997/1998; Fontijn 2002; Verlaeckt 1996). Deposition of a single object was the rule, just as elsewhere in Low Countries, and axes are the predominant object that figured in depositional practices. Cultivated areas generally seem to lack bronze items, but bronzes are known from 'natural' places including marshes. If deposition was a practice that was governed by widely-shared cultural rules, how then does the Voorhout hoard fit into the patterns discussed so far?

Voorhout in the light of depositional practices

The Voorhout hoard can be considered as an example of the widespread practice of depositing axes into watery places, but it certainly represents a somewhat uncommon one.

Firstly, this is in view of the large quantity of axes deposited in one event. Deposition of a single axe seems to have been the rule in both the Netherlands, Belgium and the adjacent parts of Germany. There are only a few examples of multiple-axe hoards and they are modest in the numbers of palstaves they contained when compared to the eighteen axes and one chisel that have been deposited in the Voorhout marsh (Butler 1963; Fontijn 2002; Kibbert 1980).

Secondly, axes deposited in wet sites in the Low Countries were as a rule used but often have their cutting edges resharpened shortly before they were finally given up, suggesting that this was considered the appropriate way of offering axes (maybe there was a belief in an future use? (Fontijn 2002: 212). The situation of most axes in the Voorhout hoard was much different; we have seen that many were damaged or straightforward scrap. This brings us closer to a theory that the Voorhout items were less valued for a role of implement, but rather as a source of foreign-convertible, recyclable- metal.

Thirdly, one of the most surprising recent realizations is the observation that most of the North Welsh palstaves and the lugged chisel in this hoard are by far unknown in the Low Countries, even though hundreds of palstaves have now been recorded. In this way, the 'alien' character of the content of the Voorhout hoard recalls the offshore find of Langdon Bay. Just in front of the coast of Dover (UK), divers found a huge collection of mid-winged axes (59) and other objects, many in a damaged state (Muckelroy 1981). Just like in the case of the Voorhout North Welsh palstaves, these mid-winged axes are foreign (east-French) products that are practically unknown from the British mainland and clearly outside their normal area of distribution. Muckelroy interprets this find as a scrap assemblage that was traded overseas but accidentally sunk just in front of the British coast (see also Samson 2006). Muckelroy supposes that these items were meant to be remelted and converted into local types when they reached the British shore. This would explain why mid-winged axes were traded into Britain in considerable quantities, but never entered the ground. He argues that bronzes found in other 'wreck assemblages' in the Mediterranean like Huelva and Rochelongues also contain objects outside their usual distribution area which must have been traded as scrap intended for local remelting.

Confronting 'trade' and 'ritual'

Whereas a case has now been made to explain the 'alien' character of the items in the Voorhout hoard and their damaged condition, it still leaves one crucial question unsolved. If we are dealing here with a collection of scrap shipped across the sea and along the coast for recycling, why then was it buried in a marshy place in the dunes? Although it is now generally accepted that large numbers of bronzes were deliberately deposited in watery places, authors kept on seeing the Voorhout hoard as a temporary cache of objects that only by some whim of fate stayed in the ground permanently, regardless of the increasing unlikeliness of such an interpretation. Is this because the content of the hoard so strongly evokes an image of trade stock, and that 'pragmatic', 'down-to-earth' trade is apparently considered as irreconcilable to permant 'ritual' deposition of valuables? This may well be a problem of our own making. Apparently, we tend to see the massive exchange of bronze items in overseas trade as a process that is completely detached from the 'ritual' uses of axes in deposition. But is it? There are also arguments supporting the view that trade or the circulation of commodities cannot exist without a higher level of exchange, where objects become imbued with special values and figure in 'ritual' practices.

Let us start by stating what we observe and what can be logically assumed on the circulation of metalwork. The Low Countries are a non-metalliferous region where Bronze Age communities nevertheless had adopted and integrated bronze for the manufacture of specific categories of implements and items. Some items, axes for example, were indispensable tools that are since c. 2000 B.C. only known in bronze. Many others are new objects like swords or spears or specific types of ornaments. Bronze did not replace other materials in all categories of implements, but its impact must have been profound (Fontijn 2002: 141-2). From c. 2300 B.C. onwards a thriving local bronze industry came into existence that must entirely have been based on reworking imported bronze. Foreign bronzes, most likely in the form of scrap, was transformed into locally-acceptable styled axes. The Late Bronze Age Drouwen hoard in the northern Netherlands (Butler 1986), consisting of broken objects of types that are completely alien to the Low Countries, underlines that imports of scrap did take place, and so does the Voorhout hoard or- further away- the Langdon Bay assemblage. This is essentially the situation for the entire Bronze Age in the Low Countries and from it we can logically infer that a steady and systematic importation of bronze from abroad was a conditio sine qua non. The Low Countries, just like many other non-metalliferous regions, must have been structurally integrated in widespread long-distance bronze exchange networks. Of all the bronze in circulation, only a small amount will have entered the ground. Large-scale settlement excavations, for example, hardly yield bronzes even if we know that bronze was produced there (e.g. Oss-Horzak: Fontijn 2002, app. 8; Fontijn *et al.* 2002). We might see this as evidence for an economic attitude in which discarded objects and even tiny pieces of scrap re-entered the melting pot. This is in marked contrast to the situation in, for example, Roman legionary camps in the Netherlands, where it is common to find thousands of bronze items (Van Enckevort & Zee 1996: 16). An analysis of the Bronze Age metalwork that has been found in the Low Countries shows that the majority thereof entered the archaeological record as deliberate depositions (Fontijn 2002). As set out earlier, they were placed in the landscape in a highly structured, selective way. Estimates of its frequency make clear that this 'giving-up' of valuables was exception rather than norm (Fontijn 2002: 214-5). Also, it is clear that only specific types of objects were deposited in such a way; local types were treated differently from certain imports. Although it can not be proven, it might well be that there were even distinct classes of artefacts that were not selected for such depositions and, as a consequence, had a low chance of ever entering the archaeological record.

For 'importing' communities foreign material must have had some ambiguity, because its creation is beyond control of these communities themselves and denotes their dependency on others (Fontijn 2002: 273-4; Helms 1993: 99; Sørensen 1987). Importing communities therefore may have had procedures of conversion to cope with the ambiguity of this foreign material. After all, it was often to play specialized socio-political and ritual roles in the local community, and in order to achieve this, any foreign material needs some sort of appropriation and recontextualisation. One way in which such conversion of imported material might have been established is by melting it down and shaping it into locally-acceptable forms. The clear emphasis on a distinct local identity, which is for example conspicuous in the ornamentation of socketed axes in the northern Netherlands, underlines the social significance such transformations had. The local styles of palstave axes in the southern Netherlands, on the other hand, are more adaptive to styles of foreign Atlantic palstaves which also figured in depositions. It is nevertheless distinguishable as local (Butler & Steegstra 1997/1998; Fontijn 2002: 121-5).

Another way in which foreign trade stock is often made acceptable for fulfilling specialized roles in a community was discussed in a cross-cultural anthropological study by Maurice Bloch and Jonathan Parry

(1989). They show how in every society there are procedures for converting objects acquired by short-term exchange (commodity exchange, trade) into the long-term transactional order (involving valuables and gift-giving with ancestors and the supernatural). Objects acquired in trade with foreigners are strongly determined by motives of individual gain and profit (Sahlins 1986). Here, the objects are 'alienable' commodities, often acquired in significant numbers. Still, due to its association with individual purposes and transactions with foreigners, the thus acquired goods can to some extent be seen as 'polluted' or immoral material. At any rate: it cannot directly be transformed into objects that are to fulfil important social or ritual roles as an –inalienable- valuable in the local community itself. The role of bronze ornaments and implement in burials and depositions shows that once imported (and eventually reshaped), some objects did end their life as such valuables. Bloch and Parry argue that such a transformation of meaning can only come about when what has been acquired in the process of individualistic trade is converted to serve the reproduction of the long-term cycle thus becoming 'morally positive'. The way in which such a conversion takes place can be highly variable, but essentially involves the inclusion of (a part of) the foreign material in some ritual (long-term transactional order) after which it is considered as fit for fulfilling more specialized roles. The donation of wealth to temples by the Romans are a good example. After a small part was burnt in a temple for some time (conceived of as a gift to a God), the entire load could subsequently be used as finance for down-to-earth economic advantage (Needham 2001: 288).

Back to the Voorhout hoard. Most archaeologists were probably right in seeing this assemblage as traded material brought here from across the sea, even though it was probably more likely as a collection of worn material from different sources intended for remelting rather than a one-type set of finished products. In the light of what is now known on depositional practices, it is much more likely that this hoard represents a deliberate deposition rather than a forgotten store of material.

With the above theory on conversion of traded material in mind, it might be argued that we are dealing here with a situation in which traded scrap bronze entered the Dutch coast, where a sample of the material was deliberately deposited (seen as some sort of exchange with gods, ancestors or however conceptualized) in order to make the entire load of foreign material acceptable for the importing community. This would explain the alien, uncommon character of this material as well as the fact that this clearly, much-travelled, collection of scrap and objects was deliberately deposited in a watery place. An argument against this view is that Voorhout is still a rather unique find: if such pars pro toto sacrifices took place we would expect more examples (there are indications that it was a patterned phenomenon in the last phase of the Late Bronze Age; Fontijn 2002, chapter 13). The value of this hypothesis may at least be heuristic. It calls for a rigorous reconsideration of other hoards that now figure as neat examples of scrap and 'traders' hoards' in other regions. In what context were they deposited? Do they exist of objects outside their normal distribution area (as for example already argued for by Bradley 1990)? And what about the metal composition of 'local types'? Mixing of scrap from different sources may have led to entirely new metal types, but a more straightforward remelting of British imported material may also lead to local axes made of British metal (cf Butler's observation that British forms of (Midgdale) axes on the continent were made of continental Singen metal; Butler 1995/1996:172) In this way, and as suggest by the Voorhout assemblage, 'ritual'deposition may be much closer to 'down to earth' trade and the economy of commodity exchange than we usually think.

References

ARNOLDUSSEN S. & FONTIJN D. 2006. Towards familiar landscapes? On the nature and origins of Middle Bronze Age landscapes in the Netherlands, Proceedings of the Prehistoric Society 72, 289-317.

BLOCH M & PARRY J. 1989. Introduction: money and the morality of exchange, In BLOCH M. & Parry J. (eds), Money & the morality of exchange, Cambridge, Cambridge University Press, 1-31.

BRADLEY R. 1990. The Passage of arms. An archaeological analysis of prehistoric hoards and votive deposits, Cambridge: Cambridge University Press.

BRIARD J. 1965. Les dépôts Bretons et l'Âge du

bronze Atlantique, Rennes (Travaux du Laboratoire d'Anthropologie Préhistorique. Faculté des Sciences de Rennes).

BRÜCK J. 1999. Ritual and rationality: some problems of interpretation in European Archaeology, European journal of Archaeology 2: 313-344.

BUTLER J.J. 1959. Vergeten schatvondsten uit de Bronstijd. In BOGAERS J.E. & CALS J.M.L.Th. (eds), Honderd Eeuwen Nederland ,'s-Gravenhage, Luctor et Emergo (= Antiquity and Survival II, no. 5-6), 125-142.

BUTLER J.J. 1963. Bronze Age connections across the North Sea. A study in prehistoric trade and industrial relations between the British Isles, The Netherlands, North Germany and Scandinavia, c. 1700-700 B.C., Palaeohistoria IX: 1-286.

BUTLER J.J. 1969. Nederland in de Bronstijd, Bussum: Fibula-Van Dishoeck.

BUTLER J.J. 1986. Drouwen: end of a Nordic Rainbow?, Palaeohistoria 28: 133-168.

BUTLER J.J. 1990. Bronze Age metal and amber in the Netherlands (I), Palaeohistoria 32: 47-110.

BUTLER J.J. 1995 / 1996. Bronze Age Metal and Amber in the Netherlands (II:1). Catalogue of the Flat Axes, Flanged Axes and Stopridge Axes, Palaeohistoria 37 / 38: 159-243.

BUTLER J.J. & STEEGSTRA H. 1997 / 1998. Bronze Age Metal and Amber in the Netherlands (II:2). Catalogue of the Palstaves, Palaeohistoria 39 / 40: 163-275.

CHILDE V.G. 1930. The Bronze Age, Cambridge: Cambridge University Press.

ENCKEVORT H.L.H. & ZEE, K., 1996, Het Kops Plateau. Prehistorische grafheuvels en een Romeinse legerplaats te Nijmegen, Abcoude: Uniepers.

ESSINK M. & HIELKEMA J. 1997 / 1998. Rituele depositie van bronzen voorwerpen in Noord-Nederland, Palaeohistoria 39 / 40: 277-321.

FOKKENS H., 2005. De positie van West-Friesland in de Nederlandse Bronstijd, In VAN DEN DRIES M.H. & WILLEMS W.J.H. (eds), Innovatie in de Nederlandse Archeologie, Gouda, Drukkerij Van Ketel, 71-83.

FONTIJN, D., 2002: Sacrificial Landscapes: cultural biographies of persons, objects and 'natural' places in the Bronze Age of the southern Netherlands, c. 2300-600 B.C., Analecta Praehistorica Leidensia 33/34: 1-392.

FONTIJN, D.R., FOKKENS, H. and JANSEN, R., 2002. De gietmal van Oss-Horzak en de inheemse bronsproductie in de Midden-Bronstijd. Enkele voorlopige resultaten, In

FOKKENS H. & JANSEN R. (eds), 2000 jaar Bewoningsdynamiek. Brons- en ijzertijdbewoning in het Maas-Demer-Scheldegebied, Leiden, Haveka BV, 63-72.

HEERINGEN R.M. van, VAN DE VELDE, H. & VAN AMEN, I. 1998. Een tweeschepige huisplattegrond en akkerland uit de Vroege Bronstijd te Noordwijk, prov. Zuid-Holland, Amersfoort: Print X-Press (= Rapportage Archeologische Monumentenzorg 55).

HELMS M.W. 1993. Craft and the kingly ideal. art, trade, and power, Austin: University of Texas Press.

HOLWERDA J.H. 1908. Bronsdepotvondst bij Voorhout, Oudheidkundige Mededeelingen Rijksmuseum van Oudheden te Leiden 2: 45-6.

KIBBERT K. 1980. Die Äxte und Beile im mittleren Westdeutsland I, München: Beck (= Prähistorische Bronzefunde IX: 10).

KOPYTOFF I. 1986. The cultural biography of things: commoditisation as process, In APPADURAI A.(ed.), The Social life of Things, Cambridge, Cambridge University Press, 64-91.

LANTING J.N. & J. VAN DER PLICHT 2001/2002. De 14C-chronologie van de Nederlandse pre- en protohistorie IV: bronstijd en vroege ijzertijd, Palaeohistoria 43/44: 117-262..

LORIÉ J. 1908. Geologische beschouwingen over de vondst der bronzen bij Voorhout, Oudheidkundige

Mededeelingen Rijksmuseum te Leiden 2: 46-50.

LOUWE KOOIJMANS L.P., VAN DEN BROEKE P., FOKKENS, H. & VAN GIJN, A.L., 2005 The Prehistory of the Netherlands Volume 2. Amsterdam: Amsterdam University Press.

MUCKELROY K., 1981. Middle Bronze Age trade between Britain and Europe: a maritime perspective, posthumously published by Sean Mc Grail, Proceeding of the Prehistoric Society 47: 275-297.

NEEDHAM S. 2001. When expediency broaches ritual intention: the flow of metal between systemic and buried domains, The Journal of the Royal Anthropological Institute incorporating Man 7: 275-298.

NORTHOVER P. 1982. The exploration of long-distance movement of bronze in Bronze and Early Iron Age Europe, Bulletin of the Institute of Archaeology 19: 45-72.

O'CONNOR B. 1980. Cross-Channel relations in the Later Bronze Age. Relations between Britain, North-Eastern France and the Low Countries during the Later Bronze Age and the Early Iron Age, with particular reference to the metalwork, Oxford: British Archaeological Reports International. Series 91.

SAHLINS M. 1986. Stone Age economics. London: Routledge.

SAMSON A., 2006, Offshore finds from the Bronze Age in NW Europe – the shipwreck scenario revisited, Oxford Journal of Archaeology, 371-388.

SCHMIDT P.K. & BURGESS C.B. 1981. The axes of Scotland and northern England (Prähistorische Bronzefunde IX: 7), München: Beck.

SØRENSEN M.L.S. 1987. Material order and cultural classification: the role of bronze objects in the transition from Bronze Age to Iron Age in Scandinavia. In, HODDER I. (ed.), The archaeology of contextual meanings, Cambridge: Cambridge University Press (New directions in archaeology), 90-101.

SPROCKHOFF E. 1941. Niedersachsens Bedeutung für die Bronzezeit Westeuropas. Zur Verankerung einer neuen Kulturprovinz, Bericht der Römisch-Germanischen Kommision 31 (II): 1-138.

VAN DEN BROEKE P.W. 1991. Nieuwe materialen, groeiende afhankelijkheid, In BLOEMERS & VAN DORP T. (eds), Pre- & Protohistorie van de Lage Landen, Houten, Unieboek Uitgeverij, 237-249.

VAN DEN BROEKE P.W. 2005. Gifts to the gods. Rites and cult sites in the Bronze Age and the Iron Age, In LOUWE KOOIJMANS L.P., VAN DEN BROEKE P., FOKKENS, H. & VAN GIJN, A.L. (eds), The Prehistory of the Netherlands Volume 2, Amsterdam, Amsterdam University Press, 659-677.

VERLAECKT K. 1995. Sociale evolutie tijdens de metaaltijden in Denemarken. Analyse en interpretatie van «depotvondsten» als basis voor een modelvorming van de samenleving in de late bronstijd en de vroege ijzertijd (ca. 1000 B.C. - 0), Gent (unpublished Ph.D. thesis University of Gent).

VERLAECKT K. 1996. Between river and barrow. A reappraisal of Bronze Age metalwork found in the province of East-Flanders (Belgium), Oxford: BAR Publishing. British Archaeological Reports International Series 632.

Acknowledgements

Thanks are due to Jay Butler, H. Steegstra and the Groningen Institute of Archaeology for allowing me to use their drawings of the Voorhout axes. Roosje de Leeuwe, Alice Samson and Stijn Arnoldussen (all Leiden University) provided me with much appreciated comments on an earlier draft. Stijn also assisted in the production of the figures. Thanks are also to the editors for inviting me to write this down, and for their admirable patience when awaiting the outcome.

Contact

David Fontijn
Faculty of Archaeology
University of Leiden
PO Box 9515
2300 RA Leiden
the Netherlands
D.Fontijn@Arch.LeidenUniv.nl

THE SYMBOLIC VALUE OF GRINDINGSTONES HOARDS: TECHNICAL PROPERTIES OF NEOLITHIC EXAMPLES.

Caroline HAMON

Abstract:
Seven settlements of the Paris Basin and Hainaut have delivered grindingstones hoards dated from the Linearbandkeramik and Villeneuve-Saint-Germain-Blicquy culture, between 5,200 and 4,600 B.C. These hoards are always linked with domestical areas (houses or village), and are of undoubtefoul symbolic value. The disposition of the lowertools, in circle or in pile, associated to their coupled handstones and to several hammerstones, can be assimilated to a codified act. The study of the grindingtools technical and functional properties brings new data of interpretation of this phenomenon. The shapes, dimensions and stages of maintenance and use of the grindingtools are slighltly different in hoards and in detritic lateral pits of the houses. The symbolic value of such hoards is discussed in relation with the agricultural identity of the earliest neolithic of these regions. Hoards may be either an evolution of the previous symbolic of grindingtools from burial contexts, or an expression of the status of the house or its inhabitants, towards the social organisation of the whole village, or be assimilated as a ritual of abandonment of the village, linked with the owning of the land.

Resumé :
Sept sites d'habitat du Bassin parisien et du Hainaut ont livré des dépôts de meules datés des cultures Rubanée et Villeneuve-Saint-Germain-Blicquy, entre 5200 et 4600 B.C. Ces dépôts sont systématiquement liés à une zone domestique (maison ou village), et sont chargés d'une dimension symbolique indéniable. La disposition des meules, en cercle ou empilées, associées à leur molettes respectives et quelques percuteurs, peut être assimilée à un acte codifié. L'étude de leurs caractéristiques techniques et fonctionnelles apporte de nouvelles données pour interpréter ce phénomène. Les formes, dimensions et étapes d'entretien et d'usage de ces meules diffèrent légèrement entre les dépôts et les contextes détritiques classiques. La valeur symbolique de ces dépôts est ici discutée en relation avec l'identité agricole des premières populations néolithiques de ces régions. Les dépôts peuvent soit constituer une évolution de la symbolique de ces meules depuis le contexte funéraire, soit exprimer le statut de la maison et de ses habitants en regard de l'organisation sociale du village, soit enfin être assimilés à un rituel d'abandon du village, en lien avec la propriété de la terre.

Introduction

Despite the central role played by grindingstones in neolithic subsistance, their study appeared quite recently in archeological research. Main informations about these tools come from lateral pits of danubian houses, mostly used as detritic areas. Focusing on the earliest neolithic of western Europe, grindingstone hoards constitute a source of informations, as much as a specific type of archeological structure. Their study is for this reasons of most importance for both the understanding of grindingstones technical properties and their insertion in neolithic activities.
Hoards appear as a new kind of symbolic expression and a new kind of behaviour, specific to neolithic communities. The disposition of two to five lowertools, in circle or in pile, associated to their coupled handstones and to several hammerstones, can be assimilated to a codified act. The main feature of these grindingstone hoards is their systematic association with settlements, which bring a new evidence of the thin link which associate grindingstones to domestic activities or areas. The comparison of tools from classical detritic contexts, and tools from hoards, help us definite the specific properties of these selected tools, which have not been manufactured for this special purpose.

Our study of this pratice relies on about eleven grindingstone hoards, located in Belgium and northern part of France (Hamon 2006). These hoards are dated from the earliest neolithic of these regions, which corresponds to the late Linearbandkeramik and the Villeneuve-Saint-Germain-Blicquy culture, between 5,200 and 4,600 B.C. (fig. 1). Five hoards are coming from four sites of the Paris Basin (France), the two Linearbandkeramik sites of Berry au Bac 'le Vieux Tordoir' (Allard *et al.* 1995 and 1996) and Cuiry-lès-Chaudardes 'les Fontinettes' (Ilett & Hachem 2001), and the two Villeneuve-Saint-Germain sites of Ville-

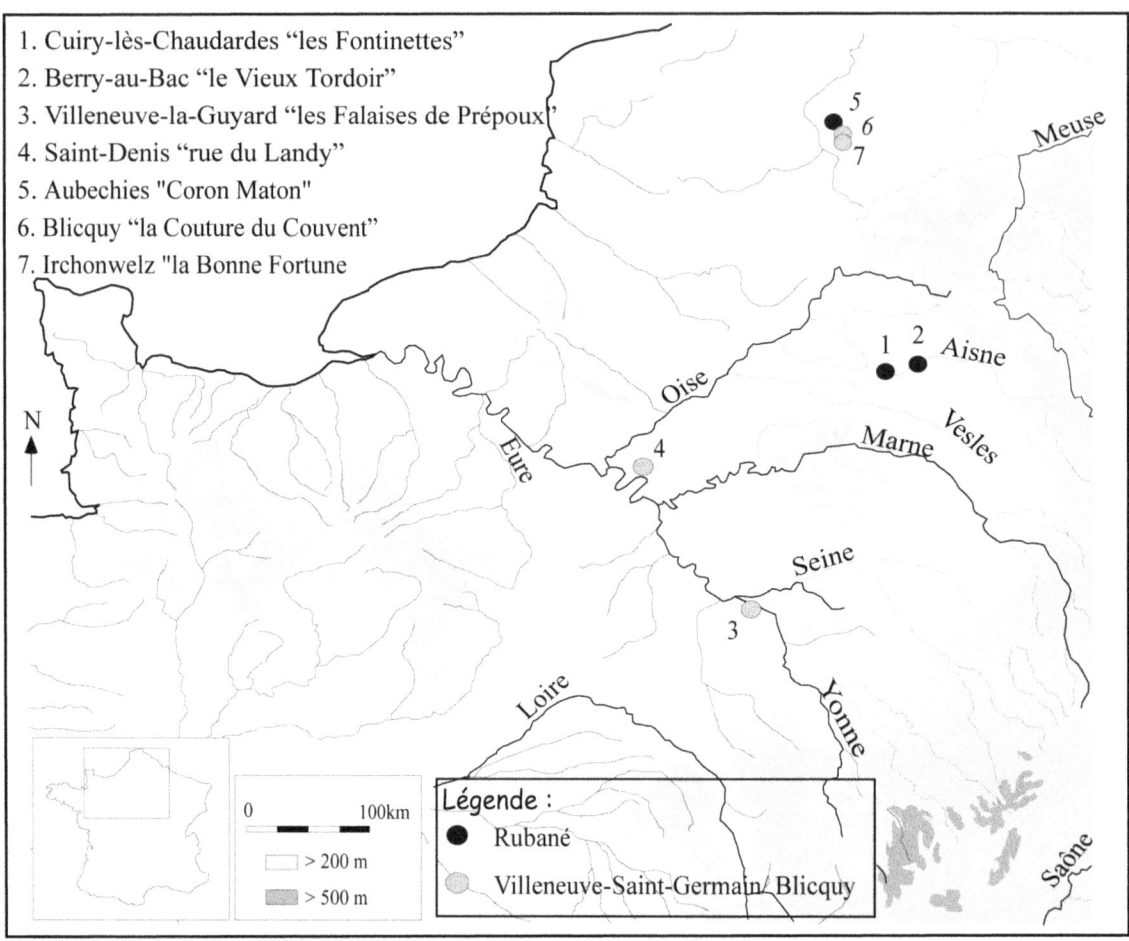

Fig. 1. Map of localization of Linearbandkeramik and Villeneuve-Saint-Germain Blicquy grindingstone hoards studied in Paris Basin and Hainaut

neuve-la-Guyard 'les Falaises de Prépoux' (Prestreau 1992) and Saint-Denis 'Rue du Landy' (Hamon & Samzun 2004 a and b); six others have been found on three sites in Hainaut (Belgium) in Aubechies 'Coron Maton', Bliquy 'la Couture du Couvent' and Irchonwelz 'la Bonne Fortune' (Constantin *et al.* 1978).

From the raw material reserve to the ritual of fundation or abandonment of a house, several hypotheses have been proposed to explain such practices (Constantin *et al.* 1978). May these hoards only be temporarily cache or can we demonstrate that they correspond to a definitive act of abandonment of the tools? Must we interpret these hoards at the light of grindingstones's symbolic, that is to say as an expression of the new agricultural identity of these early neolithic communities? The technical and functional analysis of these tools help us discuss once more grindingstone hoards signification.

Definition of the ritual signification of grindingstone hoards

Location of hoards pits

Contrary to many Neolithic or Bronze age hoards discovered in several types of contexts such as humid or borders areas, grindingstone hoards are definitely linked with settlements and living areas. Grindingstone hoards are more or less linked with the wood and mud houses of about 25 to 60 meters long which constituates the danubian villages, or to the lateral pits digged along the external walls of these houses. Nonetheless, grindingstone hoards are neither present in every houses nor in every villages, that's why they constitute precious archeological informations for both the understanding of the organization of activities in the village, and for the knowledge of grindingstones technology.

Three main location of grindingstone hoards may be definite in relation with the houses (fig. 2). Grindingstone hoards may be located in pits, digged especially for this purpose. These pits may be located inside a house: in this case, they are digged at the back of it, near an hypothetic cereals and food storage area. Grindingstone hoards pits can also be settled in part of a former lateral pit. In this case, stratigraphy clearly shows a new digging of the previous lateral pit, which first function was more likely assimilated to a detritic area.

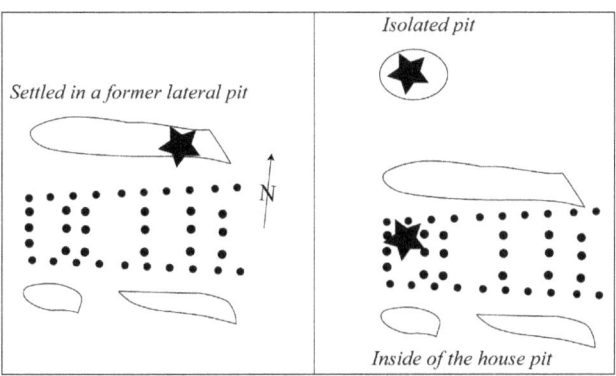

Fig. 2. Location of grindingstones towards the domestic area: village, houses and lateral pits included

The third case includes isolated pits, still located in the village area, which filling is very close to traditional lateral pits (flint, ceramic and bone rejections). Hainaut grindingstone hoards have one main specificity: two or three of them can be associated to the same house, or even to the same lateral pit, whereas no more than one grindingstone hoard can be linked with a house in the Paris Basin. Even if for the moment the logic of these hoards distribution is not clearly understood, their localisation is in any case not fortuitous.

Tools disposition

The disposition of the tools in the pits does not correspond to the spreading of objects in classical lateral pits of a house (Hamon 2005). Grindingstones lay in a codified position at half of the pit depth. Between three and six lowergrindingstones are generally deposited together with their associated handstones and a couple of hammerstones (table 1). Their disposition reflect a deliberate and single moment of deposition, and doesn't evok any later removal: for these two reasons, these archeological structures may be considered as hoards.

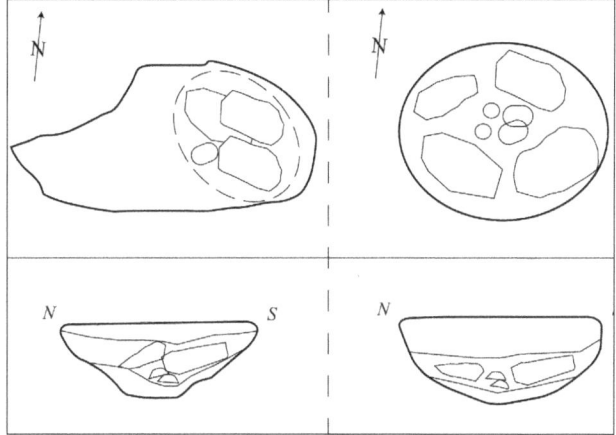

Fig. 3. Two main types of tools disposition in a hoard

Two main types of disposition can be observed (fig. 3). In the first type, the lower tools are put one on another in order to build a 'pile' under which their coupled handstones are lying. Following the second model, lower grindingstones are deposited in circle, in the center of which the coupled handstones and several hammerstones can be found.

	n° pit	location of pit	disposition	lowerstones	upperstones	hammerstones
Berry au Bac	598	back of house	circle	3	4	-
Berry au Bac	641	back of house	circle	3	2	-
Cuiry les Chaudardes	382	lateral pit	none	1	2	-
Villeneuve la Guyard	248	isolated pit	circle	3	3	1
Saint Denis	1	isolated pit	circle	5	2	3
Aubechies	10	lateral pit	circle	3	2	-
Irchonwelz	1	lateral pit	unknown	3	3	-
Irchonwelz	2	lateral pit	none	2	1	-
Irchonwelz	3	lateral pit	pile	4	4	-
Irchonwelz	7	lateral pit	pile	1	1	-
Irchonwelz	9	lateral pit	pile	2	4	-
Blicquy	30	lateral pit	none	3	1	-

Tabl 1. Brief description of the main characteristics of hoards from the Paris Basin and Hainaut

Their working surface is generally facing the soil or is more rarely in position of use. This particular position indicates a wish to protect the working surface of any alteration or dammage. Sometimes, grindingstones are found lying on their side. This tool's treatment may correspond to an habit, a 'custom' of protection of the tool during its normal cycle of use; it may also express the wish of a further reuse of the tools, like if the hoarding position was only temporary.

Which tools?

The selected grindingstonetools are always entire, contrary to the rare examples generally found in classical detritic contexts. Both lower and upper parts of the grinding system are deposited together: the curvature of the working surfaces are always corresponding one with another. These grindingstone hoards constitute the only posibility to study entire grinding systems, as only isolated upper or lower parts are found in most classical detritic contexts. The two parts of the 'neolithic mill' are generally accompagnied by hammerstones.

Two types of 'mills' are found in such hoards. They may be definite by the type of handstone used, that is to say an overflowing or a short handstone (fig. 4).

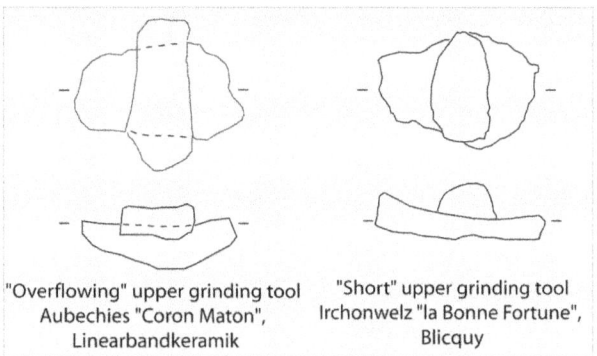

Fig. 4. Two types of early neolithic "mills", with their overflowing handstones or short handstones (after Constantin 1978).

On one hand, the handstone is far more long than the width of the thin lower tool, whereas on the second hand, the handstone's lenght correspond to or is shorter than the width of the lower grindingstone. Those two types correspond to both chronological and geographical spreading. The overflowing type exists only in the Belgium part and seems only occuring in Linearbandkeramik settlements; the 'short' type is met in the whole area, from the late Linearbandkeramik to the end of the Villeneuve-Saint-Germain in the Paris Basin and in Blicquy settlements in Belgium. But whatever their functional or chronological signification may be, both types have been chosen for hoarding.

The ritual features of such archeological tools rely on the codification of the deposition of the tools, together with the repetition of the phenomenon through a large geographical area. These structures reflect one single and meaningful moment of the life of a human group, despite we cannot determine whether the whole or only part of the community is concerned, and at which scale (the house, the village or the community).

Tool's properties

Morphology and dimensions

Shapes and sections of the lower grindingstones are mainly angulous (rectangular, rhombus), and correspond to a specific type of grindingstones, comparing to the ones found in lateral pits which are mainly ovoïd in shape (Hamon 2006). The back of lower grindingstones is generally flat and natural, while the sides are shaped by large flaking: they are more often made on fragmented blocs than on alluvial pebbles. The back and sides of upper grindingstones are generally well prepared, and regularized by pecking or even polishing of the asperities. The shaping of both lower and upper grinding tools is generally of high quality. The working surfaces are flat or concave, but never convex, which means that they have already been used quite a long time before their deposit.

Grinding tools' dimensions are generally longer than those found in classical detritic contexts (fig. 5).
Few entire examples are coming from lateral pits. Their average dimensions is of 40 by 22 cm for lowertools, and 23 by 12 cm for upper ones. Handstones from hoarding contexts are of about 20 to 25 cm long, while lowertools are from 40 to 50 cm long. Nevertheless, some regional differences occur between the Paris Basin and the Hainaut. Linearbandkeramik lower grindingstones from the Paris Basin are between 33 and 44 cm long, whereas Hainaut ones are between 38 and 48 cm long. Besides, and although their width appear stable, lowergrindingstone's thickness decrease between the Linearbandkeramik and Villeneuve-Saint-Germain-Blicquy culture. An opposite evolution can be observed for

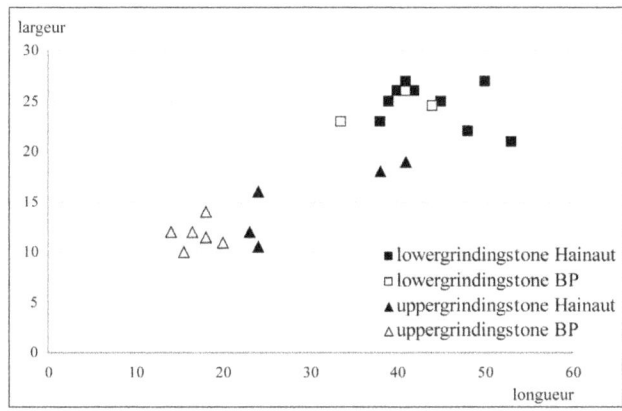

Fig. 5. Comparison of the dimensions of Paris Basin and Hainaut lower and uppergrindingstones, from Linearbandkeramik and Villeneuve-Saint-Germain Blicquy cultures (after Constantin 1978).

handstones, which length increases from 14 to 24 cm for the Linearbandkeramik to 23 or 24 cm for Blicquy examples. These differences could be interpreted in terms of chronological evolution between Linearbandkeramik and Villeneuve-Saint-Germain-Blicquy culture.

Management of the tools

In classical detritic contexts, grindingstones show traces of deliberate breaking, generally at half or two thirds of their length, while their working surfaces are still usable. The preservation of the integrity of the deposited grindingstones is at last deliberate.

A high rate of concavity featureizes most of the lower grinding tools's working surface and indicates a long duration of use. Nonetheless, the surfaces are rarely completely polished ; some surfaces are even in a 'fresh' state of preparation.

Fig. 6. Traces of obvious repecking of the working surface ; see the previous aspect of the polish (photograph C. Hamon)

The study of the states of preparation and use of the working surfaces brings new clues to understand the 'life' of these tools (Hamon 2006). Several stages of preparation, use and maintenance can be observed on a large majority of them. The tools from Irchonwelz and Aubechies hoards show obvious traces of repecking (fig. 6). The polish is destroyed by some transversal furrows of pecking. Only part of the working surface are concerned, that is to say the sides and secondly the basis of the lower grindingtools. This stage of tools maintenance can barely be observed on tools from classical detritic contexts.

Fig. 7. Hammerstone found in Saint-Denis "Rue du Landy" (photograph C. Hamon)

The deposition of one or more hammerstones among grindingstones may be linked with these stages of pecking and repecking of the working surfaces (Hamon & Samzun 2004 a and b) (fig. 7). These considerations enhances the technical feature of these grindingstones hoards.

Tool's function

Several examples of lower grindingstones in Saint Denis show several successive stages of preparation and use on one working surface (fig. 8). The initial shaping out can be identified by a coarse hammering of the working surface. The primarily working surface can be distinguished by a fine pecking of preparation ; its general shape and preparation must be linked with a back-and-forth movement of grinding. A third stage, corresponding to a secondary use or reuse, can be identified through the polish distribution on a circular area on the center of the grindingstone; it evoks a circular gesture of grinding with a small rounded handstone or maybe with one of the hammerstone

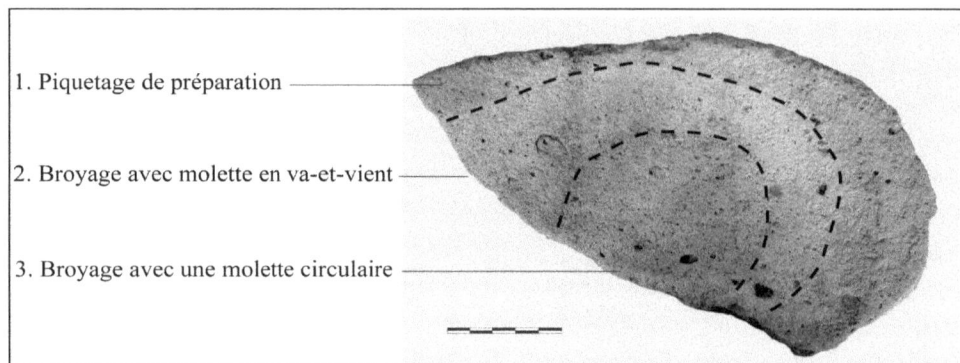

Fig. 8. Lowergrindingstone from Saint-Denis 'Rue du Landy': see the three distinct stages of preparation, use and reuse of this lowergrindingtool (photograph C. Hamon).

composing the hoard. This example of a complex lifecycle bring new clues for the understanding of the technical properties of hoarded grindingtools. This sample shows how a tool may be used several times, successively in back-and-forth and circular grinding, and sums up the technical specificities of tools found in hoarding position.

The life stages of these tools can also be definite by a functional approach. The determination of the function of the tools is based on an optical method of observation of use-wear traces on both experimental and archeological grinding tools and at low magnifications (till 120x) (Hamon 2003, 2006). Considering Saint-Denis examples, the different stages of use observed are linked with different functions. One lower grindingstone, with a long duration of use and a undoubteful back-and-forth movement of use, was definitely used for the transformation of cereals (fig. 9). A second grindingstone tool, which working surface has been clearly reused in a circular gesture, seem to have grind a hard animal matter, certainly bone (fig. 10). This secondary use may have associated a slight pounding by throwing percussion and a finer grinding for the production of small particles, corresponding to a dietary goal or to the production of some ceramic temper.

This analysis shows how either functional specific reuse or technical specific stages of maintenance characterize hoarded tools.

Fig. 10. Traces of hard animal matter grinding (bone?) on a reused lowergrindingstone grinding x30 (Saint-Denis 'Rue du Landy', photograph C. Hamon)

Hypothesis of interpretation

The codification of grindingstones deposition exclude the hypothesis of a simple act of rejection of the tools, according to the systematic location of hoards near domestic contexts and the specific disposition of the tools. The choice of entire and coupled lower and upper tools, with large dimensions and a normalized shaping out, also reinforce this idea.

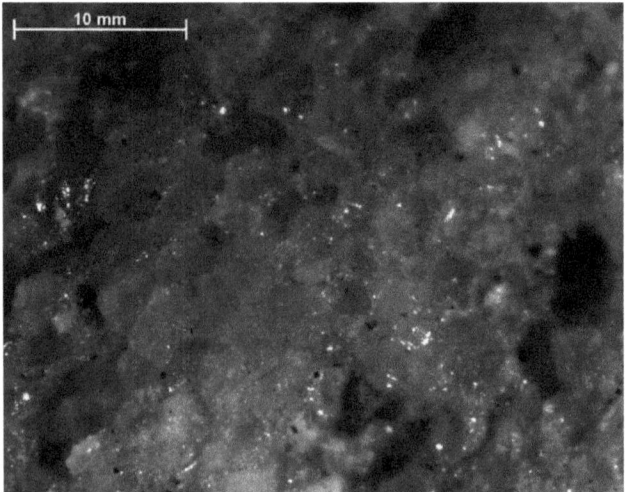

Fig. 9. Traces of cereal grinding by lowergrindingstone grinding x30 (Saint-Denis 'Rue du Landy', photograph C. Hamon)

1	ritual of fundation	location in domestic contexts
		repetition of tools disposition
2	ritual of abandonment	location in domestic contexts
		repetition of tools disposition
		new digging of lateral pit
		reuse
3	raw material reserve	repetition of tools disposition
		coupled tools
		entire tools
		already used tools
		large dimensions
		protection of the active surface
		maintenance stages
4	transfer of symbolic from dead burials to living sphere	frequency of this practice in western Linerabankkeramik
		disparition of grindingstone deposition in burials
5	territorial sign	location in domestic contexts
		repetition of tools disposition
		frequency of this practice in western Linerabankkeramik
6	expression of neolithic agricultural identity	location in domestic contexts
		coupled tools
		entire tools
		frequency of this practice in western Linerabankkeramik

Table 2. Synthetic representation of grindingstones main features with their related hypothesis of interpretation

Symbolic of the living and the dead

Nonetheless, we may ask ourselves about the status of these grindingstones. All studies show that the deposited tools have had a previous life before their 'burial': they have not been made especially for this purpose. A selection among everyday grindingstone tools has been made. The difficulty to determine the definitive or temporary feature of the deposit of these tools lays in the domestic nature of hoards, which induce nearness between hoards and people (table 2). Must we consider that these tools have been 'sacrified' and deducted from any further use, as an abandonment? Can we imagine that these tools have been temporarily deposited here, with the aim to take them back?

We may even consider that these hoards express a transfer of grindingstones symbolic from the dead world to the living one. The frequency of grindingstone hoards is higher in Northern France and South Belgium (see also Caspar *et al.* 1993 and Jadin 2003) than in any other part of the Linearbandkeramik sphere (Brink-Kloke & Meurers-Balke 2003; Pavlu 2000). In parallel, another phenomenon can be underlined in these regions: no more grindingstones are deposited in burials although this practice is largely spread in Linearbandkeramik cemetery, till the Rhein region for example (Farruggia 1992; Spatz 1999). As a matter of fact, a change of the symbolic meaning or value of grindingstones have happened. Despite no evidence, these two phenomenons may be the consequence of an evolution of the symbolic status of grindingstones between the beginning of the Linearbandkeramik in Central Europe to its late stages as they appear in north-western Europe. Grindingstone hoards may participate or be the expression of such an evolution.

A technical hypothesis

Among the first interpretations, a raw material storage has been proposed (Constantin *et al.* 1978). This hypothesis, in slight opposition with hoards codified and ritual feature, must be reexamined at the light of the technical clues observed. Several observations could be used to reinforce this hypothesis. At first, both lower and upper parts are deposited together, in a wish to preserve the integrity of the grinding system. Then, the working surfaces seem to have been object of great care, as they are always facing the ground or more rarely lying in position of work. The codified disposition of the tools may also be understood as a wish to preserve the working surfaces from any breaking or alteration. This position has at last often been observed in nowadays 'traditional' societies where grindingstones are still used: their lying face to the ground or to a wall corresponds to a wish of protection of the working surface from any spoil or any damage (Gast 1968; Champault 1991).

The state of tool working surfaces are linked with

several maintenance and use stages. Maintenance can be deduced from the repecking, even partial, of a working surface. Raw material optimisation is also obvious when the sides and ends of lowergrindingtools are deliberately broken, in order to change their general shape, enlarge their working surface or even modify the orientation of the working surface. We can also deduce from the few examples described above that tools are frequently reused or show multiple stages of use; these technical observations may be assimilated to a wish of enhancing as much as possible the duration of life of each blank and optimizing the investment put in the collecting of such blanks. The selected tools have entered a specific and certainly late cycle of maintenance and use, which may represent the main reason of their hoarding.

On the basis of these technical observations, grindingstone hoards may be reconsidered as a raw material reserve. The most 'functional' grindingtools may have been kept apart for further reuse, in a temporary cache. They may be kept in earth in order to enhance the properties of sandstone: this technic -still used by nowadays schist workers- may have been used by neolithic people, considering some engraved piles of schist circular sketch found in a Villeneuve-Saint-Germain bracelet workshop in Normandy (Marcigny *et al.* 1999). Following such hypothesis, hoards may be in relation with the house or building, where a 'craftman' could be speciliazed in the maintenance of grindingtools. Hoards may express a valorization of the know-how of a living or dead craftman, in charge of the maintenance of the grindingstones of the whole village for example. According to ethnographical datas, the number of grindingstones in a hoard overflows the number of grindingstones generally depending of one single house: no more than two or at most three lowergrindingstone tools are used at a time in the same house (Roux 1986; David 1998). Hoards may at last express an early sharing of the tasks, as one single person of the village could be in charge of the manufacturing and maintenance of the grindingstones of a whole village. The technical and functional features of hoards may finally be related to a social meaning.

Territoriality and agricultural identity

The systematical localisation of grindingstone hoards near danubian houses, and more generally, the domestic sphere, brought the first hypothesis of interpretation of this practice. Such hoards may evok a ritual of fundation or abandonment of the house, which would lead to a definitive act of hoarding (Constantin *et al.* 1978).

These hoards could be linked with a wish to signify the achievement of the building of one house or of the whole village. They may materialize the establishment of a new settlement for the community, or of a new house for one large family at the occasion of a 'wedding' for example. It could also be linked with the building of a new house dedicated to a specific collective purpose, in relation with the social organization (house dedicated to meetings or to women), the food procurement (storage, preparation of collective meal) or even a more religious function. At last, these hoards may be linked not with the buildings, but with the people: they may symbolize the specific status of its inhabitants, in relation to cereal procurement (Lindström-Holmberg 1998). Nonetheless, the archeological material found in lateral pits don't seem to be different from other lateral detritic pits. That's why we think, on the contrary, that they signify more the abandonment than the fundation of a house or a whole village. This idea is supported by one stratigraphical observation: in some cases, the pit or area dedicated to these hoards are installed, or digged, in former lateral pits. In such cases, hoards seem to happen after the complete filling of the lateral pit, that is to say long after the beginning of the occupation or even the abandonment of the house.

We can even go further in this hypothesis, and interpret hoards as a way to let a territorial print. As buried, these hoards can only have a symbolic, and non visible, charge and meaning. This type of deposit can express the colonization of a new territory by agricultural communities, who want to express by this act their new owning of the land. If we consider that this 'colonization' has happened on territories intially occupied and shared by mesolithic groups, we can imagine why grindingstones have been chosen among all objects. Grindingstones may symbolize three aspects of agricultural communities's new way of life: their high consumption of cultivated cereals, their sedentism and their technical innovations among which ceramic technology and polishing technics. This object also demonstrates a real attachment to the domestic area, which could be the reflect of a new social order.

All these data lead to an interpretation of these hoards in relation with the abandonment of their settlement by agricultural communities, who wanted to leave a meaningful trace of their settling in direction to contemporaneous hunting groups or agricultural communities. Besides, this hypothesis could explain the relatively high frequency of hoards in these regions, where the relationship between mesolithic and neolithic communities may have been more intense than in the heart of the Linearbandkeramik sphere.

Conclusion

Considering the quite scarcity of these hoards in neolithic contexts, we can underline the high symbolic value of the selected objects. At last, neolithic hoards concern the most symbolic tools and objects of theses agricultural societies, such as polished axes for the french middle Neolithic, and long pressignian blades for the late stages of Neolithic. All these objects can be assimilated both as the main technical innovations of each period and among the most significant tools for the exploitation of the environment and the development of the agricultural way of life.

This alternating could also be linked to a new social structuration and to new economical networks. Grindingstones hoards could symbolize a real attachment to the domestic cellar, as the economical and social base of social structuration. Axes hoards could express a higher rate of structuration of the society, relying more on the conquest of new lands and on the circulation (or even exchange) of productions. Long pressignian blades, which constituate a stage of sophistication and a high technicity level, may represent a new social order based on skillness and specific know-hows, annoucing the further change linked with the apparition of copper metalurgy.

Relying on tools and technical productions among the most meaningful and symbolically charged for each stage of the Neolithic, hoards could at last be an expression of Neolithic people's identities and social structuration.

References

ALLARD P., DUBOULOZ J., HACHEM L., ILETT M. et ROBERT B. 1995. Berry-au-Bac «le Vieux Tordoir»: la fin d'un grand sauvetage et la fouille d'un nouveau site rubané, *Les Fouilles Protohistoriques dans la Vallée de l'Aisne*, 23: 11-95.

ALLARD P., CONSTANTIN C., DUBOULOZ J., FARRUGGIA J-P., HACHEM L., ILETT M. 1996. Berry-au-Bac «le Vieux Tordoir» ultimes fouilles du site rubané, *Les Fouilles Protohistoriques dans la Vallée de l'Aisne*, 24: 7-54.

BRINK-KLOKE, H. & MEURERS–BALKE, J. 2003. Siedlungen und Gräberfeld am Oespeler Bach (Dortmund) – eine Kulturlandschaft im Wandel der Zeiten, *Germania* 81: 47-146.

CASPAR, J-P., CONSTANTIN, C., HAUZEUR, A., BURNEZ-LANOTTE, L. 1993. Nouveaux éléments dans le groupe de Blicquy en Belgique: le site de Vaux-et-Borset «Gibour» et «à la Croix Marie-Jeanne», *Helinium* XXXIII: 67-79.

CHAMPAULT D. 1991. La pierre qui dure. De quelques usages contemporains d'objets préhistoriques (Sahara, Yémen), *Techniques et culture 17-18. Préhistoire et ethnologie, le geste retrouvé*, Editions Maison des sciences de l'homme, Paris: 319-330.

CONSTANTIN C., FARRUGGIA J.-P., PLATEAUX M., DEMAREZ L. 1978. Fouille d'un habitat néolithique à Irchonwelz (Hainaut occidental), *Revue archéologique de l'Oise*, 13: 3-20.

DAVID N. 1998. The ethnoarcheology of grinding at Sukur, Adamawa state, Nigeria. *African review*, 15 (1): 13-63.

FARRUGGIA J-P. 1992. *Les outils et les armes en pierre dans le rituel funéraire du Néolithique danubien*, 581, BAR International Series, Oxford.

GAST M. 1968. *Alimentation des populations de l'Ahaggar. Etude ethnologique*. Mémoires du centre de recherche anthropologique, préhistorique et ethnologique VII, Paris.

HAMON C. 2003. De l'utilisation des outils de mouture, broyage et polissage au Néolithique en Bassin parisien: apports de la tracéologie, *Bulletin de la société préhistorique française*, 100 (1): 101-116.

HAMON C. 2006. *Broyage et abrasion au Néolithique ancien. Caractérisation technique et fonctionnelle de l'outillage en grès du Bassin Parisien*, BAR International Series 1551, Oxford, 342 p.

HAMON C. 2005. Quelle signification archéologique pour les dépôts de meules néolithiques dans la Vallée de l'Aisne ? in Auxiette G. et Malrain, F. dir., *Hommages à Claudine Pommepuy, N° spécial 22 de la Revue archéologie de Picardie*: 39-48.

HAMON C. & SAMZUN A. 2004 (a). Découverte d'un dépôt d'outils de mouture et de broyage daté du Néolithique ancien (culture Villeneuve-Saint-Germain récent v. 4700-4600 avant notre ère) à Saint-Denis « Rue du Landy » (Seine-Saint-Denis), *Bulletin de la société préhistorique française*, tome 101 (3): 611-613.

HAMON C. & SAMZUN A. 2004 (b). Une fosse Villeneuve-Saint-Germain final à Saint Denis « Rue du Landy »: un dépôt de meule inédit en Ile-de-France, *Internéo 4*:17-28.

ILETT M. & HACHEM L. 2001. Le village néolithique de Cuiry-lès-Chaudardes (Aisne, France), in GUILAINE J. dir., *Communautés villageoises du Proche Orient à l'Atlantique*, Errance, Paris: 171-184.

JADIN I. 2003. *Trois petits tours et puis s'en vont... la fin de la présence danubienne en moyenne Belgique*, ERAUL 109, Liège.

LIDSTRÖM-HOLMBERG C. 1998. Prehistoric grinding tools as metaphorical traces of the past, *Current swedish archeology* 6: 123-141.

MARCIGNY C., GUESQUIERE E., GIAZZON D., GAUME E. 1999. Un site de production de parures en schiste dans le nord du département de la Sarthe à Champfleur, «Bois de Barrée», *Bulletin de la société préhistorique française* 93 (3): 635-648.

PAVLU I. 2000. *Double querns, in Life on neolithic site, Bilany. Situational analysis of artefacts*, Académie des sciences tchèques, Prague: 73-98.

PRESTREAU M. 1992. Le site néolithique et protohistorique des Falaises de Prépoux à Villeneuve-la-Guyard (Yonne), *Gallia Préhistoire*, 34: 191-207.

ROUX V. 1986. *Le matériel de broyage. Etude ethnoarchéologique à Tichitt (R.I) Mauritanie*, Edition Recherches sur les civilisations, mémoire n° 58, Paris.

SPATZ H. 1999. *Die Mittelneolithische Gäberfeld von Trebur, Kreis Gross-Gerau. Materialen zur vor- u. frühgeschichte von Hessen* Band 19, Wiesbaden.

Acknowledgments

All my sincere acknowledgements go to Claude Constantin and Leonce Demarez who let me study the Hainaut material, to the team and the UMR 7041 of the CNRS for the study of the Aisne Valley hoards and to Anaïck Samzun in charge of Saint-Denis "rue du Landy" site.

Contact

Caroline Hamon
Post-doctorante
UMR 7041 ArScan
Protohistoire européenne
Maison de l'archéologie
21 allée de l'Université
92023 Nanterre cedex
France
caroline.hamon@mae.u-paris10.fr

NEOLITHIC DEPOSITIONS IN THE NORTHERN NETHERLANDS

Karsten WENTINK and Annelou van GIJN

Abstract:
The aim of the present paper is to explore the nature of the Dutch Middle Neolithic flint axe depositions and interpret these on a cultural level. These axes associated with the Funnel Beaker Culture are often retrieved from waterlogged places either single or as part of multiple object hoards. By means of a metrical, micro-wear and spatial analysis it will be demonstrated that these objects are remnants of a highly structured phenomenon that was practiced throughout the research area.

Samenvatting:
Het doel van het huidige artikel is een overzicht te geven van de Nederlandse midden-neolithische deposities en deze te interpreteren op een cultureel niveau. Deze bijlen, welke toegeschreven worden aan de Trechterbeker cultuur, zijn vooral gevonden in moerassige plekken, zowel alleen of als onderdeel van een meervoudig depot. Door middel van een metrische-, gebruikssporen-, en ruimtelijk-analyse zal worden aangetoond dat deze objecten onderdeel uitmaken van een uiterst gestructureerd fenomeen dat ten uitvoer werd gebracht in het gehele onderzoeksgebied.

Introduction

Already in the 19th century discoveries of groups of large axes puzzled those confronted with them. The fact that most were found in waterlogged places in particular formed the basis of speculation as to the nature of these objects. Surely people would not have been living in such inhospitable areas. Such axes were believed to represent hidden trade-goods, left there by merchants to be retrieved later. Or perhaps they were treasures hidden in times of trouble. A ritual explanation was only proposed, when all 'profane' explanations could be excluded. Presently such interpretations, so clearly devised by minds influenced by western capitalism, are widely dismissed (Fontijn 2002: 19). However until now, new studies focusing on the nature and interpretation of the Dutch Neolithic depositions remained absent.

The earliest intentional depositions known in the Netherlands were dated to the Late Mesolithic. These concerned pottery vessels that were buried in pits together with pieces of antler, bone and wood (Louwe Kooijmans 2001: 512). Although some other Early Neolithic finds are known that could be interpreted as intentional deposition, these are still a subject of debate (pottery vessel and red-deer antler from Bronneger (Louwe Kooijmans 2001: 112), three clusters of flint at Hoge Vaart (Hogestijn & Peeters 2001: 41).

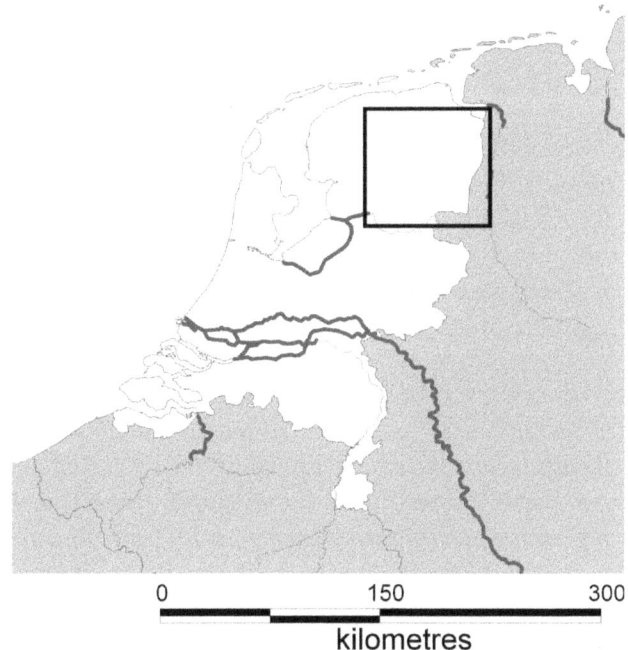

Fig. 1. Research area (black square).

It was not until the Middle Neolithic that depositional practices became more structured and common.
The focus of this paper will be the depositional practices associated with the Middle-Neolithic Funnel Beaker Culture (TRB - 3400-2850 cal. B.C.). The Dutch TRB (part of the TRB-Westgroup) has the advantage of a more or less restricted geographical distribution within the Netherlands, being mostly confined

to the northern half of the country. The most dense concentration of TRB finds however, are found on the Drenthe Plateau (fig. 1) located in the province of Drenthe (Bakker 1982). This till plateau was formed in the Saalian ice-age. In the Holocene period it was for the greater part surrounded by large peat areas of which the 'Bourtanger Bog' is one of the biggest in Europe. Although evidence of earlier TRB activity in Northern Germany concentrates in the wetlands formerly exploited by the Mesolithic predecessors (Midgley 1992: 311), the Dutch TRB finds from the large bogs are basically confined to peat track ways and finds of an alleged ritual character. As of yet no evidence is present to suggest that the bogs were actively exploited as part of the subsistence strategy by the TRB. Most settlements and megalithic tombs were located on the Drenthe Plateau. Although the till contains many large boulders that were used for the construction of the passage graves, it rarely contains good quality flint. This caused TRB people to be dependent on exchange contacts to acquire good quality flint axes, which were mainly produced in Northern Germany and Denmark. There is no evidence to suggest that high quality flint axes were locally produced (Beuker 2005: 277).

TRB flint axes share a very distinct technological feature; they are rectangular in cross-section, making them easily distinguishable from the oval axes made in the Atlantic tradition. The latter are predominantly found in the southern half of the Netherlands. Although some of these southern axes did reach the Plateau and were found in graves, they are completely absent from hoards (Bakker 1982: 95). The imported northern TRB axes, however, are found in numerous depositions containing either single or multiple objects that were retrieved from waterlogged places. It is the aim of the study to investigate and interpret this phenomenon of deposition on a cultural level. Do these remarkable finds from waterlogged places indeed reflect prehistoric ritual behaviour. If so, which patterns can be observed and how should these be interpreted? What was the life-history of these objects and how can these be linked to the lives of either individuals or groups? The present paper presents preliminary results of the Research Master thesis of the first author (Wentink 2006), and forms part of the second author's research project "The social significance of flint for Neolithic and Bronze Age communities"(Van Gijn *in prep.*). The compilation of the database, as well as the spatial and metrical analysis was performed by the first author, whereas the microwear analysis was done in cooperation.

The Dutch hoards, general patterns and interpretational framework

At present 20 multiple object hoards are known from the Netherlands containing multiple axes, rough-outs, flint nodules and other tools (Achterop 1960; Ter Wal 1996). Ter Wal has convincingly argued for the existence of single object hoards containing only one large axe deliberately placed in the peat (Ter Wal 1996). Furthermore, several other types of objects were placed in the peat in Neolithic times, such as horns of cattle, pottery vessels (probably containing foodstuffs) and disc-wheels. Although the former occurred during the TRB period, the depositing of disc-wheels is exclusively dated to the Single Grave Culture (SGC) (Van der Waals 1964).

Although several multiple object hoards consist of only 2 axes (n=7) most contain 3-5 axes (n=9) with only a few containing more. The latter however don't only consist of axes but also of flint nodules, long blades or other flint tools. Nine hoards, based on typology, can be placed in the TRB period and eight can be attributed to the subsequent SGC, the remaining three were unfortunately not of a distinguishable character (Achterop 1960; Ter Wal 1996). Many of the hoards were discovered during peat-cutting activities at the end of the 19th and beginning of the 20th century. Although many axes ended up in museum collections, contextual information is often of poor quality or completely lacking. Several objects were left in the field, lost, stolen or destroyed, and on one occasion the complete hoard was lost and is only known from 19th century written sources (see Pleyte 1882: 52). The reclamation of peat began as early as the 17th century and continued well into the mid 20th century. The fact that all known hoards have been found during the last 50 years of this reclamation one can only imagine what has been lost.

One of the problems in dealing with depositions and rituals is determining when a find should be considered as such. For a long time, researchers distinguished between several different categories of finds. Finds could be interpreted as hidden treasure, unretrieved traders stock, votive hoards, workshop hoards, etc. (Schuhmacher 1914). However, interpretations like these present us with a number of problems. How do we determine to which category our finds belong and more importantly, do these categories, which mainly reflect modern western logic, conform to prehistoric ones? The latter question in particular should be answered negatively. Before a find could be labeled as being 'ritual' one had first to dismiss any 'logical', profane interpretation. However, many anthropological sources have shown that profane and ritual are two things that are often intertwined and that no real distinction can be made between the two (Hermkens 2005; Hampton 1999; Stout 2002; Fontijn 2002).

When dealing with deposition Fontijn therefore proposes to abandon these outdated attempts to align prehistoric behaviour with our own categories and to look instead at patterns within aspects of the objects themselves and the context in which they are found (Fontijn 2002). Although Fontijn's research deals with Bronze Age depositions, this approach should be equally suitable for Neolithic depositions. If these finds reflect prehistoric ritual behaviour, there should be consistencies that are shared by all finds which are remnants of that ritual. These patterns might be reflected by the context in which the objects are found, namely deposition in a certain context and the lack thereof in others. Moreover, the use-life of these objects may display patterning such as originating from the same source, having had the same treatment before deposition or showing wear-traces of specific activities, or the lack thereof. In order to interpret selective deposition one should not just look at a single hoard or object, but at all the evidence and at the patterns this evidence brings to light. This applies not only to depots, but also for that matter, to any other type of archaeological data. Interpretation should therefore be based on these patterns and not on individual objects. The question whether or not a specific object is a ritual deposition therefore becomes less relevant and more dependent upon the entire material context from that place and period.

Sources & Methodology

Database
The main tool used to gain access to patterns and subsequent interpretations of depositional practices was the compilation of a database (MS Access) containing information on hoards, single finds and sites related to the TRB culture. The definition of a site here being a location where multiple finds, not related to a single act, were recovered, thus excluding multiple object hoards. Numerous sources were used for the compilation of the database. Site information was retrieved from literary sources and the Dutch National Archaeological Database (Archis) and included amongst others all known megalithic monuments, stone cists, TRB flat-graves, peat trackways, excavated settlements and many find-scatters. Object information was partly retrieved from literary sources and partly from museum collections. From the latter, axes were examined and contextual and metrical information was recorded. Sites or objects from the above sources were only incorporated when the find-location could be pinpointed with at least 2 km. Many of the older finds, for which only a rather vague description of the find-location was available were therefore ignored. Presently the database contains 1645 records, 1038 of which describe individual axes.

Micro-wear analysis
From the recorded objects 69 axes were selected for micro-wear and residue analysis. The axes of several multiple object hoards in the collection of the Drents Museum were part of a travelling exhibition and were therefore not available for this research. Axes from a variety of contexts were examined, among which objects from multiple object hoards, supposedly single object hoards, finds from megalithic tombs and a collection of stray finds. Two excavated TRB settlements were included; they contained no complete flint axes, only some axe fragments (Van Gijn, *in prep.*).

The selected sample has been subjected to residue and use-wear analysis at the Laboratory for Artefact Studies, Leiden University. For the analysis a stereo-microscope (magnifications 10-160x) and an incident light microscope (magnifications 100-500x) were used. The incident light microscope used was attached to an adjustable stand, thus enabling high-power functional analysis on large objects. Photographs were taken with a Nikon DXM1200 digital camera. With the aid of the stereo-microscope a general survey of the object was carried out and obvious traces of residue located. For examination with the incident light microscope some objects were partially cleaned with alcohol to remove finger grease after the absence of potential residue was attested using both microscopes. Phenomena such as edge-removals, rounding, polish, striations and residues were recorded (Van Gijn 1990). Comparison of recorded phenomena with experimentally used tools led to the interpretation of the object's functional life. The aim of the residue and micro-wear analysis was to obtain information on the use of flint axes in general and also to gain information on the use-life of individual axes.

Spatial analysis

For each object or site in the database coordinates (Netherlands National System) were recorded, making it possible to plot them onto a series of maps using the GIS software MapInfo (Version 7.0). The records were combined with cartographical information including geological maps, soil maps, historical maps, land-use maps and a detailed digital elevation model of the province of Drenthe (AHN). Of many of the objects in the database only an approximate find location was known. For this reason an additional variable was added to each set of coordinates, describing the accuracy of the record. This could vary from an accuracy in the range of 1-10 m, 10-100 m, 100-1000 m or more than 1 km. The latter could only be used to give an approximate overview of find distributions. The aim of the analysis was to obtain information on the relation between sites and finds and also to investigate their relation to the landscape.

Metrical analysis

General observations

The most conventional way of studying stone or flint axes is by means of a metrical analysis. Ter Wal carried out an extensive metrical analysis on a sample of 433 axes from the Drents Museum in Assen and concluded that it appears that axes from a wet context are generally much larger than those from a dry context (Ter Wal 1996). Although the current dataset is much larger, the patterns are similar to Ter Wal's observations. At present the database contains records of 1038 axes, these however cannot all be used in a metrical analysis. The older find descriptions in particular do not contain detailed metrical information about the axe, and in the light of the nature of this research it would take too much time to measure all available axes manually. Also a number of axes had to be dismissed from the analysis due to their being incomplete. For the variable 'length' 789 axes could be used in the analysis which is 76% of the total number of axes in the database and can therefore be seen as a representative number.

As can be seen in table 1, both stone and flint axes are similar in terms of length, although stone axes tend to be a bit larger with the exception of a few extremely large flint axes. However axes of different lengths they are not evenly distributed over the landscape. Axes from dry contexts are generally smaller than the average 128 mm, while axes from wet or border contexts are larger than average. Flint axes from border contexts (i.e. transition zones from dry to wet places) are almost double the length of the average. It is precisely this context from where most multiple object hoards seem to originate. The problem here is that many older finds are often only described as coming from the peat whereas their vertical position relative to the underlying sand is not mentioned. This vertical position is of interest as the peat gradually grew over time, making the contemporary land-peat border unrepresentative of the Neolithic situation. Depositing an object at the edge of the peat would mean that the axes would be positioned near the underlying sand, which would subsequently be covered by a layer of peat up to several meters thick. In the cases where the vertical position is mentioned, it is clear that these axes are often found in, on or near the underlying sand. This suggests that at the time they were deposited at the edge of the peat, something that is also observed in Denmark (Tilley 1996: 101).

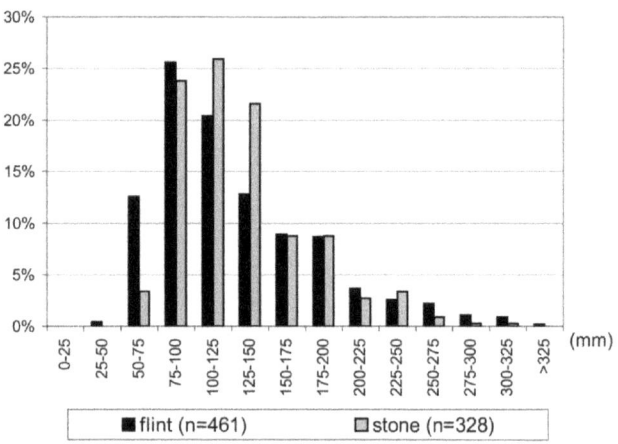

Fig. 2. Frequencies of length relative to raw material.

It should be noted that the observed length of the axes represents the end-stage of the 'life' of each individual axe (marginalizing lost axes). The number of discarded flint axes, as can be seen in figure 2, shows a gradual increase as length decreases, with a peak in the 75-100 mm range. Stone axes however show a more extreme pattern of discarding which already starts in the 125-150 mm range, to peak at the 100-

context material	dry n	Av.length	wet n	Av.length	border n	Av.length	total n	Av.length
stone	19	115	27	142	19	143	328	130
flint	51	102	57	153	25	229	461	127
total	70	105	84	149	44	192	789	128

Table 1: Number and average length of stone and flint axes from varying geological contexts.

125 mm range. While a fair number of flint axes are still used into the 50-75 mm range, stone axes in that range are virtually absent. It seems that stone axes are discarded slightly bigger than flint axes. For this pattern a functional explanation can be offered.

Olausson showed, with the aid of experiments, that the main difference in usage between flint and stone axes lies in the configuration of their edges and inherent qualities of the raw material (Olausson 1983). A flint axe blade is generally sharper and thinner resulting in a deeper penetration with each blow, making it more suitable for fine carpentry. Stone axes have a blunter edge, but their raw material is less susceptible to damage. This, together with the total weight of the tool makes it more suitable for heavy work. Reduced length and therefore weight of the stone axe has a negative effect upon its effectiveness as a tool. With flint axes it is predominantly the sharp edge which makes the tool functional, resulting in an overall pattern of slightly bigger discarded stone axes relative to the flint axes whose effectiveness is less linked with tool length or weight.

TRB axes

The dataset used above reflects a palimpsest situation as no distinction has been made between axes belonging to different cultures or periods. In fact this is quite difficult to do since many axes cannot be attributed to a specific Neolithic culture apart from the larger axes - the imported objects - which can often be assigned to either the TRB or SGC. The smaller - locally produced - axes do not have any defining characteristics. As they were produced from poor quality flint, the raw material defined to a greater degree the eventual shape of the artefact. This local flint was moreover transported by the Saalian glaciers from Denmark and Northern Germany to the Netherlands. Therefore the local raw material itself, although of poor quality, is indistinguishable from the raw material used for the production of the imported axes. Based on the nature of the local raw material, Bakker has suggested 150 mm being the maximum length of locally produced axes (Bakker 1979). If we only consider axes attributed to the TRB, we find they are predominantly large (>150 mm), imported axes (52,5%) while these form only 26,9% of the total dataset. From the axes smaller than 150 mm 25,9% come from a grave context, while from the total database only 9,5% of the axes smaller than 150 mm come from graves. This means that among the axes attributed to the TRB culture both axes from graves and the large imported axes are over-represented. This is reflected in figure 3 displaying two distinct peaks. There are however clear patterns within this dataset that are not influenced by the over-representation of these groups.

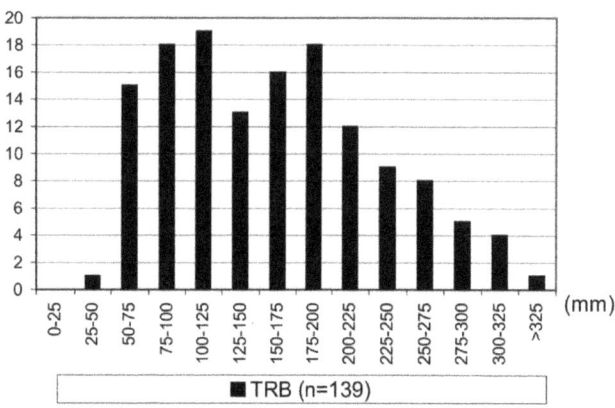

Fig. 3. Frequencies of TRB dated axes per length group.

- Grave context

Ter Wal noted that TRB axes from graves are much smaller than those derived from wet contexts (Ter Wal 1996). When plotting the relative distribution of axes from grave contexts per length group this becomes particularly clear as can be seen in figure 4.

It is evident that we can speak of a very selective distribution. Virtually all axes are below the 150 mm line which according to Bakker separates imported axes from locally produced axes (Bakker 1979). When examining the individual axes from grave contexts, it

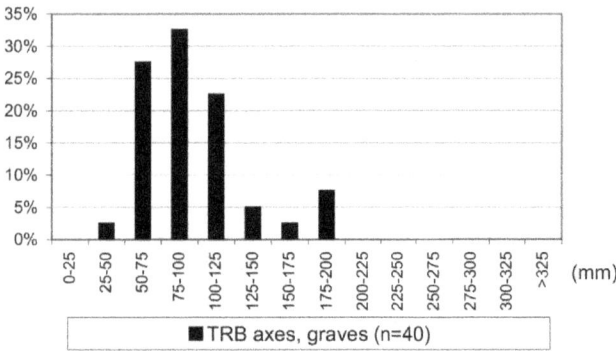

Fig. 4. Relative distribution of TRB axes from grave contexts per length group.

can be seen that many were indeed locally produced, however a number may have been worn-down remnants of imported axes. These imported axes often radically changed shape, as they were resharpened and repaired (Bradley & Edmonds 1993: 48). It is however virtually impossible to distinguish between these two groups. The overall character of this find-group suggests that predominantly, if not exclusively, used, worn axes accompanied the dead in their graves, something that will be elaborated upon below in the section dealing with the results of the micro-wear analysis.

- *Wet context*

According to the explanation presented above in section 4.1, the majority of the axes was discarded when their decreased length/weight-ratio began to counter tool effectiveness. However, a number of axes also entered the archaeological record while being still long enough to be effective (ca. 26% of the total number of axes were longer than 150 mm). This can partly be explained by people losing axes, something that would undoubtedly have occurred every now and then and which is also witnessed in anthropological contexts (White & Modjeska 1978). This, however, does not explain the presence of the more extreme cases. With the extremely large axes there is the question of functionality. Especially with flint axes the risk of breakage (due to end-shock) increases when the axe blade is longer. A hypothesis therefore might be that many flint axes exceeding the length of 200 mm were not functional, due to the imminent risk of end-shock, but also because of practical reasons related to hafting. The fact that most axes found in hoards are of extreme length (>250 mm) and in mint condition might indicate that they never served as functional tools (as usage would cause an axe to wear down). This can also be substantiated by the results of the use-wear analysis, the detailed results of which are presented below, showing that none of the axes examined longer than 218 mm displayed traces of use. Further evidence as to the non-functional role of these large axes can be found when examining the find context from which they were derived.

In figure 5 it can be seen that although a number of smaller axes was also retrieved from waterlogged places, these form only a very small proportion of the total number of axes. It is striking however that the largest axes are found almost exclusively in wet contexts (finds from border contexts are included here). This would suggest that more practical reasons generally pertain to the discard of small flint axes. The extremely large axes, however, are only found deposited in wet contexts suggesting the need for a ritual rather than a secular explanation for discard.

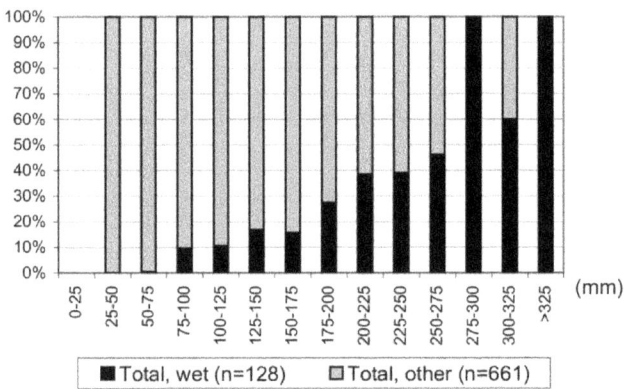

Fig. 5. Distribution of all axes from wet contexts relative to axes from other or unknown contexts.

The production of tools of extreme sizes meant for non-functional purposes is a phenomenon that is also encountered in ethnographical context. In the Kimberley region of northwestern Australia, so-called Kimberly points were manufactured. Some points were specially produced for exchange purposes. These points could be recognized as such by their being much larger than the normal, functional points (Akerman, Fullagar & Van Gijn 2002: 18). Another example comes from Malinowski (Malinowski 1961: 88) who reports the following concerning arm-shells associated with the Kula-exchange:

«[...] *by far the greater number of the arm-shells, easily ninety per cent, are of too small a size to be worn even by young boys and girls. A few are so big and valuable that they would not be worn at all, except once in a decade by a very important man on a very festive day.*»

Manipulation of size can thus be regarded as a powerful strategy to emphasize the special status of an object, and by doing so it is placed apart from conventional, profane tools.

For any Neolithic person, who would have been intimately familiar with the use of flint axes, it would have been clear-cut that the extremely large axes would shatter upon impact, when put to functional use. Their size placed them apart from functional life, an assumption which is being substantiated by the lack of use-wear traces and the almost exclusiveness of these objects having been deposited in wet places. We must also keep in mind the fact that these axes were not locally produced, but would have traveled 200-400 km before reaching the Netherlands. The lack of use-wear would therefore also prove that during the 'life' of the axe, which would undoubtedly have involved exchange and transport, at no time was the axe put to a functional use. It also suggests that the flint-knapper who created the axe, knew upon producing it that the axe had no functional purpose, a characteristic that was also recognized and respected by all people (owners?) that stood between the flint-knapper and the person/group depositing the axe 200-400 km down-the-line. Apparently some axes were solely produced for non-functional purposes and ended their lives being deposited in waterlogged places. We may therefore conclude that these axes were produced for ceremonial rather than functional purposes and also circulated in this sphere. Something that would further substantiate this interpretation, but which is not mentioned so far, is the presence of unpolished axes in the Netherlands.

Among the imported axes there are 27 specimens which can be dated to the TRB period that are either completely unpolished or partly polished, leaving the cutting edge unpolished. These unpolished axes form a well-known part of many multiple object hoards known from The Netherlands and are also often found in wet contexts with no accompanying finds. When inspected for the presence of use-wear, no traces of use were found on any of these objects. The lack of micro-wear traces, together with the find context indicates that they should be seen in the same light as the extremely large axes.

As can be seen in figure 6 the unpolished axes represent about 30-40% of the imported axes. Besides extreme length a way to clearly distinguish them from

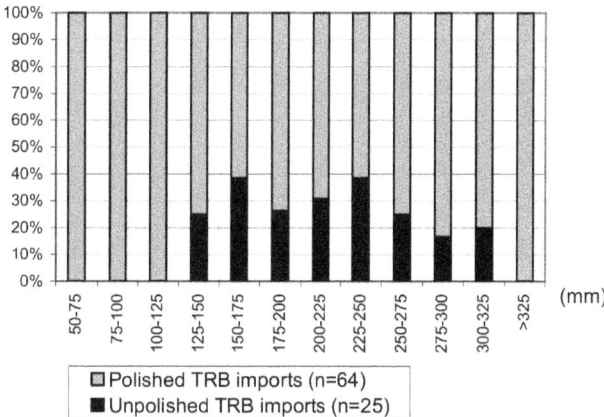

Fig. 6. Relative distribution of unpolished TRB imported axes compared to polished imported axes.

functional tools, would have been by not polishing them. This is further emphasized by some axes which are partially polished with exception of the cutting edge. The fact that all of the unpolished axes came form wet locations, lacked traces of use and were often of extreme lengths all indicate that these represent a group of axes that has never been meant for usage but were specially produced of ceremonial rather that functional-related activities. They further illustrate the fact that these ceremonial axes were not tempered with. After production their physical form was not altered.

At the production centers in Northern Germany or Denmark axes were produced specially for ceremonial (exchange) purposes. There were different ways in which it could be made visually apparent that these axes should be placed apart from the functional axes. Axes could be made to such a size they would be totally unpractical, or they could be circulated in unfinished form. Often the latter would have been partially polished with the exception of the cutting edge emphasizing the fact that they weren't meant for functional use. These axes traveled vast distances to reach the Netherlands without ever having been put to use. Moreover these axes ended their lives of exchange in waterlogged places, where they were deposited either as a single object or as part of a multiple object hoard.

Microwear and residue analysis

Introduction
The 69 objects selected came from different collections and included finds from the National Museum

of Antiquities in Leiden, The Groninger Museum in Groningen, the Drents Museum in Assen and objects currently in private ownership. The sample mostly contained flint objects and predominantly axes (59 axes, 2 chisels, 7 blades and one scraper) from several different contexts. Of the 69 objects 19 were grave finds coming from megalithic tombs, 13 were single finds (including both 'stray finds' and objects generally interpreted as single object hoards) and 37 objects were part of multiple object hoards. The axes were of differing taphonomical quality. Some axes showed signs of patination, which could to some extent influence micro-wear analysis. Moreover, many axes had been part of museum collections, sometimes for over a hundred years. The mere handling of these objects could have obscured old traces and possibly caused new traces to develop. Also a variety of recent residues were encountered including such things as white paint, ink, nail polish, and glue. Sometimes the total lack of dirt residues indicated that the objects had been well cleaned, possibly also leading to the removal of potentially present prehistoric residues.

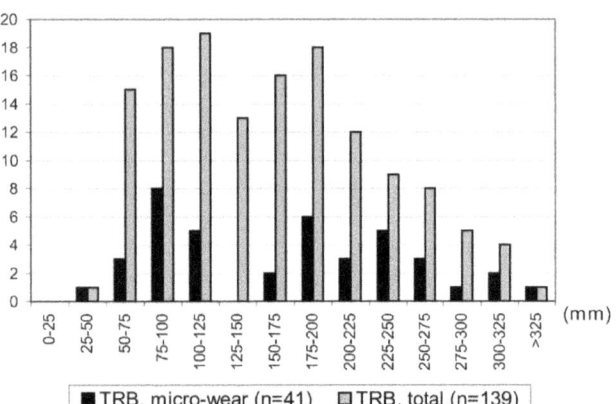

Fig. 7. Numbers of TRB flint axes selected for micro-wear analysis and to total number of TRB flint axes per length group.

The micro-wear analysis embraced axes from both TRB and SGC context. In the light of the present paper only results of the TRB axes (n=41) will be reported. The results of the analysis concerning SGC axes and their relation to the TRB axes are reported elsewhere (Wentink 2006). When plotting the length of the TRB axes selected for micro-wear analysis relative to the total number of TRB flint axes in each length group, it can be seen in figure 7 that axes from nearly each group were present in the analysis. Although the focus of the research lay with the large axes coming from supposed ritual contexts (single finds from waterlogged places, multiple object hoards and unpolished pieces), the sample also contained some of the smaller axes that were analyzed for comparative purposes.

General patterns

Use-traces were not equally present on all examined length groups. No TRB axe larger than 215 mm appeared to have traces of use. It is posited that a functional cut-off point lies around this mark. The fact that the largest SGC axe with use traces is 218mm long appears to substantiate this assumption. Many of the axes with use-traces showed clearly developed use polish which overlies the traces of grinding. Moreover rounding and micro-retouch were present indicating usage. Although on some occasions a clear polish was present which indicated wood working, often exact interpretation on contact-material level was not possible. This is most probably related to the fact that axes were used for all kinds of activities and not solely for the working of one contact-material. On occasion an axe showed traces of resharpening prior to deposition, especially in grave contexts. With the aid of the microscope differences within the grinding-traces could be observed as indicative of the use of different grindstones. These differences were often accompanied by slight differences in the grinding angle and thus interpreted as being the result of secondary resharpening of the axe. Traces of hafting could be observed in the form of friction gloss, and on occasion black residue (possibly remnants of birch-tar) could be identified.

Grave context

As was already mentioned the overall character of axes coming from grave contexts could be typified as small and seemingly worn down. This is corroborated by the results of the use-wear analysis. In total the database contains records of 54 TRB axes coming from grave contexts. Of these, eighteen objects were examined for the presence of use-traces, which is 33.3% of the complete sample. The axes came from three different passage graves (D19 Drouwen, D5 Zeyen, and G2 Glimmen). Of the eighteen axes, sixteen could be positively described as having been used, as can be seen in table 2. The remaining two were classified as unsure, since it appeared that post depositional processes had obscured possible traces of use, not definitely excluding the possibility that they in fact were used.

contexts	use yes	used unsure	total	resharpened yes	no	unsure	total
D19	12	1	13	8	4	1	13
D5	1	-	1	1	-	-	1
G2	3	1	4	1	3	-	4
total (n)	16	2	18	10	7	1	18
total (%)	88.9	10.1	100	55.6	38.9	5.6	100

Table 2: Micro-wear traces per context.

Although the majority of the axes appear to have been used, also a fair number of these were resharpened before deposition. In these cases, the cutting-edge predominantly displayed only very fresh-looking traces of polishing. However inside deeper negatives (caused by use) that remained untouched by the grindstone, use-polish could still be seen. Also on some occasions the angle used for resharpening had left the extreme edge of the axe intact including use-traces in the form of use-polish, rounding and edge-damage. Besides actual use-traces the majority of these axes (72,2%) also displayed traces of hafting. The axe from tomb D5 showed minor traces of red ochre on its cutting-edge, something that will be elaborated upon below.

It can be concluded that used axes predominantly accompanied the dead in the graves. This is also supported by the overall worn character and minimal length of axes from grave context. The resharpening of the axes seems to indicate that many were prepared for use to make sure that the deceased was accompanied by a sharp axe that was ready for use. These axes could very well have belonged to the deceased in life, therefore being intimately linked to the person who owned them. They would have been used during the clearing of fields and the construction of houses. Moreover these small axes would have often started out as being much larger, however each time the axe was resharpened their length decreased. It is therefore not improbable that axes like these were the possessions of specific people for many years.

Depositions

In an attempt to isolate finds of a potential ritual character fourteen axes coming from multiple object hoards were examined for the presence of use traces. Moreover nine single finds of large axes were selected solely upon the appearance of the axe, being either unpolished or much larger than average. For two of these axes it was known that they came from wet contexts, of the remaining seven no detailed contextual information was known, making it as yet impossible to determine whether or not these could have been deposited axes. However a very homogeneous image emerged while performing the analysis. With the exception of three single find axes, all artefacts appeared to show no traces of use. Some other quite interesting traces were found instead.

On 13 of the 20 remaining axes very clear wear-traces were found. They appeared to be caused by friction with a rather soft material, possibly hide or bark, perhaps a combination of the two. Interesting however was the overall presence of this polish. All ridges, cutting-edge and higher ribs (of the unpolished axes) displayed this gloss. Due to the overall presence of the gloss it was interpreted as having been caused by a material in which the object was wrapped in an as yet not identified material. This is not unthinkable since the axes originated some 200-400 km from Drenthe making it highly plausible that during transport the axe was wrapped in a soft material to protect it from damage. Another explanation is that since these unused axes were deposited in wet contexts, they also played a ceremonial role prior to deposition. This could have involved the object being wrapped in a certain material and being unwrapped on special occasions for display purposes, an activity that is also witnessed in ethnographic context in the New Guinea Highlands (Hampton 1999) and in Northern Australia (Akerman, Fullagar and Van Gijn 2002). Although it is impossible to tell exactly what happened, both explanations seem plausible, given the context and origin of these axes. Axes for which contextual information was available and which displayed these traces, came exclusively from wet contexts.

These traces were also witnessed on some single find axes, for which no contextual information was recorded. This might indicate that they could very well have had the same biography as those for which contextual information was present, suggesting that they would also have been deposited in wet contexts.

Another interesting phenomenon encountered while examining these axes was the presence of a red residue on over 65% of the axes (table 3), identified as being red ochre by means of X-ray powder diffraction (Dik, in Wentink 2006). The ochre seems predominantly located on the cutting-edge of the axes and was especially well preserved on the unpolished axes, probably due to taphonomic reasons. On some occasions only small fragments of red residue were encountered, however, on most axes clear traces of ochre were present all along the cutting edge. The residue was not accompanied by use-traces, which would have been the case if these axes were involved in some sort of contact with unprocessed ochre. It can thus be concluded that the ochre most probably was applied as a pigment paste.

In the preceding section it has already been argued that some axes were produced solely for ceremonial purposes. This is substantiated by the fact that the axes do not show traces of use and moreover, often do show traces of being wrapped in a soft material. Another feature that distinguished these 'ceremonial' axes was the presence of a red pigment on the cutting edge, further emphasizing the fact that these axes were not meant for usage.

Spatial analysis

Introduction
For the spatial analysis relatively few data could be used, as often objects cannot be dated to a specific culture. As mentioned before, Late-Neolithic axes are virtually indistinguishable from TRB axes, especially when it comes to the locally produced specimens. Plotting all Neolithic axes on a map would therefore result in a palimpsest in which all potential patterns would be obscured. However, when we only plot TRB dated axes, we will inevitably only see either axes coming from secure TRB contexts (mostly graves) or the large imported flint axes, which are predominantly interpreted as being ritual in character. Although we can look for patterns within the distribution of these large TRB axes, it is hardly possible to compare this with the distribution of the small, used axes, found outside graves. We know for a fact that at least a proportion of these small used axes were retrieved from wet contexts. This could indicate intentional deposition, however, since we do not know the dates of these axes, they cannot be used for interpretational purposes as to TRB cultural behaviour.

Based on the observations described above, the following characteristics can be presented to identify objects that are likely candidates of selective deposition:

- Specimens longer than 218 mm (this being the largest used flint axe from the sample selected for micro-wear analysis).
- Unpolished specimens longer than 150 mm.
- Presence of red ochre residue on cutting edge.
- Lack of use traces, but presence of traces of packing/transport.
- Found together in a hoard with other objects that conform to either of the above stated characteristics.

All objects in the database have been reviewed with the above characteristics in mind. Objects were individually evaluated, to decide whether or not they should be interpreted as an intentional deposition. Most objects labeled as intentionally deposited

treatment find type	polished yes	polished no	ochre yes	ochre no	used yes	used no	packing/ transport yes	packing/ transport no	context wet	context unknown
hoard (n=14)	8	6	7	7	1	13	8	6	12	2
single (n=9)	4	5	8	1	3	6	5	4	2	7
total (n)	12	11	15	8	4	19	13	10	14	9
total (%)	52.2	47.8	65.2	34.8	17.4	82.6	56.5	53.5	60.9	39.1

Table 3. Different treatments per find type.

conformed to more than one of the above mentioned characteristics. Objects that scored positive on the presence of ochre or presence of traces of packing/transport were only selected if they also scored on any of the other characteristics. Objects that were longer than 218mm, unpolished or coming from a multiple object hoard were automatically selected. This method resulted in the selection of 55 axes belonging to 36 depots, which could be interpreted as being of a potential ceremonial character.

Natural landscape of depositions

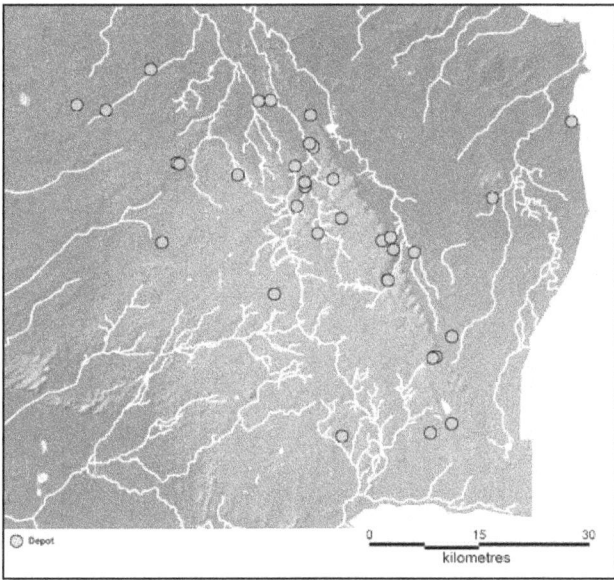

Fig. 8. Spatial Distribution of TRB depots on the Drenthe Plateau.

When the 36 depots that were selected as likely candidates of selective deposition were spatially plotted, a clear pattern emerged. When examining the spatial distribution it is striking to see that virtually all selected axes are located in stream-valleys that would have been filled up with peat (see fig. 8). It was already noted that many hoards with contextual information were found near the border of the peat, however in Drenthe peat-growth was common in many different places. The obvious lack of selected axes in the most extensive raised bogs such as the Bourtanger Bog, must therefore be noted. Depositions only seem to occur here in the direct vicinity of an intersecting stream.

Axes dated to the TRB but which were not included in the selection, showed a far more diverse distribution pattern. These were present in all zones, including the higher grounds where they are found between the megaliths and find scatters of a potential domestic nature (hardly any settlement has been excavated). Also a high proportion of TRB axes between 150 mm and 218 mm appeared to be located in the stream valleys possibly suggesting that these also concern deposited objects. This group therefore would be an interesting subject for further research. The same applies to many of the TRB battle axes that have gone unmentioned so far, but were also often found in stream valleys. Virtually no contextual research has been carried out for this group in the Netherlands. It is however known from Denmark that battle-axes appear in a variety of ritual contexts, such as at enclosures (buried in pits with pottery and flint axes at Sarup), or as part of multiple object hoards (Midgley 1992, 245; Skaarup 1990, 86; Tilley 1996, 101).

The stream valleys in which the selected axes were found formed predominantly in the Pleistocene, when at the end of the Saalian ice-age streams of meltwater eroded their way through the newly formed till plateau (Spek 2004: 203). In the Weichselian these valleys were deepened and widened. However at the end of the Weichselian the valleys were blocked by large deposits of cover-sands, resulting in the formation of large strings of small bogs and fens (Spek 2004: 203; Kuijer 1991: 23). Due to the Holocene rise in groundwater-levels (as a result of rising sea-levels) these obstructions eventually eroded and streams re-emerged. During the Atlantic, sea-levels continued to rise causing the streams to become more stable and stimulated peat growth in the stream valleys (Kuijer 1991: 23). This would have resulted in a situation during the Middle-Neolithic in which the lower parts of the valleys would be the domain of peat growth and would be flooded during winter. The lack of clear wood-remains indicate a fairly open landscape with only few trees, in contrast to the higher grounds on which a dense forest was present (Spek 2004: 209; Bakker 1982: 114). A number of depots are located near the starting point of a stream while others are found further downstream in the valleys. Within these valleys the depots are predominantly found at the border of the peat, which would have been the most practical position since then the person(s) depositing the axes would not have to enter the potentially dangerous peat zone.

Although archaeologists usually focus upon the peat itself in their explanations, Neolithic people did not necessarily do the same thing. As many depots are located at the transitional point in these valleys between the lower peat and the higher sands, the latter may potentially be equally important.

At some locations on the higher grounds in the valleys, non-permeable layers of sediment (till, loam) were present beneath the sand. It is known that in historical times at these places water would seep from the ground. These places should have been recognized by people from obvious differences in local vegetation (oak/birch forest) (Spek 2004: 206). It is impossible to predict exactly where these places would have been located in the Neolithic (due to highly variable groundwater-levels and local geology). Also groundwater levels would have been influenced by the dense forest on the higher grounds, which would have caused high evaporation rates, thus lowering groundwater levels (Spek, pers. comm.). It is striking, however, that most of the hoards in the stream valleys are located on a soil type that would be expected in the above scenario. Together with the observation that part of the hoards are located at the beginning of streams we might envisage that people were depositing items at places where water would emerge from the ground. These places would not have been clear wells, however, historical sources indicate the existence of specific names to describe such places from the Middle Ages onwards (Spek 2004: 206). This indicates that people did recognize such places and could attribute special meaning to them. At this point it is unfortunately impossible to prove such a scenario, as it would require the exact find location of each depot and also detailed geological information of that find spot. Since the first is generally lacking the latter is impossible to gather. The point being made however is that we should not solely focus on the peat as being of prime importance. For some hoards for which detailed contextual information is present, it is clearly stated that finds were retrieved from the sand, near the peat and not from the peat itself. Furthermore the rise in groundwater-levels caused the peat to grow and to cover areas that in the Neolithic would have been sand. Therefore axes recovered during peat digging or during other activities on the land that would formerly have been covered with peat, were not necessarily deposited in the peat but might well have been engulfed by it during later times.

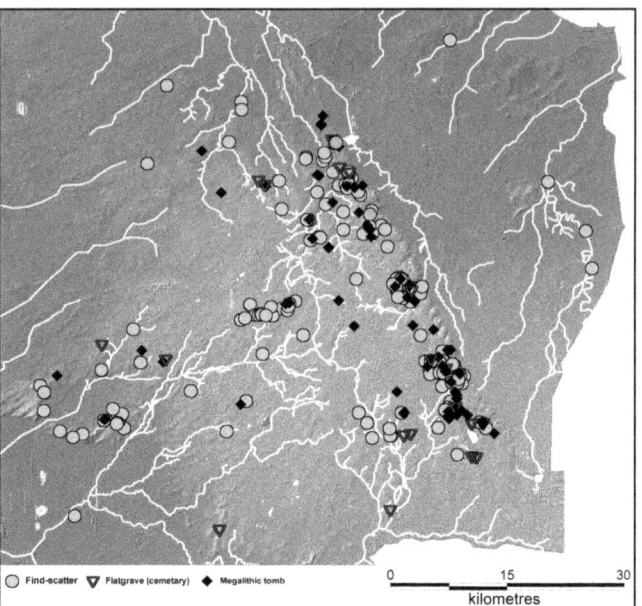

Fig. 9. Spatial distribution of TRB sites on the Drenthe Plateau.

Cultural landscape of depositions

The spatial distribution of the 36 selected depots conformed very well to the overall distribution of TRB sites, depicted in figure 9. For Denmark it was noted that half of the hoards were found within close proximity (500-1500 m) to megalithic graves (Midgley 1992: 282). This also appears to be the case in the Netherlands as clearly many locations can be found where a depot was located close to a megalithic tomb, but also proximity to flat-graves can be noted. Many flat-graves will not have been discovered, due to their naturally obscured nature. It could very well be possible that hoards that do not conform to these observations are instead located in proximity to undiscovered flat-graves.

About half of the depots (53%) could be found within a range of 600-1900 m from the nearest grave. Although this suggests a link between the two it also indicates a separation since no depot was found less than 600 m from a grave. This is in contrast to many of the find-scatters, possibly remnants of settlements, which are located within 500 m of a grave. By no means should this be interpreted as settlements being located near graves. Many find-scatters are found isolated in the landscape with no indication as to the presence of nearby graves. It does however imply that it was apparently not considered problematic to locate a settlement within 500 m from a tomb (or vice versa, assuming these find-scatters represent settlements), whereas all depots were kept well outside this range. Depots occurred relatively near graves, however at the same time a certain distance was maintained between the two.

Although the objects deposited are of a non-local origin the practice of depositing however is very much a local affair. Appropriate places where depositions took place were selected in close range of places of burial and habitation. Habitation and tomb-construction primarily took place on the higher grounds of the Drenthe Plateau. The places selected for deposition at the transition from marshes to the higher, dry grounds are therefore of a liminal nature. On the one hand these stream-valleys will have been perceived as natural boundaries between social groups as well as boundaries between people and supernatural entities (Fontijn 2002: 265). On the other hand, the higher grounds were densely forested. The many stream valleys would therefore have played an important role in water transport, thus connecting social groups. On a physical level these places can therefore be perceived as clear-cut divisions between the higher habitable grounds and the natural waterlogged stream valleys. On a cultural level these places can both be perceived as boundaries separating social groups, but at the same time also as places binding social groups.

Conclusion

The present paper set out to report the preliminary results of the research currently being carried out. Interpretation of the role these axes played within their cultural context will be the aim of further study, which will be reported upon in future publications. We can therefore conclude here with the observations that flint axes played an important role in TRB cosmology/ideology. The axes that were found in depots were probably used in rituals or ceremonies. They were kept apart from functional tools at all stages of their lives. They were specially produced and were exchanged over vast distances. These axes would often have been visually set apart from other axes by their size or by being unpolished. This separation was further emphasized by red pigments (ochre), located near the cutting-edge of the axe. During transport they would have been packed in soft material to protect them from damage. It is unfortunately impossible to tell the exact role these axes played during ceremonies and rituals. Their biographies however ended when they were deposited near the edge of the peat in one of the numerous stream valleys present on the Drenthe Plateau. Although these places were located near the places of burial and habitation, at the same time an appropriate distance between the two was observed. By doing so it was clearly emphasized again and again, that these objects had to be placed apart from profane, functional objects.

Together with the very consistent micro-wear patterns involving traces of packing or wrapping and the residue of red ochre, the spatial patterns seem to suggest the existence of a well-defined ritual. These depositions occur over the entire Drenthe Plateau, indicating that this ritual was widely adopted and performed by the TRB people. The fact that these axes were specially produced for ceremonial or ritual practices combined with the fact that they are found deposited in wet places over so vast an area of Northern Europe, seems to indicate that this ritual is closely intertwined with TRB cosmology/ideology. It would therefore be fascinating to extent this analysis to the deposited axes from Germany and Denmark. This would provide information about the homogeneity as well the local nuances of this ritual.

References

ACHTEROP S.H., 1960. Een depot van vuurstenen bijlen bij Reest, *Nieuwe Drentse Volksalmanak*: 179-89.

AKERMAN K. FULLAGAR R. & VAN GIJN A., 2002. Weapons and wunan: production, function and exchange of Kimberley points, *Australian Aboriginal Studies* 1: 13-42.

BAKKER J.A., 1979. *The TRB west group : studies in the chronology and geography of the makers of hunebeds and Tiefstich pottery*, PhD thesis Amsterdam.

BAKKER J.A., 1982. TRB Settlement Patterns on the Dutch Sandy Soils, *Analecta Praehistorica Leidensia* 15: 87-124.

BRADLEY R. & EDMONDS M. (eds.), 1993. *Interpreting the axe trade. Production and exchange in Neolithic Britain*, Cambridge: Cambridge University Press.

BEUKER J., 2005. Aanvoer uit alle windstreken - Stenen bijlen in Noord-Nederland, in Louwe Kooijmans L.P. Van den Broeke P.W. Fokkens H. & Van Gijn A. (eds.), *Nederland in de Prehistorie*, Amsterdam: Bert Bakker, 277-80.

FONTIJN D.R., 2002. *Sacrificial Landscapes Cultural biographies of persons, objects and 'natural' places in the Bronze Age of the Southern Netherlands, C. 2300-600 B.C.*, PhD thesis Leiden (Analecta Praehistorica Leidensia 33/34).

HAMPTON O.W., 1999. *Culture of Stone - Sacred and Profane Uses of Stone among the Dani*, Texas (Texas A&M University Anthropology Series; n° 2).

HERMKENS A.K., 2005. *Engendering objects. Barkcloth and the Dynamics of Identity in Papua New Guinea*, PhD thesis Nijmegen.

HOGESTIJN J.W.H. & PEETERS J.H.M. (eds.), 2001. *De mesolithische en vroeg-neolithische vindplaats Hoge Vaart-A27 (Flevoland) – Deel 20 Op de grens van land en water: jagers-vissers-verzamelaars in een verdrinkend landschap*, Amersfoort (ROB Rapportage Archeologische Monumentenzorg 79).

KUIJER P.C., 1991. *Toelichting bij kaartblad 12 West Assen, Bodemkaart van Nederland 1:50 000*, Wageningen (Stiboka).

LOUWE KOOIJMANS L.P. (ed.), 2001. *Archeologie in de Betuweroute: Hardinxveld-Giessendam De Bruin. Een kampplaats uit het Laat-Mesolithicum en het begin van de Swifterbant-cultuur (5500-4450 v. Chr)*, Amersfoort (ROB Rapportage Archeologische Monumentenzorg 88).

MALINOWSKI B., 1961(1922). *Argonauts of the Western Pacific, an account of native enterprise and adventure in the archipelagoes of Melanesian New Guinea*, London: Routledge.

MIDGLEY M.S., 1992. *TRB Culture – The First Farmers of the North European Plain*, Edinburgh: Edinburgh University Press.

OLAUSSON D.S., 1983. *Flint and Groundstone Axes in the Scandinavian Neolithic. An Evaluation of Raw Materials Based on Experiment, Scripta Minora* (Regiae Societatis Humaniorum Litterarum Lundensis)

PLEYTE W., 1882. *Nederlandsche oudheden van de vroegste tijden tot op Karel den Groote - Drenthe*, Leiden: E.J. Brill.

SCHUHMACHER K., 1914. Neolithische Depotfunde im westlichen Deutschland, *Prahistorische Zeitschrift 6:* 29-56.

STOUT D., 2002. Skill and Cognition in Stone Tool Production - An Ethnographic Case Study from Irian Jaya, *Current Anthropology* 43/5: 693-722.

SKAARUP J., 1990. Burials, Votive Offerings and Social Structure in Early Neolithic Farmer Society of Denmark, in Jankowska D. (ed.), D*ie Trichterbecherkultur, Neue Forschungen und Hypothesen, Teil I, Poznan* (Material des Internationalen Symposiums Dymaczewo 20-24 September 1988), 73-93.

SPEK T., 2004. *Het Drentse esdorpen-landschap. Een historisch-geografische studie*, Utrecht: Matrijs.

TER WAL A., 1996. Een onderzoek naar de depositie van vuurstenen bijlen, *Palaeohistoria* 37/38:127-58.

TILLEY C., 1996. *An ethnography of the Neolithic. Early prehistoric societies in southern Scandinavia*, Cambridge: Cambridge University Press.

VAN DER WAALS J.D., 1964. *Prehistoric Disc Wheels in the Netherlands*, PhD thesis Groningen.

VAN GIJN A.L., 1990. *The Wear and Tear of Flint: Principles of Functional Analysis to Dutch Neolithic Assemblages*, PhD thesis Leiden (Analecta Praehistorica Leidensia 22).

VAN GIJN A.L., in prep. *The Flourish and Demise of an Old Technology. The Meaning of Flint for Neolithic and Bronze Age Societies in the Netherlands.*

WENTINK K., 2006. Ceci n'est pas une hache. Neolithic Deposition in the Northern Netherlands, Research Master thesis, Leiden (Sidestone Press).

WHITE J.P. & MODJESKA N., 1978. Acquirers, Users, Finders, Losers: The Use Axe Blades Make of the Duna, *Mankind* 11: 276-87.

Acknowledgments

Several people of the different museums we visited through the years have shown great patience and helpfulness, notably Jaap Beuker, Benoit Mater and Vincent van Vilsteren (Drents Museum), Ernst Taayke (Archaeological Depot of the Northern Netherlands) and Leo Verhart (National Museum of Antiquities).

Harry Fokkens (Fac. of Archaeology, Leiden University) and Sake Jager (State Archaeological Service) both gave access to their unpublished data concerning axes, which was gratefully incorporated.

We would also like to thank the many people who provided data and answered numerous questions, Jaap Beuker (Drents Museum), David Fontijn (Fac. of Archaeology, Leiden University), Piet Kooi (Department of Archaeology, Groningen University), Leendert Louwe Kooijmans (Fac. of Archaeology, Leiden University), Wijnand van der Sanden (Province of Drenthe), Peter Schut (State Archaeological Service) and Theo Spek (State Archaeological Service).

Special thanks also to MA & PhD students Stijn Arnoldussen, Quentin Bourgeois, Erik van Rossenberg, Alice Samson and Corné van Woerdekom who have critically read this text.

Finally, the first author would like to thank Caroline Hamon and Bénédicte Quilliec who invited him to speak in Cork.

Contact

Karsten Wentink
Annelou van Gijn

Laboratory for Artefact Studies,
Faculty of Archaeology
PB 9515, 2300 RA
Leiden
The Netherlands
k.wentink@arch.leidenuniv.nl
a.l.van.gijn@arch.leidenuniv.nl

INTERPRETATION ELEMENTS OF HOARDS FROM LATE BRONZE AGE IN LORRAINE AND SAAR THROUGH TECHNICAL STUDIES (FORMING PROCESS AND METAL COMPOSITION)

Cécile Veber

Abstract:
The choice of a very homogeneous corpus (typology, geographic area and chronology –Late Bronze Age (LBA) = 'Bronze final IIIb'- allows to compare the deposits which make it up through the study of forming of the objects, and of the exhaustive components analysis. These investigations highlight, beyond the traditions of bronze work, common of each deposit, an image very different from each set according to the types of objects and elementary composition. Some are heteroclite where each object results of a different operation of casting, others homogeneous, are composed of groups of objects resulting from only one operation of casting. These last observations suggest that the objects had bonds between them before the deposition and kept them. Other similarities of the metal component show bonds between various deposits and let's approach the historical level of deposition phenomenon. Thus the technical investigations represent an additional means to apprehend the hoards and to open a door to their interpretation.

Résumé :
Le choix d'un corpus très homogène en typologie, dans l'espace (Lorraine et Sarre) et dans le temps (BF IIIb) a permis de comparer les différents dépôts qui le composent au travers de l'étude du formage des objets, et de l'analyse exhaustive de la composition du métal des objets. Ces investigations mettent en évidence, au-delà des traditions de travail du bronze communes à chaque dépôt, une image très différente de chacun des ensembles. Ceci suivant les objets qui y sont déposés et leur composition élémentaire. Certains sont hétéroclites et contiennent des objets issus d'une opération de coulée différente, d'autres sont homogènes, composés de groupes d'objets issus d'une seule et même coulée. Ces dernières observations suggèrent que les objets avaient des liens entre eux avant la déposition et les ont gardés. D'autres similarités dans leur composition élémentaire montrent des liens entre dépôts et nous fait saisir le niveau historique du phénomène. Ainsi les investigations techniques représentent un moyen supplémentaire d'appréhender les dépôts et de conduire à leur interprétation.

Introduction

Since already more than one hundred years the productions from the latest stage of LBA (BF IIIb) found in Lorraine's and Saar's hoards, which show a very high typological homogeneity are the subject of speculations about the origin of the metal which composes them (Simon 1852). These productions are close to lead and copper mines (Jacquot 1858).

These speculations are at the origin of the resumption of the studies of these hoards and particularly of the engagement of technical studies in order to characterize this production for a comparison with the local ores. The connection between local ore and objects is however still always difficult to establish. A project with analyses with lead isotopes is in progress (analyses by the Centre de Recherches Pétrographiques et Géochimiques (CRPG) in Vandoeuvre-lès-Nancy-France).

But the analyses of composition can be used in another manner. The aim is to characterize the production only with the composition, alloy elements and impurities. The composition and the forming process of each object are known and can be compared with the other from a same hoard, then to other hoards. Through the knowledge of the composition and forming process of the objects it is a question of understanding the choices of those which carried them out and of trying to reach the level of the interpretation of these hoards.

This paper is divided into two parts. After a short presentation of the studied corpus, we'll show some results of technical studies, forming process and analyses to show in conclusion how these results lead us to interpretations of these hoards.

The corpus

- One geographical area : Lorraine, Saar

The studied objects come from only one geographical area which includes part east of France, Lorraine and especially along the Moselle valley, completed by part of the south-western Germany, the Saar (fig. 1).

- One dating:

LBA (BFIIIb) corresponding to the end of 9th B.C. The typological study allotted the whole of the corpus to the BF IIIb of the north-alpine area but very few of them are of Atlantic tradition.

- One context: hoards

Nearly 90% of the bronze artefacts of the BF IIIb of the area come from hoards. Very few objects come from settlements, although those are now well known and excavated. Thus the whole corpus results from hoards.

Under these conditions, the conclusions of the typological study was undertaken on more than 600 objects out of copper alloy, comprising every functional categories but bronze dishes which notes the typological homogeneity of the unit will not astonish anybody. It is also one of the significant conditions to develop problems on the characterization of a corpus and to go to the elements of interpretation.

The three followings hoards are the most significant of the corpus in the number of objects, they make it possible to have a good outline of the constitution of the corpus and of the types of objects met in this geographical area.

The hoard of Farébersviller (Moselle, France) is the last hoard discovered in Lorraine, it was discovered at the time of an operation of survey archaeology.

It counts 120 objects among which are final aileron axes, small axes with round casing of Frouard type, many sickles, bracelets of the Vaudrevange type, many other hollow or full bracelets variously decorated, thread-like loops, the ingot or melts of crucible (Veber 2002).

The hoard of Vaudrevange (Saar, Germany) was found in 1850 and is conserved in the Musée des Antiquités Nationales in Saint-Germain-en-Laye (France). We find in it axes, moulds of axe, bracelets of the Vaudrevange type, thread-like loops, and especially the tintinabulum, as well as a great number of elements of the sphere of harnessing and finally, a sword (Simon 1852, Reboul & Millotte 1975).

Finally the deposit of Frouard (Meurthe-et-Moselle, France) contains a famous tintinabulum, elements of harnessing, hollow or full bracelets variously decorated and sickles (Reboul & Millotte1975).

There is a substantial difference between the last two hoards, Vaudrevange and Frouard with their objects of prestige whereas Farébersviller contains neither tintinabulum, nor elements of harnessing.

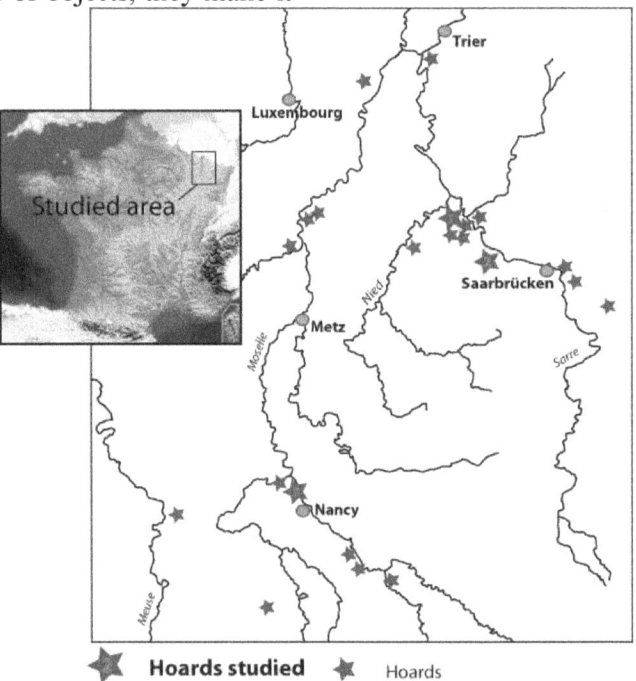

Fig. 1. Map of Lorraine with the hoards studied here.
1 : Vaudrevange ; 2 : Farébersviller ; 3 : Frouard.

Technical studies

Only half of the corpus (300 objects) was studied following a technical approach.

The purpose of the technical studies, forming process (observation by naked eye, binocular magnifying and metallographic examination with the collaboration of M. Pernot) and elementary analyses (by ICP-AES in the Centre de Recherche et de restauration des Musées de France (C2RMF, with B. Mille and D. Bourgarit) is to characterize the production.

What was the main forming process? Casting or hammering? What kind of reason determined a technical choice in the forming process or in the metal composition? Is the homogeneity, highlighted by the typo-chronological studies, comparable in the technical level?

A. Bracelet type Vaudrevange
(Hoard of Vaudrevange, Saar)

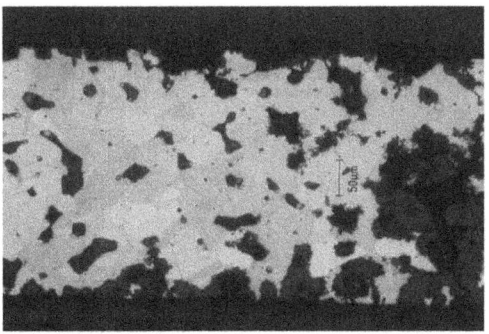

B. Metallographic examination
(Hoard of Vaudrevange, Saar)

Fig. 2. Bracelets of Vaudrevange : fine casting.
A. Bracelet of Vaudrevange type from the Hoard of Vaudrevange ; B. Metallographic examination of a bracelet of Vaudrevange type. It shows a metal which was not hammered, or in a very few percentage.

Forming process

The main results are a high majority of casting ; special fine casting (Véber & Pernot 2002) (fig. 2) and some example of secondary cast (fig. 3). That means a very good homogeneity in the forming process and some locales specialities.

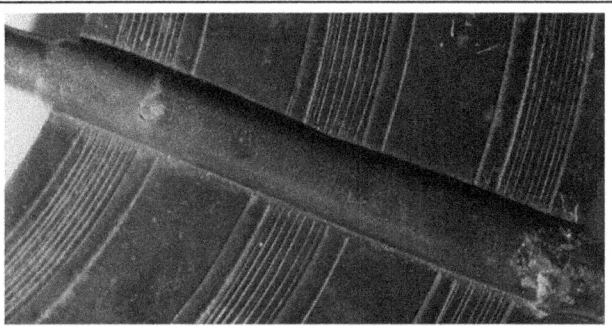

A. Tintinabulum (Hoard of Frouard, M.et M)

B. Anneaux (Hoard of Frouard, M-et-M.)

Fig. 3. Some examples of secondary casting.
A : Tintinabulum of Frouard, rivets ; B : 4 Rings.

The metal composition

The principal alloyed elements of the metal are tin (Sn: 8 to 12% on average), lead (Pb: 1.5 to 3% on average). The principal impurities are silver, arsenic, bismuth, cobalt, nickel, antimony with a global sum of 1.5% on average.

The great majority of the compositions are included in these averages. Thus we find a great homogeneity in the composition of metal. Some objects whose compositions deviated a lot from the characteristics presented above were put aside. They contained a strong alloy rate and a very weak sum of impurities. These objects as well as the characteristics of these compositions were the subject of particular work which highlighted two different alloy traditions, the Atlantic and north-alpine ones of for this period (Veber *et al.* 2003).

Hamon C. & Quilliec B. eds. 2008 - Hoards from the Neolithic to the Metal Ages : technical and codified practices

Twin compositions

The most original part of this technical study consists in looking for the twin compositions.

Twins mean same metallic composition and this terme is not restrictive and twins possibly means 3 to 8 objects with the same composition

This kind of research was tried before by Valentin. Rychner on the bronze objects from Bronze Age in Switzerland (Rychner & Klântschi 1995). The method employed is an Agglomerative Hierarchical Clustering (AHC-dendrogram) which includes results of analyses content of tin, lead and impurities.

Three types of twins could be highlighted:

- Twins of cast
(Cu, Sn, Pb =Cu, Sn, Pb)
Same copper (=same impurities from copper)-Same added elements (tin and lead).
Results: 93 artefacts or parts concerned = 1/3 of the whole corpus.

- Twins of ingot
(Cu =Cu ; Sn, Pb = Sn, Pb)
Same copper (= same impurities from copper)-different quantity of added elements (tin and lead).
Results: 33 artefacts or parts concerned.

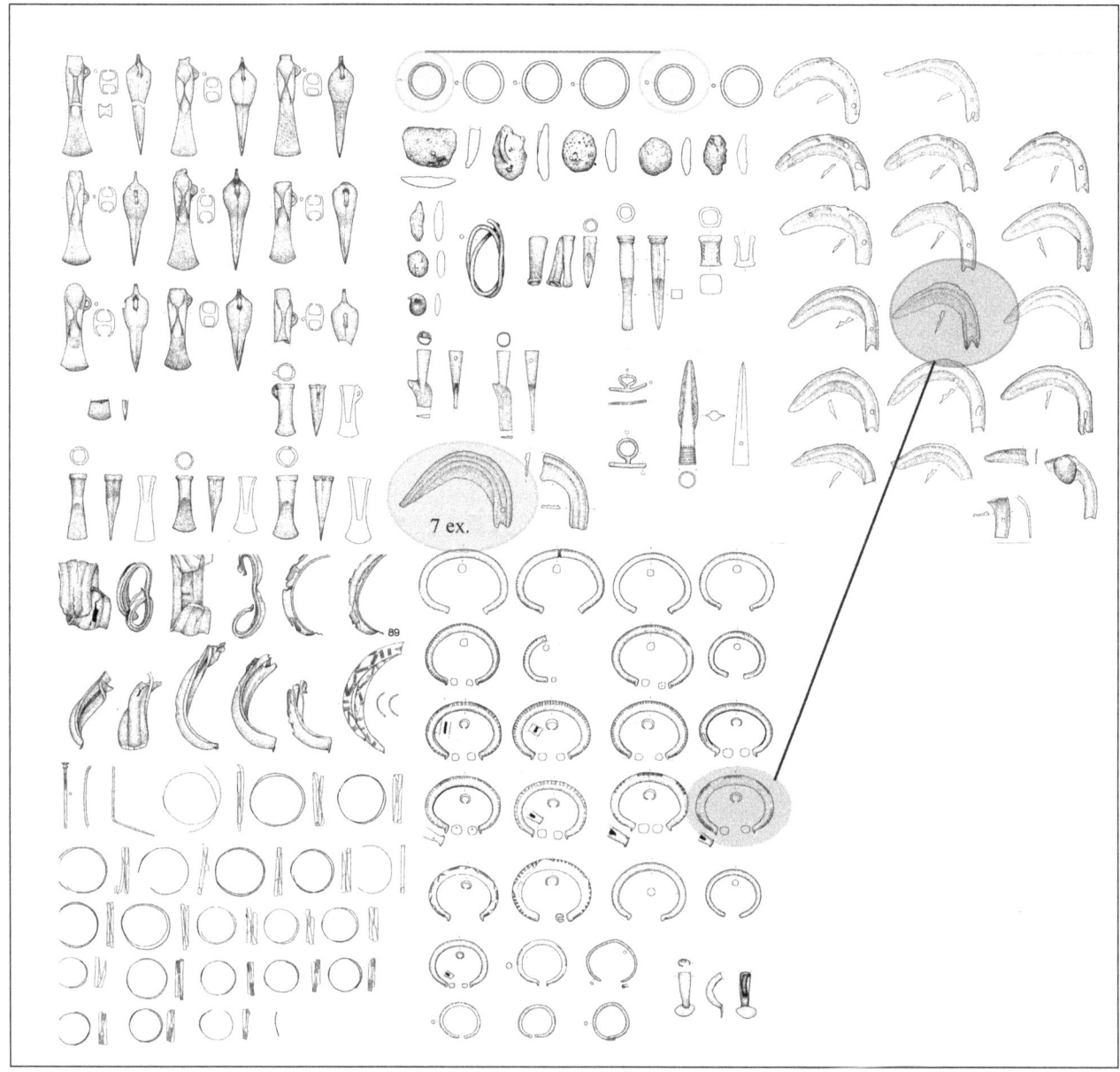

Fig. 4. Hoard of Farébersviller (Moselle, France) with twin compositions, 130 artefacts (Veber 2002).

- Twins of mixture
(% Sn+Pb = % Sn=Pb)
Mixture with tin/lead added in the copper at a second time.
Research's method: Calculation of the ratios of lead and tin on addition of there added elements.
Results: 15 artefacts or parts concerned

How the study of the forming and the knowledge of the metal of the objects contribute to the interpretation of hoards ?

The combination of the various results (forming process, metallurgical tradition and research of twins) makes it possible to have a picture of the homogeneity of the hoards (fig. 4, 5, and 6). Whereas the hoard of Farébersviller presents relatively few twins and some elements of tradition exterior to the area, the two other deposits appear much more homogeneous, in particular the hoard of Vaudrevange (Veber *et al.* 2007). Indeed, the majority of the series of objects are twins. Some bracelets are also related. In addition, several series were carried out with the same copper. Thus, the hoards were probably not constituted of the same manner. The difference in the categories of objects confirms also these remarks, some objects belong to the current corpus and other are objects of prestige. The fact of being twin of composition for the objects means that they had a bond between them before their deposition. In addition, some rare twin compositions

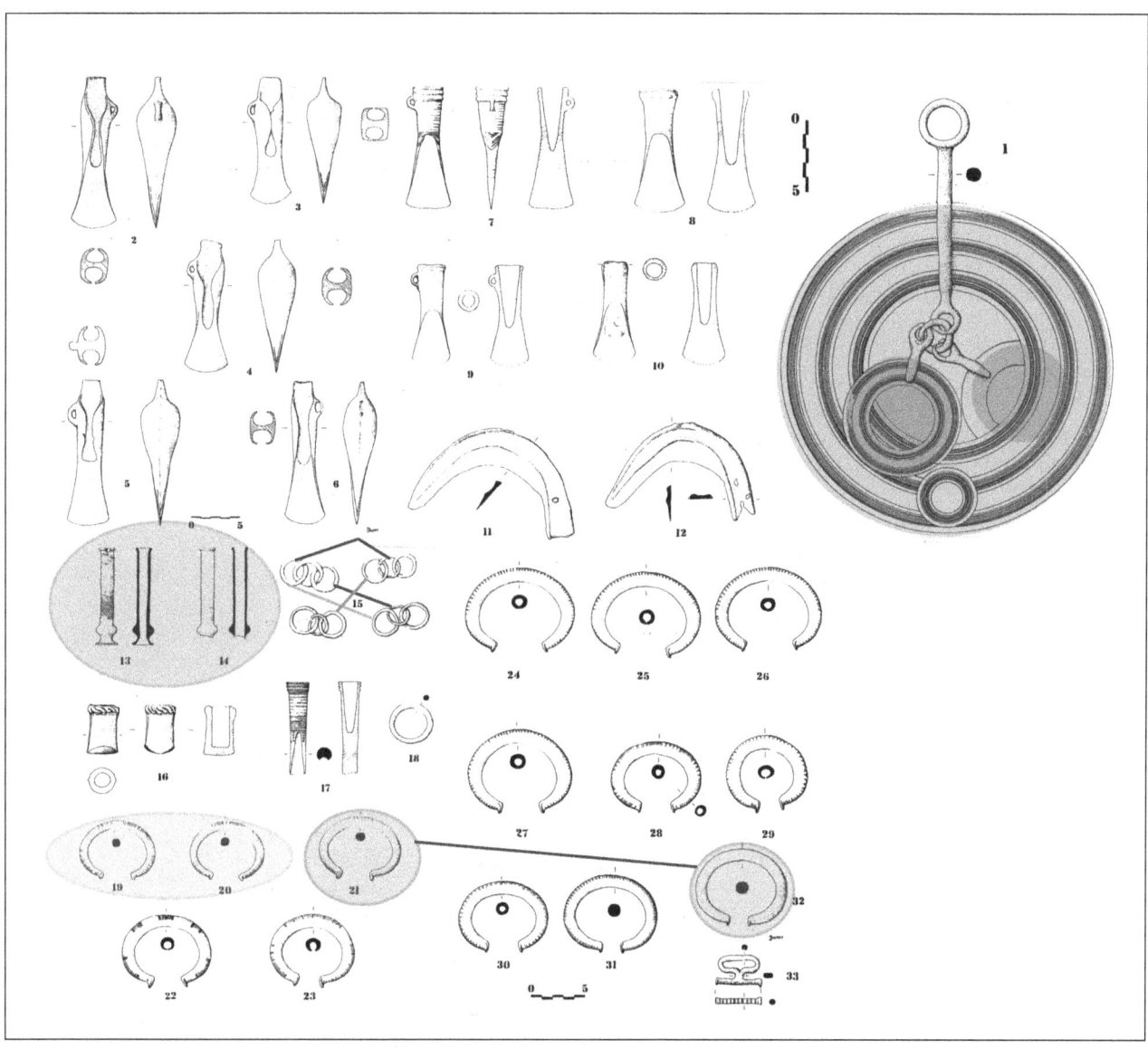

Fig. 5. Hoard of Frouard (Meurthe-et-Moselle, France) with twin compositions, 51 artefacts (Reboul & Millotte 1975).

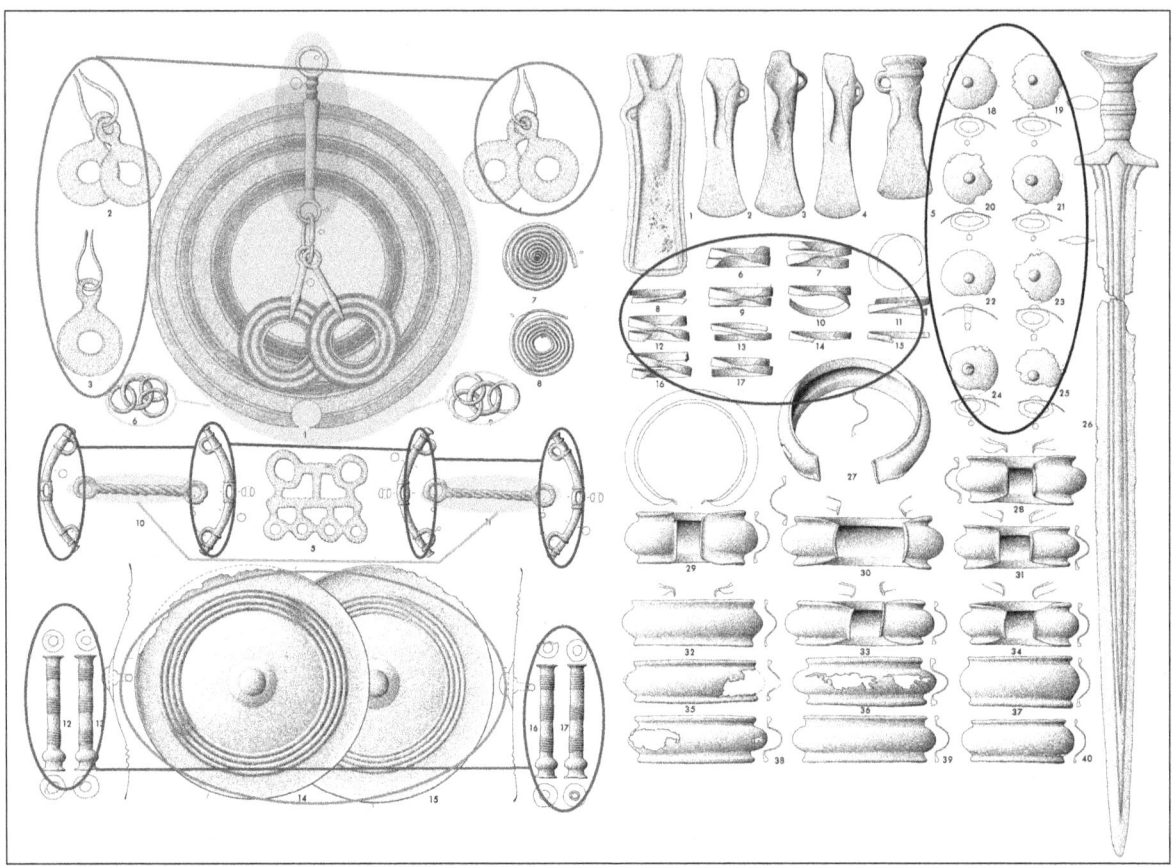

Fig. 6. Hoard of Vaudrevange (Saar, Germany) with twin compositions, 72 artefacts (Kölling 1968).

were highlighted, either inside the same deposit but between hoards. It supposes a chronological proximity of these deposits which were all found without surrounding archaeological context.

Conclusion

This example of a combination between technical observations, technology and exhaustive analyses shows for this corpus:
- A high homogeneity of the forming process which shows a high level of bronze work, specially casting,
- A high homogeneity of the composition, which is characteristic of the north-alpine area,
- Twin compositions suppose relation between artefacts before deposition,
- A clear difference in the composition of hoards with several degrees of homogeneity in metal composition. The homogeneity is in relation with the type of artefacts (prestige or not) which supposes different practices for the constitution of hoards.

This combination shows relation between several hoards in the same area, same context and same short period with an idea of a very rapid composition for these hoards. Maybe are we there close to the history and have open a door for new interpretations.

References

JACQUOT E. 1858. Notice géologique et historique sur les mines de plomb et de cuivre des environs de St. Avold, de Hargarten et de Saarlouis, *MAM* 1857-1858: 531-556.

REBOUL R. & MILLOTTE J.-P. 1975. Dépôts de l'âge du Bronze final en Lorraine et en Sarre, *Inventaria Archaeologica*, France, fasc. 4, F29-F49.

RYCHNER V. & KLÄNTSCHI N. 1995. Arsenic, Nickel et Antimoine, *Cahier d'archéologie romande 63 et 64*, Lausanne.

SIMON V. 1852. Mémoire sur les antiquités trouvées près de Vaudrevange, *Mémoire de l'Académie de Metz*, 1852, 33: 231-258.

VEBER C. 2002. Le dépôt de Farébersviller (Moselle), un ensemble du BF IIIb, *Archaeologia Mosellana*, Tome V: 37-80.

VEBER C., MILLE B., BOURGARIT D. 2003. Analyse élémentaire des dépôts lorrains : essai de caractérisation d'une production métallique de la fin de l'âge du Bronze, in : GIUMLIA-MAIR A., LO SCHIAVO F. dir., *Le problème de l'étain à l'origine de la métallurgie, Colloque 11.2, Actes du XIVème Congrès UISPP, Université Liège, Belgique, 2-8 septembre 2001*, BAR International Series 1199, 2003.

VEBER C., MILLE B., PERNOT M. 2007. Le dépôt de Vaudrevange : études techniques et éléments d'interprétation, Antiquités Nationales 37 : 69-102.

VEBER C., PERNOT M. 2002 Technical study of some Vaudrevange type bracelets found in different areas (IX/VIIIth c. B.C.) metallographical examinations experimental wax model making. In : Giumlia-Mair (A.) dir., I bronzi antichi : Produzione e tecnologia. Atti del XV Congresso internationale sui bronzi antichi / org. Dall'Università di Udine, sede di Gorizia, Grado-Aquilieia, 22-26 maggio. M. Mergoil: Montagnac 2002: 52-62.

Contact

Cécile VEBER
(INRAP/ UMR ARTeHiS Dijon)
Centre Archéologique INRAP
10 rue d'Altkirch
67100 Strasbourg
France
cecile.veber@inrap.fr

IBERIAN PSYCHO. DELIBERATE DESTRUCTION IN BRONZE AGE GOLD HOARDS OF THE IBERIAN PENINSULA

Alicia PEREA

Abstract:
Although the hoarding of gold objects in the Iberian Peninsula is a long lasting phenomenon, it gets to a peak in the Atlantic seaboard during the Late Bronze Age. What differentiates the Iberian Peninsula from the rest of Europe is the heavy weight of the gold hoarded, and the complexity of the manufacturing techniques.

We present the different kinds of gold deposits documented in the Iberian Peninsula during the Bronze Age in order to understand their social, economic and symbolic meanings. But the focus is on a particular kind of deposit consisting in one or two cylindrical bracelets which have suffered a previous segmentation by means of cutting out a part of it in a way that only ritual could explain. They belong to an archaeological type named after the well known findings of Villena/Estremoz (V/E); their manufacture includes lost wax casting and the use of a lathe for shaping the wax model. We know almost fifty examples showing a wide variability in craftmanship and weight; the one from Estremoz (Evora, Portugal) is of the few that was found in its original and complete state and weights 978 g. Till now we don't have a convincing model explanation which accounts for this ritual destruction of the object previous to its concealment.

Resumen:
Aunque los ocultamientos de objetos de oro es un fenómeno de larga duración en la Península Ibérica, alcanza su máximo en la fachada atlántica durante el Bronce Final. Lo que diferencia a la Península del resto de Europa es el elevado peso del oro depositado y la complejidad de las técnicas de fabricación.

Presentamos distintos tipos de depósitos áureos documentados en la Península Ibérica durante la Edad del Bronce para intentar comprender su significado social, económico y simbólico. Pero nos detendremos fundamentalmente en un tipo específico consistente en uno o dos brazaletes cilíndricos que previamente han sufrido una segmentación al haber cortado una sección de ellos, de tal forma que sólo la ritualización podría explicar. Pertenecen a un tipo denominado según los conocidos hallazgos de Villena/Estremoz (V/E) ; su manufactura incluye el vaciado a la cera perdida y el uso de un torno para trabajar el modelo de cera. Conocemos casi una cincuentena de ejemplares que presentan una gran variabilidad de calidad y peso; el ejemplar de Estremoz (Evora, Portugal) es uno de los pocos que apareció en su estado original y completo, y pesa 978g. Hasta la fecha no se ha encontrado un modelo explicativo para la destrucción de estos brazaletes previa al ocultamiento.

Introduction

The phenomenon of metal hoards in prehistory is common to the whole Bronze Age of Europe. What differentiates the Iberian Peninsula from other parts of the Atlantic and Mediterranean areas is the size of the hoards with gold. One example will suffice: the hoard of Caldas de Reyes (Pontevedra), in the northwest of the Peninsula, contained 27 kilos of gold consisting of ring-shaped ingots, three cups and a comb, all of solid gold, and some fragments of sheet; only 14 kilos are now preserved (Ruíz-Gálvez 1978 & 1995; Domato & Comendador 1998). It is still being debated whether the hoard should be dated to the beginning of the Late Bronze Age or before (Armbruster 1996). The only comparable phenomenon is the hoards of Irish gold of the Dowris phase (Eogan 1983).

In terms of weight, Caldas de Reyes is an exception, but if we look at the distribution of gold finds dating only to the Late Bronze Age, their concentration on the Atlantic seaboard is remarkable. In general the hoards exceed 2 kilos in weight, with an average of 500 g. The most typical objects for this period are solid gold torcs or bracelets, alone or in association, and these hoards are real accumulations of wealth. Another notable characteristic is that the gold is seldom found in association with bronze, which would seem to suggest independent manufacturing and trading systems (exception in Vilaça & Lopes 2005).

Two distinct entities or domains can be distinguished if we look exclusively at these gold hoards: the Sagrajas/Berzocana (S/B) domain and the Villena/Estremoz (V/E) domain. The hoards that characterise them display certain consistent features, both in the association of objects within the hoards themselves, and in the technology used to make them.

The standard S/B type hoard consists of one or two solid gold annular torcs with incised decoration (fig. 1); these may be accompanied by bracelets of the same type, which are not usually decorated, or annular ingots in the shape of bracelets - very rarely is scrap material present.

All these metal objects belong to what we have called the S/B technological domain system (Perea 1995 & 1999), defined by the use of plastic deformation as the basic manufacturing technique, using a pre-cast shape probably cast in an open mould.

Fig. 2. Three on a total of 28 bracelets from the hoard of Villena (Alicante, Spain).

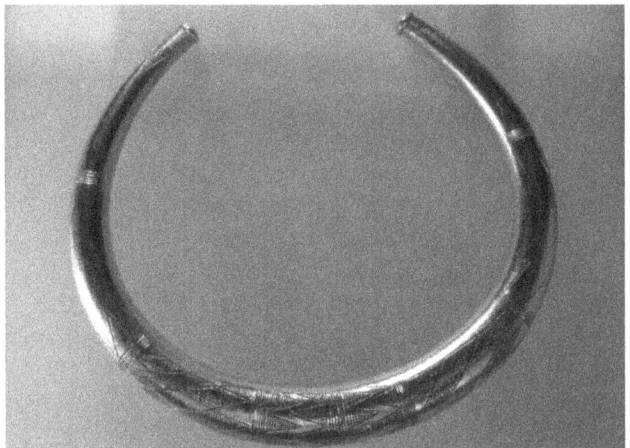

Fig. 1. One of the torcs from the Berzocana hoard (Cáceres, Spain).

Some examples of the best-known hoards of this type are the following:
- Berzocana (Cáceres): two torcs, 1,700 g.
- Baiôes (Viseu): two torcs and a bracelet, 1,559 g.
- Portel (Évora): one torc, 2,100 g.
- Penela (Coimbra): one torc, 1,800 g.
- Sagrajas (Badajoz): a double torc and a torc rolled into a spiral, with a fragment of wire to close it, and four bracelets, 2,190 g.
- Sintra (Lisbon): a triple torc, 1,262 g.
- Valdeobispo (Cáceres): a torc and four bracelets, 1,175 g.

The typical V/E hoard consists of one or two cylindrical bracelets which can vary greatly in size and complexity of ornamentation (fig. 2) by combining three structural elements in various ways: ridges, spikes and openwork (Armbruster & Perea 1994). Other material is rarely found except in cases where the hoard was deposited outside the geographical area where it was produced, that is the Atlantic seaboard. Thus the Abía de la Obispalía (Cuenca) and the Villena and

Cabezo Redondo (Alicante) hoards are exceptions to the rule. All the bracelets of this kind belong to what has been called the V/E domain system, defined by the lost wax technique and a manufacturing process that uses an alternating rotary lathe for making the wax model and for the finishing stage. They range in weight from 50 to 978 g, the heaviest item being the bracelet from Estremoz (Évora).

No piece made using S/B technology has been found -

ver, we know that they coexisted because we have found objects made from scrap pieces of both technologies, such as the Sintra torc (fig. 3) and the Cantonha bracelet (Perea 2005).

Fig. 3. The Sintra (Portugal) torc has a clasp piece made up of a scrap fragment from a Villena/Estremoz bracelet.

Deliberate breaking of the V/E bracelets

The Estremoz bracelet is both the heaviest example of a V/E bracelet and the most perfect from the technological point of view; in addition, it is one of only seven that is complete. The others, a total of forty-seven known examples, appear to have been deliberately cut after the manufacturing process.

The Villena hoard contained twenty-eight V/E bracelets, all of them cut through (fig. 4). In addition to the bracelets, the hoard contained other pieces of gold with a total weight of 9,112 g. The inventory is as follows: 28 bracelets; 11 bowls; two gold flasks and three silver flasks; 13 fragments of sheet, probably the remains of decoration on the hilts and other parts of weapons; an iron terminal covered with gold sheet appliqué; an iron bracelet or ring; and a gold-covered piece of amber (Perea 1994).

Fig. 4. One of the bracelets from the Villena hoard (Alicante, Spain).

There is absolutely no possibility that the cut bracelets were made incorporating this feature. Firstly, because the manufacturing process necessarily involved modelling a complete cylinder of wax on the horizontal axis of a lathe with alternating rotation; secondly, because marks left by the cutting process on the metal surface of the cut edges can be observed (fig. 5). The cut was produced by abrasion, probably using a flexible tool - some kind of fibre or leather, an abrasive product such as sand or powdered sandstone and a lubricant such as water or oil.

The characteristics of these cuts must also be taken into account. Firstly, the cut was made with surprising precision (fig. 6).

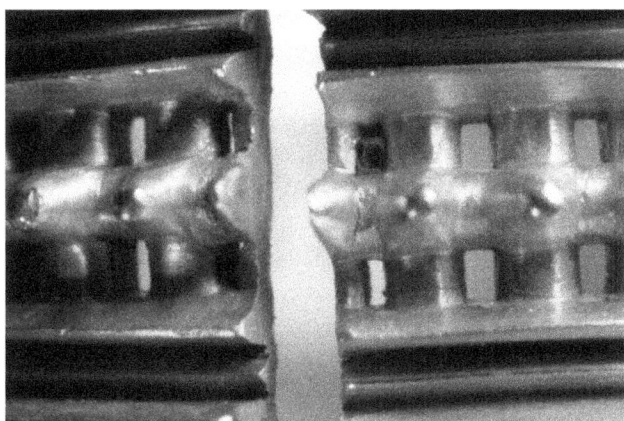

Fig. 6. Cutting line dividing a conical point with exact precision in a Villena/Estremoz bracelet.

For example, in some of the bracelets, the cutting line passes exactly through the centre of a conical point, dividing it in two.

Secondly, the size of the cut is very different in different examples: in some two cuts were made in order to remove a relatively wide piece of the cylinder (fig. 7), while in others a single cut has been made, and the edges are practically touching (fig. 6).

Fig. 7. Villena/Estremoz bracelet with a wide part of the cylinder cut out.

Finally, there are bracelets that were cut both in their place of origin and manufacture, the Atlantic seaboard, and outside it, for example close to the Mediterranean coast, where the Villena hoard was found.

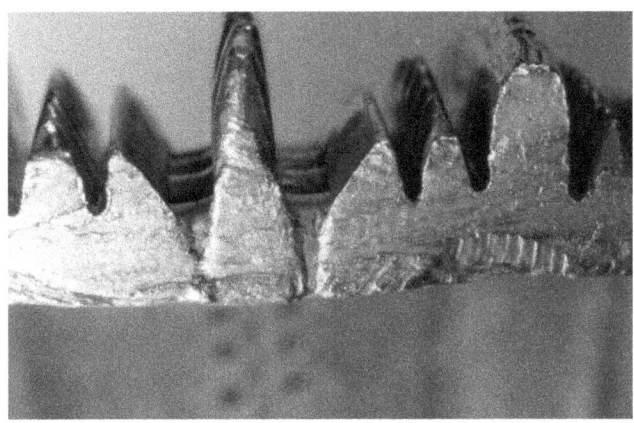

Fig. 5. Marks left by the cutting process in one of the Villena/Estremoz bracelets.

Traditional interpretations

It is surprising that virtually no author has tried to explain the feature we are describing since the twenty-eight bracelets in the Villena hoard were discovered in 1963. No reference is made to the cuts or any explanation offered for them in the lengthy description published by the archaeologist who discovered the hoard (Soler 1965) or by Almagro-Gorbea in his subsequent review (Almagro-Gorbea 1974). They implicitly assume that the opening of the bracelets is simply another morphological feature of the type.

A comment by Soler is illustrative in this respect: surprised at the cut in the first bracelet to be found (Soler 1965: 14), which was a casual find before the rest of the hoard, he thought it has been intentionally broken at the time of the discovery, an idea he subsequently rejected when he saw that the other examples were the same; he expanded on this idea by citing the publication of the bracelet from Portalegre by Cardozo (Cardozo 1959), where that Portuguese archaeologist had the same opinion (Soler 1965: note 67).

Until the 1990s, no-one offered any hypotheses to explain the systematic openings in the V/E bracelets, apart from functionalist explanations that made the size of the wearer's arm the main reason for this feature. Ruíz-Gálvez proposed a mercantilist model for what she considered an intentional division of the bracelets (Ruíz-Gálvez 1995 & 1998), which would relate to the payment of transit taxes as they were passed along livestock routes; according to this author, the weights of the twenty-eight bracelets from Villena would be multiples or fractions in a weight system of Mediterranean origin. This hypothesis was based on the examination of a single find, the Villena hoard, and on the assumption that the bracelets were of Mediterranean origin. However, today their Atlantic origin seems to have been clearly established: the technology used to make them emerged and matured on the Iberian Atlantic seaboard, and original and evolved types are broadly distributed over the same area (Armbruster & Perea 1994; Perea 2005: fig. 3).

In our opinion, Villena is a *unicum* and as such is not a valid basis for a study of this kind. The significance of the V/E bracelets must be sought in their own geographic and socio-economic context, where finds are characterised by containing one, or at the most two bracelets, and no other associated material.

Ruíz-Gálvez's hypothesis does, however, provide a starting point that can be accepted without difficulty: the differences in size and complexity of the bracelets' ornamentation, and the fact that their fragmentation is not uniform - but in some cases the bracelet has been cut without removing any material and in others varying amounts of gold have been removed - could be of accounting, although not necessarily metrological significance.

Proposal

Numerous bronze hoards have been described that display signs of deliberate damage, i.e., breakages and fragmentations that cannot be explained simply in terms of breaking up the metal in order to recycle it. According to Nebelsick (Nebelsick 2000), who describes examples from the European Urnfield period and the Late Bronze Age on the Atlantic seaboard, destruction of this kind would indicate a ritual context of euphoric hysteria and frenetic violence. Symbolism have been present in the actual selection of the objects in the hoards, in which metaphorical relationships have been seen between pieces of opposing significance, for example, male objects (swords) and female (ornaments), or even complex meanings that combine three complementary concepts, such as woman-warrior-horse. Finally, the relationship between the place of concealment and the state of the objects seems related to some type of ritual in which the complete objects, which would represent the civilized, could have been buried within the settlement itself, while the damaged objects would have been destroyed beyond its boundaries, that is in a wild place; this is the Homeric metaphor of the cultivated olive and the wild olive tree.

Although no such deliberate damage is visible in the V/E bracelets, we do believe that the cuts described above were made as part of a ritual act subject to strict ceremonial rules. Our argument is based on two fundamental considerations.

The first consideration refers to the difficulty of the chosen method of cutting: if a craftsman working with metal wanted to obtain a piece of gold from an existing object, or simply to destroy it, he would use a hammer and chisel to perform an operation requiring no more than a few minutes of moderate effort. Cuts made with a chisel have been visible on objects of both bronze and gold; for example cuts of this kind have been documented in the jumble of half-melted down gold pieces and ingots in the hoard from Bélmez, Córdoba (Perea 1991: 137). However, the cuts observed on the V/E bracelets were made using friction, in an operation that must have taken several hours and involved great effort and expertise.

The second consideration that supports the ritual character of the cuts is that the process chosen seems to have been intended to avoid at all costs disfiguring the object. Cutting it with a chisel would have destroyed its perfect circular symmetry. All the examples known maintain their perfectly cylindrical shape, except for small irregularities and defects that occurred in the course of the lost wax casting but never as a result of the cutting process.

Finally, the significance of the differences in size of the cuts must be considered: why were varying amounts of gold removed from different bracelets? On this subject we can only make purely intuitive speculations.

Considering that the depositional pattern of the V/E bracelets on the Atlantic seaboard takes the form of small hoards containing one or two bracelets at the most, we could speculate that the acts of destruction and burial were related to funerary rites that took place on the death of the owner of the bracelets, male or female.

As Nebelsick (2000: 169-170) once again reminds us, the sacrificial rite of Mediterranean origin divided the offering, or the victim, into two portions, one human and the other divine. In the Homeric sacrifice, it was the animal's bones that belong to the gods (Grottanelli 1999; Sánchez 2003). This would explain the fact that complete objects can rarely be reconstructed from bronze hoards consisting of scrap metal because particular pieces are missing. The selection of fragments from a vandalised mass would be at the base of the circulation of scrap metal and of its proto-monetary use. Similarly, during individuals' rites of passage - for example after death or when the objects changed hands - ritual sacrifice would seek divine sanction to ensure a successful passage.

The varying amounts of metal removed from the bracelets and the cuts that, without destroying them, definitively marked the object as buried can thus be explained in terms of this ideology of redistribution between the human and divine worlds.

References

ALMAGRO-GORBEA M. 1974. "Orfebrería del Bronce final en la Península Ibérica. El tesoro de Abia de la Obispalía, la orfebrería tipo Villena y los cuencos de Axtroki". *Trabajos de Prehistoria*, 31: 39-100.

ARMBRUSTER B. 1996. "Zu den technologischen Aspekten der Goldfunde aus dem bronzezeitlichen Schatz von Caldas de Reyes (Prov. Pontevedra)". *Madrider Mitteilungen*, 37: 60-73.

ARMBRUSTER B. & PEREA A.1994. "Tecnología de herramientas rotativas durante el Bronce Final atlántico. El depósito de Villena". *Trabajos de Prehistoria*, 51 (2): 69-87.

CARDOZO, M. 1959: "Joalharía lusitana". *Conímbriga*, I: 13-27

DOMATO X.M. & COMENDADOR B. 1998. *El Tesoro Desencantado: As Silgadas (Caldas de Reis)*. Santiago.

EOGAN G. 1983. *The Hoards of the Irish Bronze Age*. University College. Dublin.

GROTTANELLI C. 1999. *Il Sacrificio*. Laterza. Roma.

NEBELSICK L. 2000. "Rent asunder: ritual violence in Late Bronze Age hoards". In: C.F.E. Pare (ed.) *Metals make the World Go Round. The supply and circulation of metals in Bronze Age Europe*. Oxbow. Oxford: 160-175.

PEREA A.1991. *Orfebrería Prerromana. Arqueología del Oro*. Comunidad de Madrid. Caja de Madrid.

PEREA A. 1994. "Proceso de mercantilización en sociedades premonetales". *Archivo Español de Arqueología*, 67: 3-14.

PEREA A.1995. "La metalurgia del oro en la fachada atlántica Peninsular durante el Bronce Final: interacciones tecnológicas", in RUÍZ-GÁLVEZ, M. (ed.) *Ritos de Paso y Puntos de Paso. La ría de Huelva en el mundo del Bronce Final Europeo, Complutum, extra 5*, 69-78, Madrid.

PEREA A. 1999. "Project Au for the study of goldwork technology and the concept of Technological Domain Systems". In Young, S.M.M., Pollard, M. and Ixer, R.A. (eds.) *Metals in Antiquity*. BAR International Series 792: 68-71.

PEREA A. 2005. "Mecanismos identitarios y de construcción de poder en la transición Bronce-Hierro". *Trabajos de Prehistoria*, 62 (2):

RUÍZ-GÁLVEZ M. 1978. "El tesoro de Caldas de Reyes (Pontevedra)". *Trabajos de Prehistoria*, 35: 173-196.

RUÍZ-GÁLVEZ M. 1995. "From gift to commodity: the changing meaning of precious metals in the later Prehistory of the Iberian Peninsula". En: G. Morteani y J.P. Northover (eds.) *Prehistoric Gold in Europe. Mines, metallurgy and manufacture*. Kluwer. Dordrecht: 45-63.

RUÍZ-GÁLVEZ M. 1998: *La Europa Atlántica en la Edad del Bronce. Un viaje a las raíces de la Europa occidental*. Crítica. Barcelona.

SÁNCHEZ C. 2003. "Sacrificio, banquete y ritual en La Odisea". En: P. Cabrera y R. Olmos (eds.) *Sobre La Odisea. Visiones desde el mito y la arqueología*. Polifemo. Madrid: 171-199.

SOLER J.M. 1965. *El Tesoro de Villena. Excavaciones Arqueológicas en España nº 36*. Madrid.

VILAÇA, R. & LOPES M.C. 2005. "The treasure of Baleizâo, Beja (Alentejo, Portugal)". Journal of Iberian Archaeology vol. 7: 177-184.

Acknowledgments

This work is part of a research project entitled: "Technological and power connections in the Iberian Peninsula Atlantic Seaboard during the Late Bronze Age-Iron Age transition" (BHA 2002-00138), directed by A. Perea with financial support from the Spanish Ministry of Education and Science.

Contact

Dra. Alicia Perea
Centro de Ciencias Humanas y Sociales, CSIC
Albasanz 26-28,
28037 Madrid
perea@ceh.csic.es

VOLUNTARY DESTRUCTIONS OF OBJECTS IN MIDDLE AND LATE BRONZE AGE HOARDS IN FRANCE.

Maréva GABILLOT & Céline LAGARDE

Abstract:
Numerous destructed objects have been found in Middle and Late Bronze Age hoards in France. The objects which were really destructed can be distinguished from other objects
which were normally used. The marks of these destructions can be recognized and characterized: all the types of objects are concerned but axes are not destructed like swords or spearheads. This contribution proposes to show these destructions in Middle and Late Bronze Age hoards, by establishing a classification of the marks. This contribution also proposes an interpretation of these destructions by the statistical way, by systematic numberings of the destructed objects, of each type of objects or of each hoard. These analysis allow to approach the destruction of the objects within the Bronze Age hoards like a social characteristic.

Resumé :
Les dépôts du Bronze moyen et final en France sont composés de nombreux objets détruits. Les objets réellement détruits peuvent être distingués de ceux qui ont été utilisés «normalement». Les traces de ces destructions peuvent être reconnues et caractérisées: tous les types d'objets sont concernés par cette pratique mais les haches ne sont pas détruites de la même façon que les épées ou les pointes de lance. Cette contribution propose de montrer ces destructions dans les dépôts du Bronze moyen et final pour tenter une classification des traces. Cette contribution propose aussi une interprétation de ces destructions par la voie statistique, en proposant des dénombrements systématiques des objets détruits, par types d'objets ou par dépôts. Ces analyses permettent d'aborder la destruction des objets dans les dépôts comme une caractéristique sociale.

Introduction

Middle and Late Bronze Age hoards in France are often composed of broken objects in bronze (fig. 1). Some hoards only contain entire objects, while in some others, entire objects appear with destructed ones. Others hoards are composed only of destructed pieces.

In certain areas, during certain periods, like in the Armorican area in the Late Bronze Age, hoards are almost exclusively composed of destructed swords, axes and sickles or spearheads. It is then possible to talk about a real archaeological phenomenon.

Several studies, about different samples of many hoards, sometimes composed of tens of pieces, lead to analyse this phenomenon.

Marks of destruction

The objects who were really destructed can be distinguished from other objects who were 'normally' used. The use of objects produces damages on the blades and on the handle parts: these damages (abrasions are studied separately), present particular marks, they are usually microscopic and are studied by traceology (Klienlin, Ottaway 1998, Quilliec 2007).

Among the broken objects in a hoard, some of them are only chipped, while others are completely broken, to such an extent that they are hardly recognizable. Besides these objects really only chipped, all the others bear some very visible marks. Such breakings, on which we can see some particular 'scars' visible to the naked eye, result from specific actions of destruction.

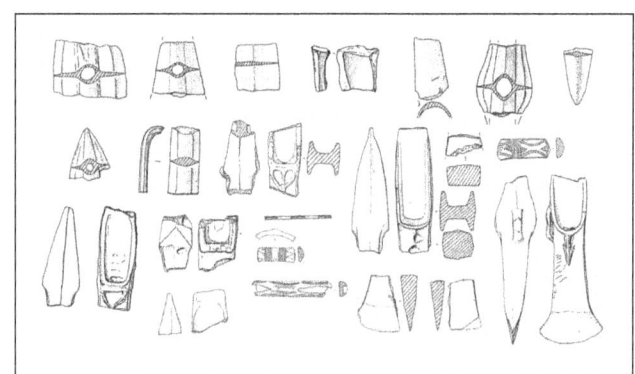

Fig. 1. Sample of destructed objects from the hoard of Sermizelles 'II' (Yonne, France).

The marks of these destructions can be identified and characterized. All classes of objects are concerned but the axes are not destructed like swords or spearheads. All types of objects bear some blow marks, but we can record two different types of blow marks. Some of them are shallow: less than 1 mm deep, but rather wide: 3 to 5mm (fig. 2). The others are deeper (1mm deep) and very narrow (1mm wide) (fig. 3).

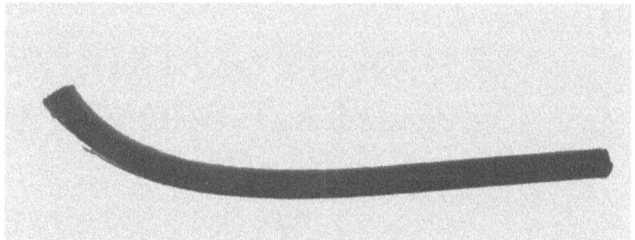

Fig. 4. Piece of sword from the hoard of Chéry 'Ferme de Malassis' (Cher, France).

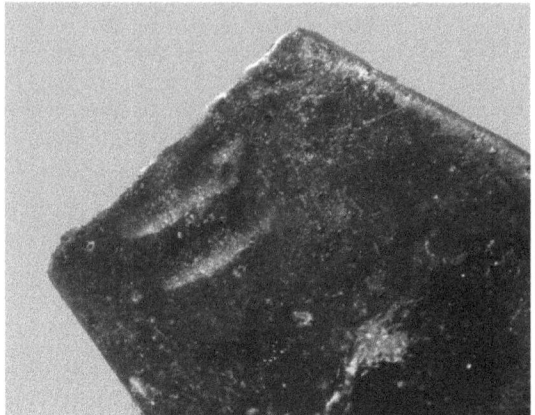

Fig. 2. Detail of a destructed axe from the hoard of Chéry 'Ferme de Malassis' (Cher, France).

These observations pose a technical problem because we don't know exactly the technical process for breaking such solid bronze objects, which are sometimes several centimeters thick (axes for example). The observations of the marks suggest the use of two different tools, corresponding to two different marks. However, the tools are not well known, neither the gestures of their use. The use of these tools is therefore only hypothetic.

The other marks of destruction are the torsions: the flat objects, particularly the swords, present these 'scars' (fig. 4). Sometimes, the torsion has not been strong enough to break the objects, which may indicate the hardness of this action (fig. 5). Othertimes, curvatures at the extremities of each fragment are visible ; these curvatures indicate that the torsion has been made until the break of the object.

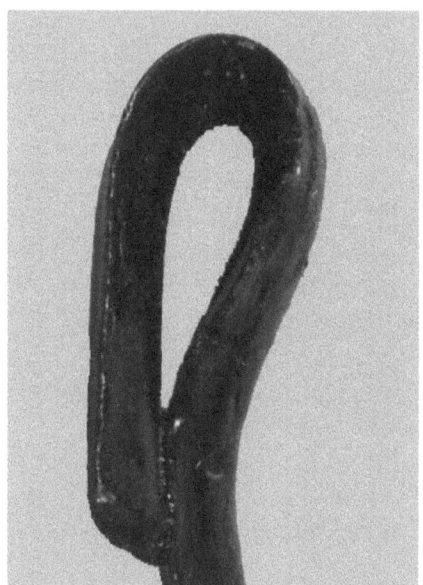

Fig. 5. Piece of sword from the hoard of Chéry 'Ferme de Malassis' (Cher, France).

After having repertoried the marks, one question is now very important. In fact, the technical process for breaking a sword or an axe of several centimeters thick is not really known. An essential question is which mechanical effort and how long is necessary to invest for its realization. *A priori*, it represents a hard action, which would significates that the breaking of bronze objects is not an innocent action.

Examples of statistical interpretation

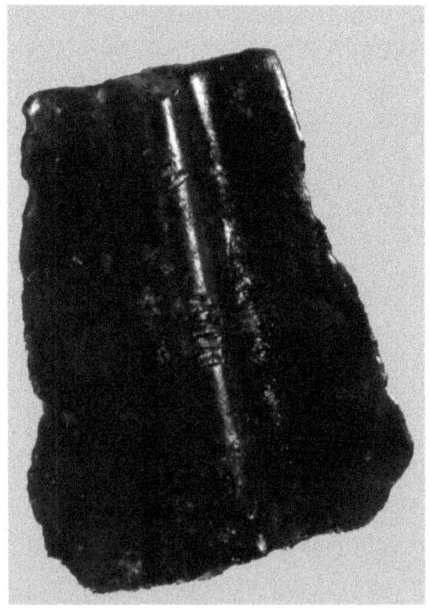

Fig. 3. Detail of a destructed spearhead from the hoard of Chéry 'Ferme de Malassis' (Cher, France).

The other very important question after the technical one is the reason of the destruction of such objects. A beginning of answer can be given by the statistical analysis. The numbering of destructed objects may be instructive.

To compare easily the proportions of each type of objects, a previous study has proposed the calculation of a rate of 'deposed metal' for expressing the quantity of 'kept metal' in hoards (Gabillot 2004). This calculation is based on the assumption that all broken objects have been, one day, entire. Then it is possible to calculate the quantity of metal that is kept with regard to the beginning of the objects's life. This is the 'rate of deposed metal' (indice de métal déposé –IMD- in french).

In the Sermizelles hoard for example (Yonne, Centre-East of France), axes are well represented, which significates that they are globally not very destructed, compared to the swords, which rate of deposed metal is smaller, which indicates that swords are more concerned than axes by this phenomenon of destruction (fig. 6).

Then, in the case of one hoard, we can see that the different types of objects are not destructed with the same intensity.

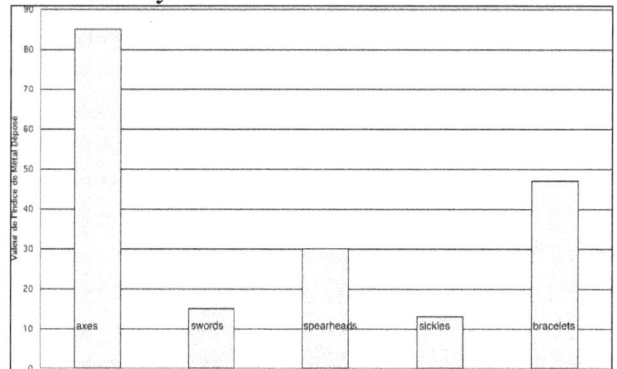

Fig. 6. Representativeness in quantity of metal of each type of objects in the Sermizelles «II» hoard (Yonne, France).

Different interpretations can be given to explain these results, like the fact that it is more difficult to break a sword than an axe.

However, it seems necessary to go after the numbering of these destructed objects in the hoards because of particular phenomena noted during several analysis.

For example, during the second millenium B.C., in the armorican area, the proportion of destructed objects varies from one period to another (fig. 7).

Another example shows that at the same time, two areas don't present the same quantity of destructed objects in the hoards: at the end of the Bronze Age, the hoards contain many broken objects in the armorican area while they contain very less in Burgundy (fig. 8).

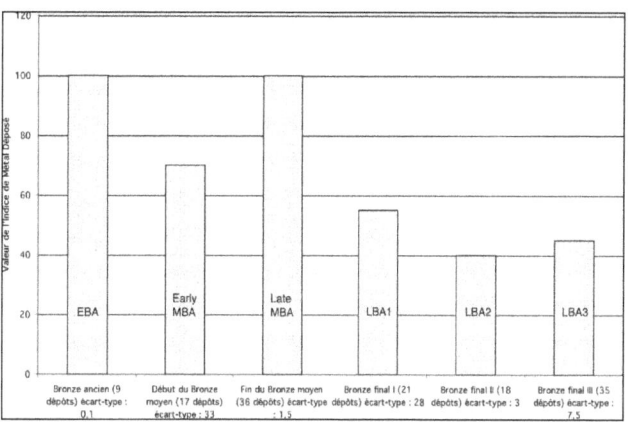

Fig. 7. Representativeness in quantity of metal from all amorican hoards during the second millenium B.C.

Other analysis in progress show particular phenomena too: at the end of Middle Bronze Age in the north-west France for example, a type of hoards contains bracelets, always entire, but with broken axes, while in Burgundy, axes are less broken but bracelets are widely destructed.

With such cases of variability, the quantity of destructed objects seems to be a characteristic element for classifying the hoards, like the number of objects, their total wealth, the proportion of each class of objects.

Late Bronze Age hoards in the South-West of France

Another study deals with Late Bronze Age hoards in the south-west of France (9th century B.C.). In the Atlantic Complex, Late Bronze Age is divided into three stages, characterized by metallic horizons. No dry hoard was evident during the Late Bronze Age 1. In the Late Bronze Age 2, a dozen hoards, from Saint-Denis-de-Pile area, show the influences from Saint-Brieuc-des-Iffs area. At the beginning of Late Bronze Age 3, there is a particular metallic group : Créon/Saint-Loubès area. At the end of Late Bronze Age, Vénat area is known in Aquitaine by some hoards (Coffyn 1971, Coffyn 1985).

The aim of this work is to identify the marks observed on the bronze objects deposited (Lagarde 2005). Moreover it is related to the rate of destructed objects in the hoards.

The objects are selected from four hoards: Braud-et-Saint-Louis, Cézac, Cubzac-les-Ponts (Gironde) and Saint-Front-de-Pradoux (Dordogne). A meticulous observation highlights particular marks which show the practices and gestures combined with these

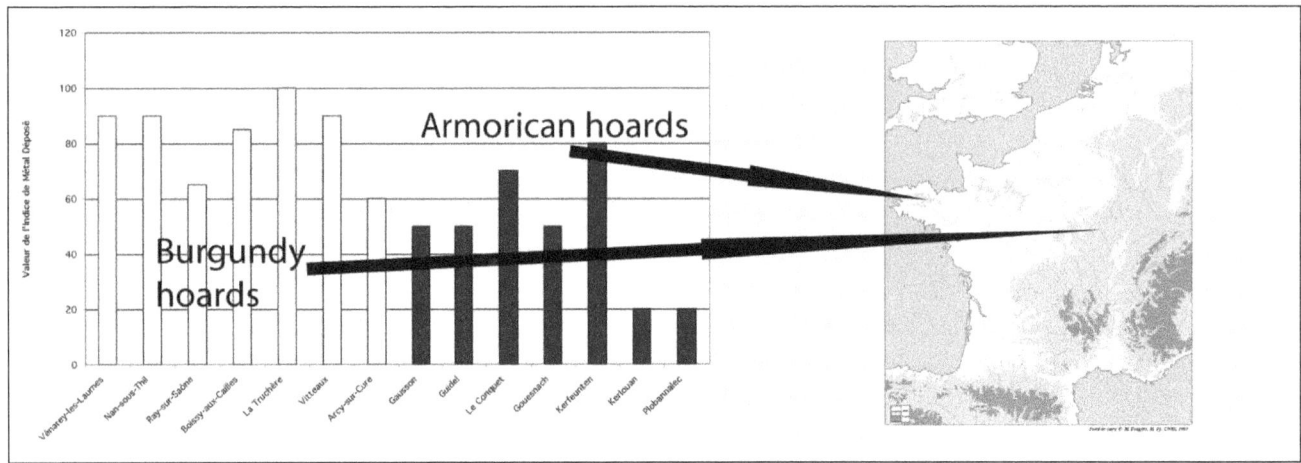

Fig. 8. Breaking of bronze objects and spatial analysis:
the objects are 'less' broken in Burgundy than in Armorican area.

objects. Three types of marks were identified corresponding to different actions: to break, damage or destroy.

Fragmentation

Many objects are broken. These breaks are not produced by a normal use of the objects. On the contrary they concern a voluntary act aiming at breaking the object. Several types of fractures have been observed. It acts first of the break of a small part of the artefact

Fig. 9. Edge of a broken axe. The remains of the axe was not deposited. Hoard of Cubzac-les-Ponts (Gironde, LBA 3).

(edge of an axe for example, fig. 9). In the second case, the objects are systematically broken down in several fragments. The swords are almost exclusively concerned; their blades are broken in many pieces (fig. 10). In all the cases of fragmentation, the break is sharp and precise. The blow was made by a sure, measured and precise gesture. This gesture requires knowledge of the metallurgy and handling of the tools only by coppersmith masters. By this gesture, the craftsman expresses all his know-how. For certain blades of swords, torsion was used to break the object. The craftsman takes part actively to the stages before the deposition (Lagarde *et al.* 2007). What are the goals of this fragmentation: facilitating the recycling, taking the right quantity of metal or a ritual act?

Fig. 10. Sword broken in several pieces, two of which have been deposited. Hoard of Cubzac-les-Ponts (Gironde, LBA 3). The end of the blade was folded.

Deterioration

Among the objects observed, a small number shows marks of blows which did not break the object. These damages do not come from a normal use of the object. For example, an axe in the Braud-et-Saint-Louis hoard wears the marks of two important blows which caused a deep notch in the metal matter (fig. 11). On another example, the blade of sword in the Cubzac-les-Ponts hoard is notched on several occasions along the median bulge (fig. 12); the marks are regular and parallel.

Fig. 11. Deep blows marks. Axe of the Braud-et-Saint-Louis hoard (Gironde, LBA 2).

Fig. 12. Many blows marks on the median bulge. Piece of sword of the hoard of Cubzac-les-Ponts (Gironde, LBA 3).

In rare cases, multiple blows related to the edge of axes were recorded. It is a gesture going further in the deterioration. The blows are carried with obstinacy, destroying this part of the object little by little (fig. 13). The remainder of the axe are intact. These marks are very different from those intended to split up the object. Do they illustrate a different technique or a particular rite?

Fig. 13. Edge of an axe broken by blows. Hoard of Braud-et-Saint-Louis (Gironde, LBA 2).

State of fragmentation

The 'rate of deposed metal' (IMD) was applied to the hoards of the LBA in the south-west of France when the composition and the state of the objects were known. In the Saint-Denis-de-Pile hoard for example, the IMD for each category of objects shows inequalities (fig. 14). First, all the categories of objects are broken. However the tools are less broken than the other categories and in particular the weapons. This difference is even more visible between the axes (68%) and the swords (11%). When the object is broken there is thus a distinction according to the category. This phenomenon can be found in the other hoards, the axes being rather deposed entire and the broken swords in great majority. Using this calculation, we can make comparative studies between the hoards of the same area, but also with hoards of different geographical and chronological contexts (with the Sermizelles II hoard for example). To have a general view, we have calculated the proportion of destructed objects for each hoard. Then we make groups according to various metal groups (groups of

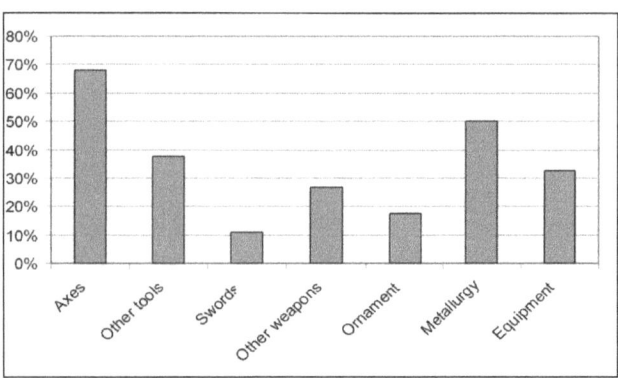

Fig. 14. Representation by category of objects of the quantity of deposed metal in the Saint-Denis-de-Pile hoard (Gironde, LBA 2). The axes and the swords are individualized in tools and weapons categories. Average quantity of deposed metal of the hoard is 34%.

Saint-Denis-de-Pile, Créon/Saint-Loubès and Vénat). With the LBA 2, the group of Saint-Denis-de-Pile shows an important average of fragmentation (fig. 15). As we precisely saw for the Saint-Denis-de-Pile hoard, all the categories of objects are broken, according to different degrees. At the beginning of LBA 3, the small group of hoards of Créon/Saint-Loubès contains only axes in great majority entire. Finally at the end of Late Bronze Age, the group of Vénat shows an important IMD which is necessary to moderate. Indeed there are differences between hoards. For example the hoard of Cubzac-les-Ponts consists of broken weapons and small pieces of equipment or harnessing which are intact. The hoard of Terrasson contains entire pieces of equipment.

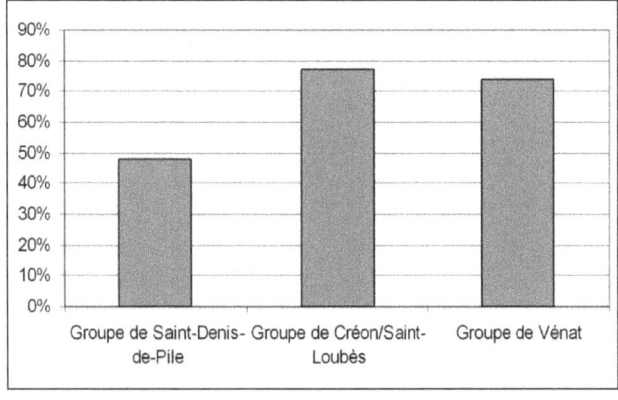

Fig. 15. Representation of the quantity of deposited metal during the Late Bronze Age by metallic groups.

Conclusion and perspectives of research

The fragmentation of the objects is a complex phenomenon in which interact many parameters (category of the object, composition of the hoard, geographical and chronological contexts). This analysis shows that the presence of destructed objects within the hoards and then certainly the destruction itself before the deposition, would be, in this case, a social or cultural practice, a constitutive element of the hoards themselves, which characterizes human groups living in the atlantic area in the second millenium B.C.

For going after these analysis and into too much detail, it would be necessary to test the technical process of breaking for estimating the degree of technical difficulty (know-how, time investing) with experimental analysis and to go after the numberings of each class of objects within each hoard, of each hoard in each period, each geographical area ; these numberings made in order to know the degree of breaking of bronze objects corresponds to a social wish, characterizing a human community bounded by the time or/and by a geographical area.

References

COFFYN A. 1971. Le Bronze final et les débuts du premier Âge du Fer autour de l'estuaire girondin, thèse de doctorat de 3e cycle, Université de Bordeaux III.

COFFYN A. 1985. Le Bronze final atlantique dans la péninsule ibérique, Paris.

GABILLOT M. 2004. La fragmentation des objets : critère d'étude des dépôts de l'âge du Bronze, Actes du 25ème Congrès Préhistorique de France : Approches fonctionnelles en Préhistoire, Nanterre, 24-26 novembre 2000 : 1-9.

KLIENLIN T. L. & OTTAWAY B. S. 1998. Flanged axes of the north-alpine region: an assessment of the possibilities of use wear analysis on metal artifacts, in Mordant, Pernot, Rychner (eds.), L'atelier du bronzier en Europe du XXe au VIIIe siècle avant notre ère, actes du colloque international Bronze' 96, Neuchâtel et Dijon, tome II : du minerai au métal, du métal à l'objet, Paris, CTHS : 271-286.

LAGARDE C. 2005. Production métallique en Aquitaine à la fin de l'âge du Bronze, Master 2 Recherche «Mondes anciens et médiévaux», Université de Bourgogne, juin 2005.

LAGARDE C., GABILLOT M. & PERNOT M. 2007. Technical study from the hoards of Sermizelles (Yonne, France), 2nd International Conference: Archaeometallurgy in Europe, Aquileia, 17-21 juin 2007: 1-12 (CD-Rom).

QUILLIEC B. 2007. L'épée atlantique : échanges et prestige au Bronze final, Mémoire de la Société Préhistorique Française; 42.

Contact

Maréva Gabillot
CNRS, UMR 5594,
Université de Bourgogne
6, bd Gabriel,
21000 Dijon
France
mareva.gabillot@u-bourgogne.fr

Céline Lagarde
Université de Bordeaux 3
CNRS, UMR 5060
Maison de l'archéologie
33607 Pessac cedex
France
celtine1@yahoo.fr

USE, WEAR AND DAMAGE:
TREATMENT OF BRONZE SWORDS BEFORE DEPOSITION

Bénédicte T. QUILLIEC

Abstract:
On the whole Atlantic Europe, after the reconstitution of the different stages of sword forming and uses processes, we underline a high frequency of damage traces. This kind of traces is more important on swords that were unearthed in the ground than in wetlands, settlement and funerary contexts. Metallic objects from the Late Bronze Age like swords, discovered in hoards were very often broken, more than isolated discoveries. A large number of swords is broken and this important aspect lead me to examine in more details the relationship between the damages and the contexts of finds: the frequency of damage traces and deposit in hoards is especially quite similar in all the regions of West Europe, above all in the South Anglia, North and West France. As regards to the technological traces observed on swords different interpretations can be proposed, such as precise and codified acts. The high frequency of damage traces lead to the suggestion of the deliberate breaking and destruction of the weapons. The technical signification may correspond to social and cultural practices, based upon the object and its representation or its signification (as functional object, raw material). Having the will to damage a weapon which also symbolise a person can result from a deliberate action to annihilate the person owning this destroyed object. Although damages were certainly done by a technician, for example a craftsman (because high know-how and technicity were necessary to break metal since traces of damages are systematic actions), the decisions may have been taken by the whole community.

Résumé :
Dans toute l'Europe atlantique, nous pouvons, d'après la reconstitution des différentes étapes de la chaîne opératoire de fabrication des épées et de leurs usages, souligner la très grande fréquence de traces de destruction. Ce type de traces est plus fréquemment retrouvé sur les épées retrouvées en contexte terrestre que sur celles découvertes en contexte aquatique, funéraire ou d'habitat. Les objets métalliques de la fin de l'âge du Bronze comme les épées, découverts dans des dépôts sont très souvent cassés, et beaucoup plus que les découvertes isolées. La grande quantité d'épées cassées et endommagées m'a conduite à étudier en détail les relations entre destructions volontaires et contextes de découvertes : la fréquence des traces de destruction et de mise en dépôts est comparable dans toutes les régions d'Europe occidentale, surtout dans le Sud de l'Angleterre, le Nord et l'Ouest de la France. Concernant les traces techniques observées sur les épées, différentes interprétations peuvent être proposées, comme des actes précis et codifiés. La fréquence importante des traces de destructions sur les armes, sur les objets et leur représentation ou leur signification (comme objet fonctionnel ou matière première), conduit à suggérer que ce sont des actes délibérés, correspondant à des pratiques sociales et culturelles. Vouloir endommager une arme, qui symbolise aussi une personne, peut résulter d'une action délibérée d'annihiler la personne à travers ses effets personnels. De plus, les destructions ont certainement été réalisées par un technicien, le bronzier par exemple (un haut niveau de savoir-faire et de technicité sont nécessaires pour casser le métal, d'autant que les traces de destructions sont des actes systématiques), les décisions pouvant avoir été prises par l'ensemble de la communauté.

Introduction

In this paper is exposed a research about the treatment of bronze swords before their wet or dry deposition. Indeed on the whole Atlantic Europe, from Scotland to Andalusia, similar sword types have been found and repetitive practices were associated to their abandonment. Studies of the Atlantic swords are based on technical attributes and location discoveries. A large number of swords is broken and this important aspect leads to examine in more details the relationship between the damages and the contexts of finds. After the geographical and chronological context of this study, the technological traces of uses and damages observed on swords and their interpretations are presented. Each regional group in Europe and its modes of deposition is exposed. Finally I set out different hypothesis about weapons which look deliberately damaged before burring. It shows intervention of different actors in these social practices.

Geographical and chronological context

Currently, nearly four thousand Atlantic swords are listed for the three stages of the Late Bronze Age (Quilliec 2007 a). We observe an evolution of the shapes of weapons (offensive and defensive weapons like swords, spears, shields, helmets or breastplates) and we underline the marked increase in numbers of swords and hoards during the three stages of Late Bronze Age (from about 1,350 to 800 B.C.). Although chronological systems are different in each European country, the Late Bronze Age system with three stages considered is the one of Patrice Brun (Brun 1984: 263 ; Brun 1988: 599), who had systematized Jacques Briard system (Briard 1965). Stage 1, from c. 1,350 to 1,150 B.C. (that could be equivalent to the Late Bronze Age I-IIa of the J.-J. Hatt system); stage 2, from c. 1,150 to 930 B.C. (Late Bronze Age IIb-IIIa) and stage 3, from 930 to 800 B.C. (Late Bronze Age IIIb). My intention is not to define regional groups as Patrice Brun done it in his article (Brun 1991). In this work, regional groups of the Atlantic complex were based on countries where high rate of discoveries trying to make them with approximate equivalent number of swords to compare (Quilliec 2007 a: chapter 3).

Metallic objects like swords were unearthed in wetlands (rivers, lakes and bogs) or in the ground. Deposits, in hoard or isolated discoveries, are the most important contexts of sword discoveries (fig. 1). However a constant can be noticed: the extreme rarity of discoveries in settlement and funerary contexts: it represents less than 2% of the all corpus (Quilliec 2001). Discoveries in funerary contexts represent less than 0.5% of the corpus (16/3,909) and in settlement contexts, it is hardly even 1% (46/3,909).

In the different European museums where they are stored, I studied in detail one thousand swords. This sample is a significant corpus to make a frame of reference and these observations can be used to identify regional variations, as well as technological groups covering very wide geographical areas.

Technical studies

As regards to the interpretation of technical traces noted on swords, 'chaîne operatoire' could be reconstructed from hypothesis of conception to abandonment (Quilliec 2007 b: fig. 3). The craftsmen or

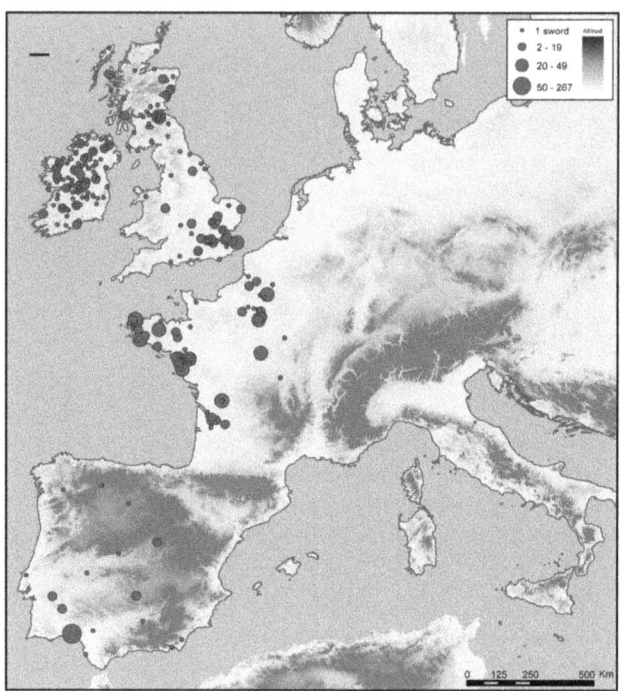

Fig. 1. Atlantic swords distribution during the Late Bronze Age (c. 1,350-800 B.C.) in West Europe.

the users have made traces or faults which are still visible on the objects, that were noted and expounded. With a detailed analysis of technical aspects, we try to understand how the objects were produced in spite of difficulties of the material. Indeed, bronze conserves traces of forming made by the craftsman, but faults or traces of forming are more often than not erased by the bronze craftsman. Sometimes traces are worn away. The use and wear of the swords lead to make other traces. Besides workshops and scraps from the Late Bronze Age are uncommon and most of the metallic objects due to recycling are lost for us. The steps of the 'chaîne opératoire' are forming, uses and damages and deposition. The observations came from macroscopic and microscopic exams and gave information about the forming processes and the uses. Others metallurgical artefacts like clay moulds, experimentations in wax, X-rays, some component analysis and metallographic exams were used too (Quilliec, Pernot 2003). They were essential to understand a complex craft like bronze metallurgy.

The earliest swords of the Late Bronze Age were in bronze, copper alloy with tin only or tin and lead. They were mainly manufactured by casting but traces before and after casting have been detected. Before casting, a model or a pattern and a mould, like a clay mould were made. Traces are for example marks made in wax, visible casting seams or rough surfaces (Quilliec 2007 c). Traces of casting were identified for example by holes on the surface. After casting, swords were polished or burnished. In most of cases a hilt was joined to the tang by riveting. Occasionally, swords were deposited without ending acts.

The reconstitution of the different stages of sword forming processes conduces to identify traces of uses and to rediscover acts and gestures too (Leroi-Gourhan 1943 and 1945). We underline a very high frequency of break and damage traces before deposit. Lot of swords are broken and it seems evident they come from intentional actions. As for recycling, even if we have no proof, we suppose that a part of old metallic object was melt down again. Deposition of rough-out swords without ending treatment like burnishing was very exceptional.

In spite of corrosion which can be very abundant (for example bronze objects from Brittany, because of the composition of the ground) traces of use can be separate from traces of forming and in any cases from damages traces. In this way, even if lots of them were worn away by regular polishing of the blade, traces of uses which are proof of fighting are very common (93.6%).

As Kristian Kristiansen highlighted it in a previous studies a variety of tracks of fighting has been identified on swords (Kristiansen 2002). An important comment was about the reconstitution of the gestures which correspond to the act that made the traces. In the same field others studies about interpretation of uses traces on axes were carried out by Ben Robert and Barbara Ottaway and some kind of traces are similar to sword's (Robert, Ottaway 2003).

We can make distinctions with nature of scars on the blade or on the edge which are signs of different uses. My intention is not to explain or argue each traces but only to expose them to illustrate my purpose. Others technical studies focus on fragmentation (Gabillot 2003) and on types of damages (Nebelsick 2004) and specifically on swords (York 2002). For example we observe nicks on the edge of the blade (fig. 2) and a stroke on the blade which has deformed the ornament on the blade (fig. 3) that could had happened when knocking or giving a blow or conversely striking back or warding off it. A variety of nicks or tears suppose different kind of impact and certainly different kind of fighting techniques.

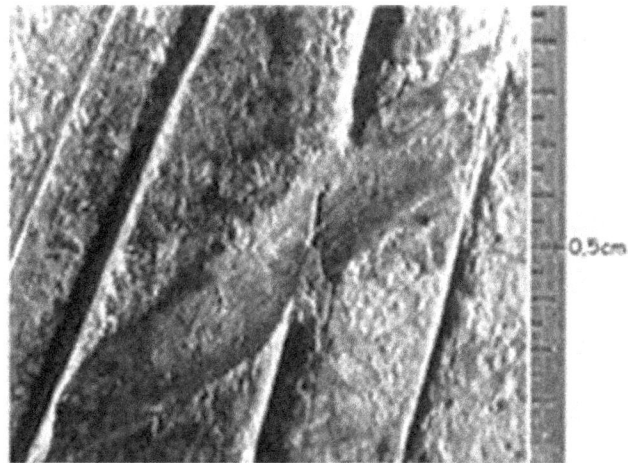

Fig. 3. A stroke on the blade with a deformed ornament: Challans, 'La Villate', Vendée, France, (M.A.N. Saint-Germain-en-Laye inv. n°81.446).

Cracks (fig. 4) and scratches on the blade (fig. 5) indicate traces of fight too. We can consider that a broken sword in two parts is not apparently a deliberate break. We suppose that it could be accidental and consequently interpreted as a scar of use.

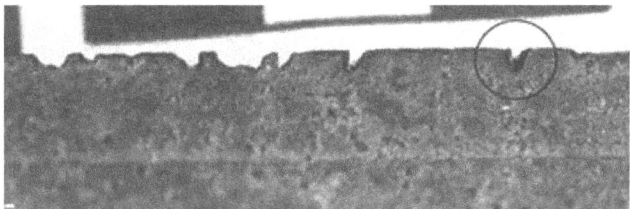

Fig. 2. Nicks on the edge of the blade: Neuvy-sur-Barangeon, Cher, France (M.A.N. Saint-Germain-en-Laye inv. n°29.377)

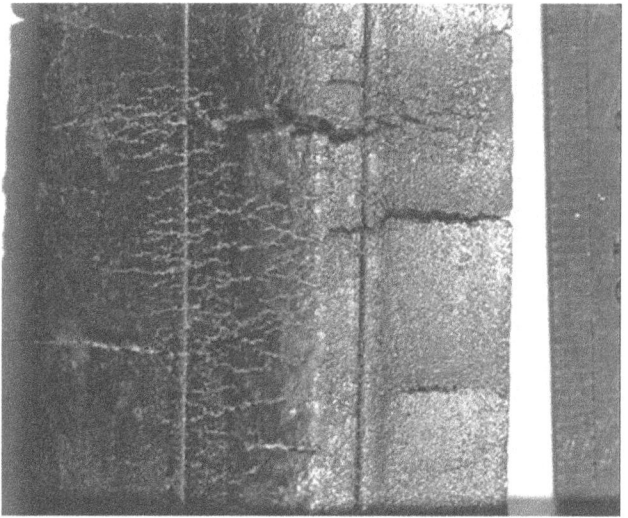

Fig. 4. Cracks on the blade: Vénat hoard, Saint-Yriex, Charente, France, (S.A.H.C. Angoulême, inv. n° Ch.20 -A. & R.16).

Fig. 5. Scratches on the blade: Puertollano, Camino de Santiago, Ciudad Real, Spain (Archaeological Museum Ciudad Real).

Frequent or intensive wear and uses of a sword without stages of sharpening, the point and the edges of the blade become to get blunt (fig. 6).

All these example of wear and use traces can be found in association. Nevertheless sometimes when many traces have been detected on a same weapon it appears evident to be a deliberate rather than a fortuitous action. For these reasons and in order not to confuse as far as possible the only used weapons with the damaged weapons, we consider that a weapon is damaged when we note several traces which render it unusable like a sword (as its initial function).

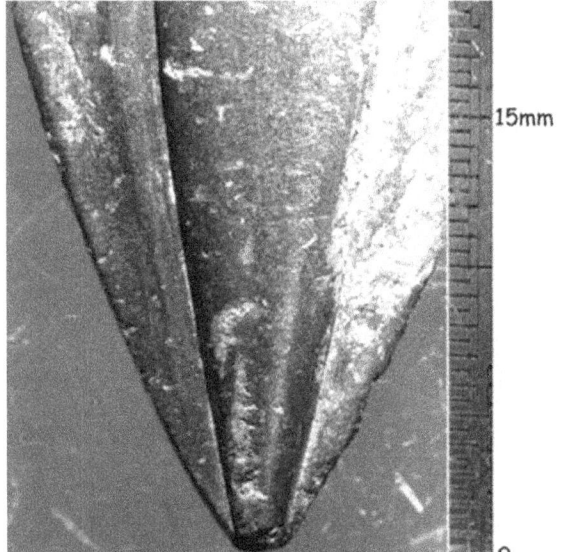

Fig. 6. The point of the blade is blunt. Challans, 'La Villate', Vendée, France (M.A.N. Saint-Germain-en-Laye inv. n°81.425).

Different examples of traces of intentional damages were distinguished. Lots of swords are broken and it is obvious that breaking a sword on three or four or even up to eight fragments can not be an accident.

Besides only some fragments of swords were found in hoards and the other fragments of these swords are missing. A selection of just a part of the weapon (it is valid for all kinds of objects) had been made (fig. 7). But in the present state we can not explain these deliberate lacks of material.

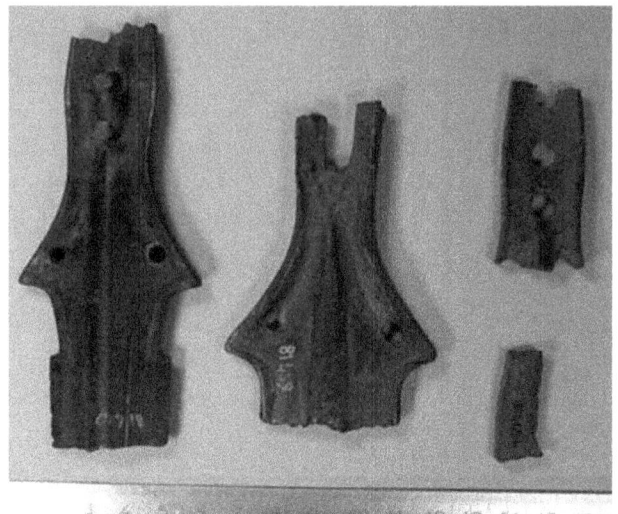

Fig. 7. Several fragments of swords. Challans' hoard, 'La Villate', Vendée, France (M.A.N. Saint-Germain-en-Laye inv. n°81 449; n°81.449b; n°81.447 and n°81.459).

The systematic breaking argues to intentional actions like twisting (fig. 8) or hammering –with large scar (fig. 9). A bent blade of a sword can be related to a fight but when it is winded like in this example (fig. 8) we have to envisage a intended act. Similarly repetitive bows of hammering on blade which have distorted the edges (fig. 9) or nicks and tears (fig. 10) demonstrate a furious energy to destroy the shape of the edges and to the render the weapon out of order.

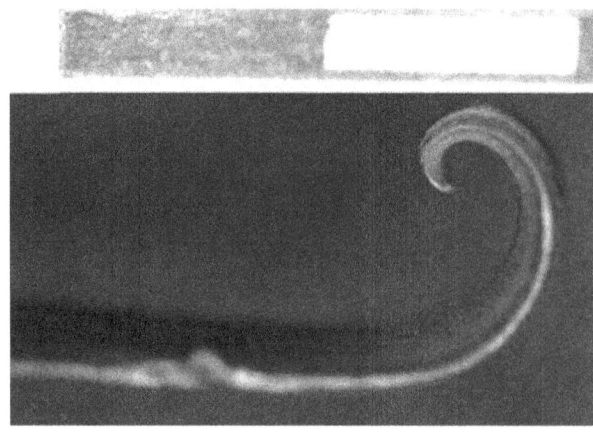

Fig. 8. The end of the blade had been twisted so far as to wind the point: Dolwyddelan, Worcester, Wales (British Museum, London inv. n°1851.12.30.1).

Fig. 9. Traces of hammering are obvious on the edges of the blade:
'Forêt de Compiègne', Oise, France
(M.A.N. Saint-Germain-en-Laye inv. n°28.951).

Fig. 10. The shape of the edge of the blade is completely bend (nicks): Saint-Ygeaux, Kerboar, Côtes d'Armor, France (S.R.A. Rennes, inv. n°32-4).

Discoveries contexts

With a sample of one thousand swords studied in detail, we have a significant corpus to make a frame of references and these observations can be used to identify regional variations of deposition (table 1). By combining technological analysis with contextual information we try to understand complex rituals. It is no accident that repetitive actions are widespread on the entire Western Europe. The frequency of bronze swords with traces of manufacturing, use, damage and their context of deposition determines regional groups with common technical and cultural behaviour patterns that shows organisations of prehistoric societies are complex and probably reveal correlations between economical world and mental world.

On the whole Atlantic Europe we underline a very high frequency of traces of uses (93.6%). It becomes apparent that swords were really functional and not only intended to demonstrate prestige status, to be shown at the time of ceremonial representation or to be offered to deities (fig. 11A). It is worth mentioning the very important number of swords with traces of damages that represent 65.4% of the corpus (fig. 11B). The association of uses and damages traces are widespread too (61.2%), that consequently should prevent us to think that swords were only meant to be votive, especially made as offering to divinities (we can not either rule out possible ritual fights!).

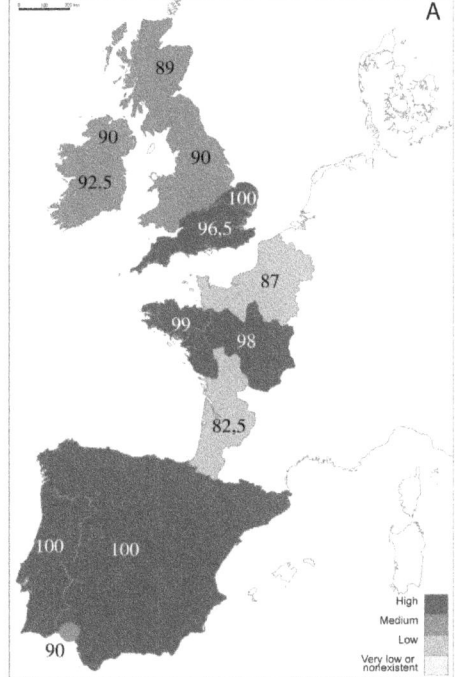
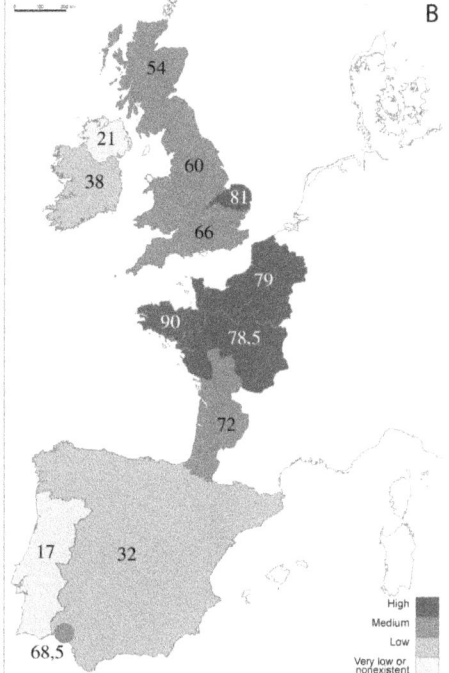

Fig. 11. Percentages of swords from the LBA found with traces of:
A- Uses (total = 93.6%); B- Damages (total = 65.4%).

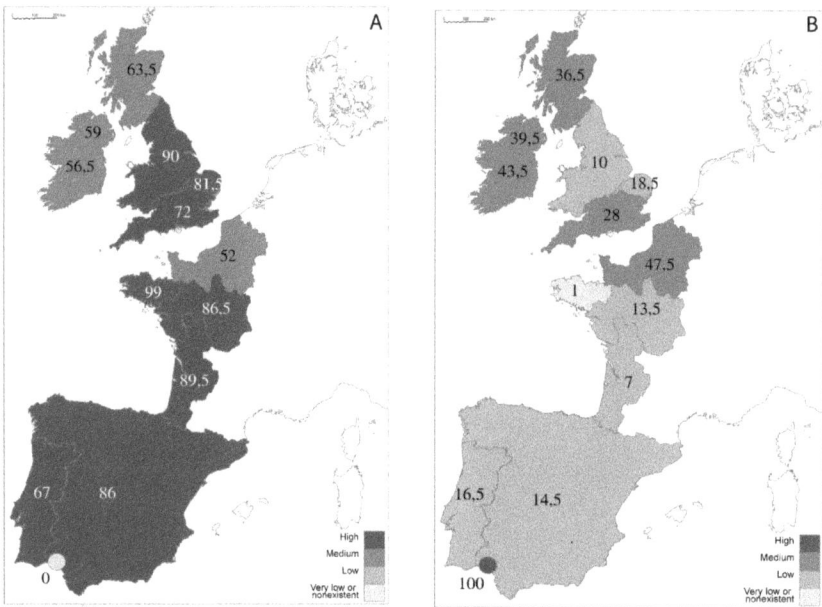

Fig. 12. Percentages of swords from the LBA found in:
A- Ground context (total = 69.7%); B- Humid context (total = 29.8%).

Specific deposition of swords in earth or water was a very frequent and recurrent practice during all the Bronze Age and above all during the Late Bronze Age (Bradley 1990: 9). Swords discoveries in ground are more important (69.7; fig. 12A) in all over Western Europe than discoveries in humid context (29.8; fig. 12B).

The frequency of damage traces and deposit in hoards is especially quite similar in all the regions of West Europe. Swords found in hoards were very often broken, more than isolated discoveries. We can add that technical traces on bronze are more important on swords that were discovered in hoard (buried in the ground than in wetlands), settlement and funerary contexts. Swords found in ground context are more damaged (fig. 13A) than swords found in humid or wet context (fig. 13B). We is likely to explain this phenomenon by the will not to get back the weapons and not to be able to use it (like object and like symbol).

On the whole Europe we underline a high frequency of wear traces. The dominant trend we observe is that this kind of traces is more important in the 'interior' (South Anglia and North-West of France) than in the

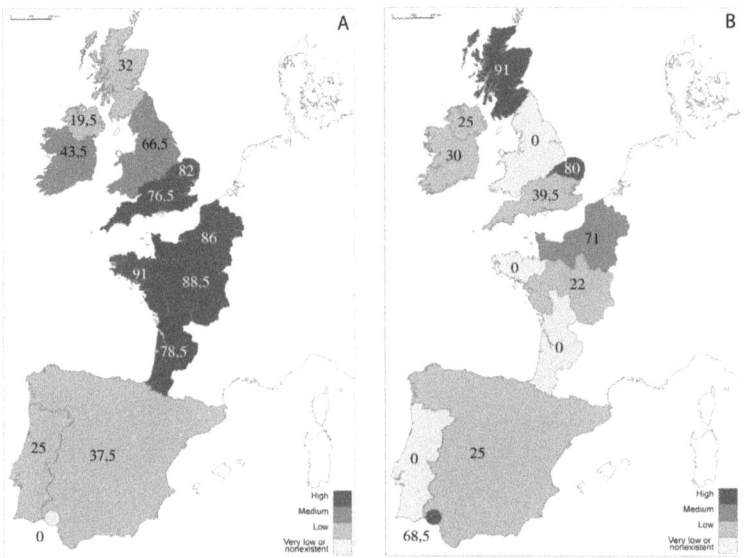

Fig. 13. Percentages of damaged swords from the LBA found in:
A- Ground context (total = 71.2%); B- Humid context (total = 52.4%).

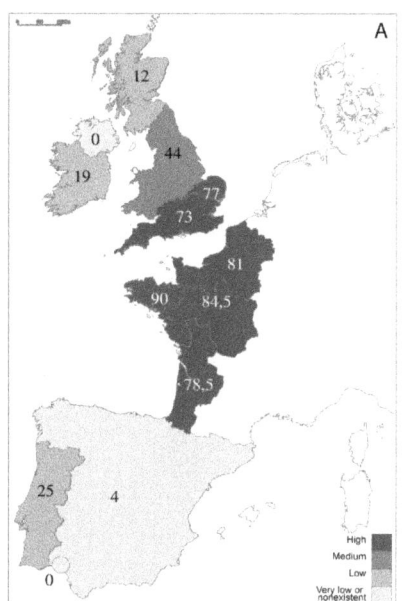
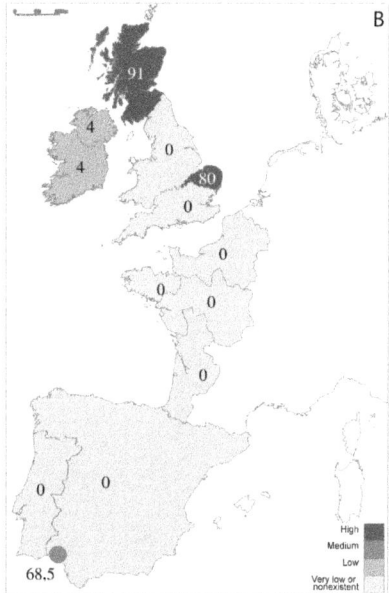

Fig. 14. Percentages of damaged swords from the LBA found in:
A- Ground Hoard context (total = 63%) ; B- Humid Hoard context (total = 28%).

periphery of the Atlantic Complex, but less in South-West of France. The North of France is once more an exception. Others investigations focused on each regional group will help us to understand these specificities.

As to the frequency of damage traces and deposit in hoards, the results are quite similar: an opposition between the 'centre' and the surrounding areas (in the extreme South and North of the Atlantic Complex, like the Iberian peninsula or Scotland). Thus, in the borders, frequency of damages and hoards is less common. We underline that metallic objects like the swords, discovered in hoards were broken very often, more than the isolated discoveries. A large number of swords is broken and this important aspect requires further investigations, especially in relationship to the context of finds (land or water). Altogether 63% of swords of the LBA found in ground hoards have damages traces (fig. 14A) while there are only 28% from humid hoards (fig. 14B).

Social interpretation

By combining morpho-typological and technological analysis with contextual information, we have a better understanding about metalworking and the consequences, showing a more complex organisation of proto-historic societies. Studies of the Late Bronze Age swords based on technical attributes aim to identify interaction between cultural groups and then, were used to examine how elite of the Late Bronze Age societies may have been organised in Western Europe. As regards to the technological traces observed on swords different interpretations can be proposed, such as particular and codified acts. The high frequency of damage traces lead to the suggestion of the deliberate breaking and destruction of the weapons.

Discovery contexts of swords are so original that we suppose ritual gestures with deposits. They could be at the same time sacred and profane gestures. The choice of a place and the choice of the conditions of deposition are probably determined by specific and codified knowledge (Quilliec 2007 d).

These results reveal that actors were different. Then, at the scale of a community, and perhaps more widely, we can notice interactions between the different actors around the sword as objects and as symbol (fig. 15).

Swords in the centre of the diagram were discovered in various contexts, buried or submerged. It appears very frequent to find them damaged and, looking carefully, we notice that swords were used too. Of course before their use and wear, swords were produced. We can associate technical gestures to these traces of manufacture. But, to carry out these gestures, it is necessary to have specifically knowledge and know-how. Traces of use show particular gestures too, directly linked to the function of the sword and their owners. They are warriors but we should

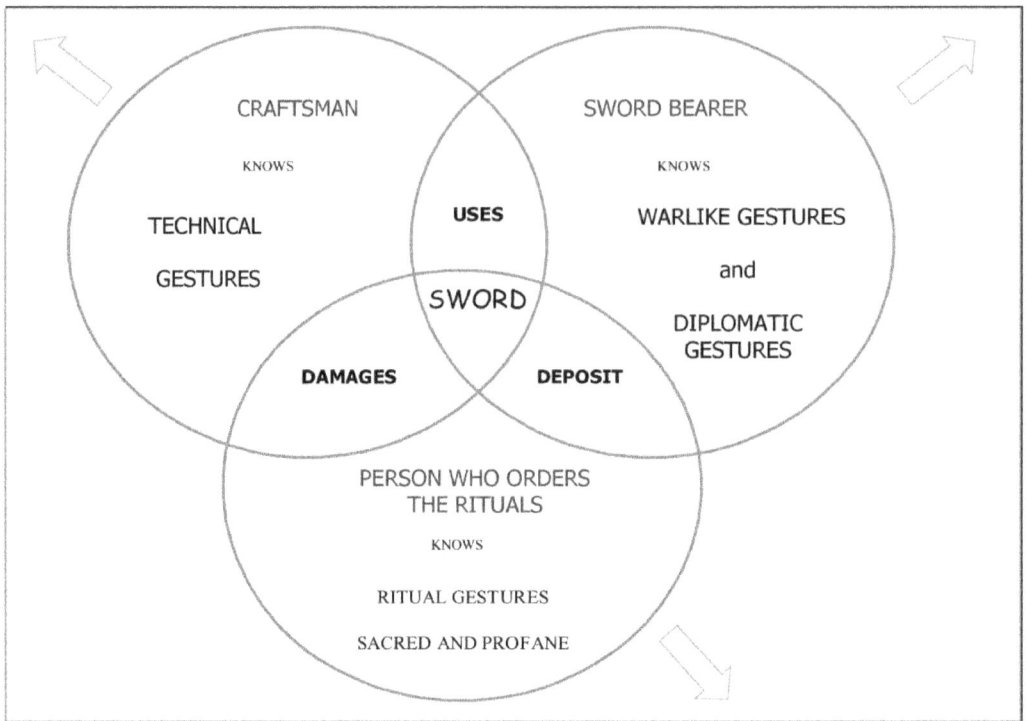

Fig. 15. Hypothesis of 'Late Bronze Age social organisation' based on sword studies.

not forget that in the Late Bronze Age swords have a social and identity status (Quilliec 2007 e). As well, we can suppose diplomatic gestures, although they are not physically perceptible. We perceive the social position and knowledge of the person who uses the sword (appearance and knowledge).

Because of these codes a specialist probably carried out these damages. But regarding damages and hoards, they are cultural actions: although I think that they were done by a technician as a craftsman, because high know-how and technicity were necessary to break metal since traces of damages are systematic actions in all the regions. And the most competent person to carry them out is certainly the bronze craftsman. Production can not be made without an exchange with the user, to have a weapon which meets esthetical and functional needs. The weapon bearer has also a role in the abandoning of the weapon and deposit can be determined with the agreement of all the actors.

Therefore, at the community level each individual intervenes in different spheres: traces left on swords are the proof of different actions and they show several ways of intervention: forming, uses and damage and deposit. We can deduce spiritual actions (sacred and profane rituals), technical actions and political actions.

Different actors made these voluntary or involuntary gestures and actions (fig. 15). These actors are not only individuals but also people whom hold a social role. It is possible to distinguish three steps of intervention around the sword found in hoards:

- technical gestures, which are from the bronze craftsman (bronze craftsman);
- warlike and diplomatic gestures, which are from the sword bearer (sword wearer, warrior);
- sacred and profane ritual gestures, which are from a 'person who orders the rituals' (ritualist).

Also, this people probably made trades in each sphere with their 'homologous' from other villages or countries. Traces were made by craftsmen and users during the life of the swords: production, maintenance, wear, damage, deposit; the various interactions involving swords, whether spiritual, technical or political are complementary.

Therefore we have a physical link with people of the Late Bronze Age, underlining the immaterial links which exist in all the societies. Individuals acted in different but complementary areas. It's an hypothesis of the Late Bronze Age community organisation. Regional links of bronze technologies, which are decisive in the construction of group identity and in the development of trade, and it is probably significant that there were privileged alliances are essential to understand and to define the relations between the different countries.

Traditional hypothesis of hoard' interpretations can be reserve to raw material, social and territorial markers of identity, and sacred offerings to divinities or secular people. But these hypothesis are associated to specific rules and social and cultural needs.

Discussion

Several interpretations depending on the location and on the composition of deposits (Needham 2001). I will accentuate on contexts of deposit in engraved or wet areas. Deliberate breaking and destruction of swords are codified gestures that lead to social and ritual action. For this reason, isolated or associated objects were a selection and should be considered as hoards. And I do not think people wanted to get back objects or raw material. Removing objects or fragments of objects from a group aim to restrict the circulation field, to maintain the shortfall of the metallic production in order to keep a high value of exchange (Gálan-Domingo 1993). It contributes to control the production (Needham 2001, fig. 8) and to balance the flow of metal supply (Verlaeckt 2000: fig.13.3).

But why break a sword and bury it in ground? And why deposit only a fragment selecting a part of the object? As for 'funeral interpretation' of hoards like cenotaphs, parts of objects can be associated to someone. As for fragment of sword, which is consider to be a male symbol, is likely to 'represent a man', to embody a warrior as individual or to personify a leader with the aim in symbolise his function, his power and influence in the society for example. Sword represents in this case the function of his possessor, who has rights and duties to protect, to defender and to dispense justice: sword is a war symbol too.
To deposit a fragment of sword in association with others can be to break up of the symbolic character of the sword. Break a sword is equivalent to break its bearer and all its representations: statute of warrior and his identity. The objects can be deposited during public ceremonies. There is no doubt that swords belong to many warriors. Fragments can represent a died warrior or discharge character or even an enemy killed during a fight, a war.

Historical or mythological examples are known with a personification of the weapon as the sword which has a name. Sword is a personal weapon, for example, Excalibur and the King Arthur. The power of the weapon can turn against his bearer if it does not belong to him. During the Celtic period, we know that weapons of the enemies were sacrificed and were deposited in sanctuaries from the Iron Age. Nobody was allowed to touch them (Julius Caesar, The Gaul War). It was a taboo. We can suppose that these kinds of ritual practices were embedded in Bronze Age cultures.

Of course to part with sword can conduce to be discredited and perhaps deposit a weapon can have a similar function. Discredit a chief of his functions during his life or prepare his succession at his death. When sword disappears of the living world, it takes off metal circulation, as functional and symbolic object but as raw material, economical material too (Needham 2001).

Functions of destruction could have been done to remove a part of raw material, part of an object, because of its function or its representation (weapon, tool, and ornament). They could have been done to give off impossible to use the objects. One of the objectives seems to prevent anyone from getting it back. Otherwise, why did prehistoric human take metallic objects off their eyesight?
We can not find again immersed swords that can explain why they were less destroyed than when they were buried. In the ground, objects could have been getting back, but it is impossible to use them if they were damaged.

The technical signification may correspond to social and cultural practices, based upon the object and its representation or its signification (as functional object, raw material). Having the will to damage or 'to kill' a weapon, which also represents or symbolises a person can result from a deliberate action to annihilate the person owning this damaged object. Functional practical and technical actions seem to be ideological, sacrificial and / or economical actions. Although damages were certainly done by a technician like a craftsman but the decisions may probably have been taken by the whole community.

Destruction was not a specificity of swords and I am conscious of this exclusive study. It could be different with others weapons and all the component of hoards.

But as to sword only results show that it is a particular weapon (and for ages) and it is on the centre of complex interactions and only retain one interpretation would occult a part of its significance and its rules for the men of the Bronze Age.

References

BRADLEY R., 1990. T*he passage of arms. An archaeological analysis of prehistoric hoards and votives deposits*, Cambridge University Press, Cambridge.

BRIARD J., 1965. *Les dépôts bretons et l'âge du Bronze atlantique*, Faculté des Sciences de Rennes, t. 38, n° 224, 352 p., 113 fig.

BRUN P., 1984. Modèles diffusionnistes et systèmes chronologiques in : *Transition Bronze Final Hallstatt Ancien : problèmes chronologiques et culturels, Actes du 109e Congrès National des Sociétés Savantes, Dijon 1984, Section d'archéologie et d'histoire de l'art, T. II*, p. 262-277.

BRUN P., 1988. L'entité «Rhin-Suisse-France orientale» : nature et évolution, in BRUN P., MORDANT C. (dir.), *Le groupe Rhin-Suisse-France orientale et la notion de civilisation des champs d'urnes, Actes du colloque international de Nemours, 1986, Mémoires du Musée de Préhistoire d'Ile-de-France n° 1, 1988*, éditions A.P.R.A.I.F., Nemours, p.599-618.

BRUN P., 1991. Le Bronze Atlantique et ses subdivisions culturelles : essai de définition, in CHEVILLOT C. et COFFYN A. (dir.), *L'Âge du Bronze Atlantique, ses faciès, de l'Écosse à l'Andalousie et leurs relations avec le Bronze Continental et la Méditerranée, Actes du 1er Colloque du Parc Archéologique de Beynac, 10-14 Septembre 1990*, Association des Musées Sarladais, 11-24.

GABILLOT M., 2003. La fragmentation des objets : critère d'étude des dépôts de l'âge du Bronze, *XXVe Congrès Préhistorique de France, Approches fonctionnelles en Préhistoire, Nanterre, Novembre 2000*, Paris, Société préhistorique française, 193-201.

GALAN-DOMINGO E., 1993. Estelas, Paisaje y Territorio en el Bronce Final del Suroeste de la Penìnsula Ibérica, *Complutum, extra*, n° 3.

KRISTIANSEN K., 2002. The Tale of the sword - swords and swordfighters in the Bronze Age Europe, *Oxford Journal of Archaeology* n° 21 (4), 319-332.

LEROI-GOURHAN A., 1943 (1992). *Évolution et Techniques, tome I : L'homme et la matière*, A. Michel, Paris.

LEROI-GOURHAN A., 1945 (1992). *Évolution et Techniques, tome II : Milieu et techniques*, A. Michel, Paris.

NEBELSICK L., 2004. Rent asunder: ritual violence in Late Bronze Age hoards, in PARE C.F.E. (dir.), *Metals make the world go round, The supply and circulation of metals in Bronze Age Europe, Proceedings of a conference held at the Université of Birmingham, June 1997*, Oxbow Books, 160-175.

NEEDHAM S., 2001. When expediency broaches ritual intention: the flow of metal between systemic and buried domains, *The Journal of the Royal Anthropological Institute*, vol. 7, n° 2, 275-298.

QUILLIEC B., 2001. Les épées du Bronze final et les voies fluviales et maritimes, In *Systèmes fluviaux, estuaires et implantations humaines de la Préhistoire aux grandes invasions, Actes du 124e Congrès National des Sociétés Historiques et Scientifiques, Nantes 1999*, Paris, CTHS, 241-252.

QUILLIEC B., 2007 (a). L'épée atlantique : échanges et prestige au Bronze final, Mémoire de la Société préhistorique française n°42, 172 p, Cédérom.

QUILLIEC B., 2007 (b). Technologie des épées à l'âge du Bronze final en Europe atlantique : reconstitution des chaînes opératoires, Actes du Congrès du Centenaire de la Société Préhistorique Française, Avignon, Septembre 2005, 401-411.

QUILLIEC B., 2007 (c). Les épées en bronze protohistoriques : conçues pour détruire ; conçues pour être détruites, Annales de la Fondation Fyssen, n°21, 38-47.

QUILLIEC B., 2007 (d). Fabrications et usages des épées en bronze en Europe atlantique, c. 1350 et 800 B.C., Table ronde «Spécialisation des tâches et sociétés», ArScAn UMR 7041, Nanterre, 2003/2004, Technique et Culture, 46/47, 235-251.

QUILLIEC B., 2007 (e). La production des armes à l'âge du Bronze : maîtriser des savoir et affirmer son appartenance culturelle, in ROUILLARD P. *et al.* (dir.), Mobilités, Immobilisme, imitation, transfert et refus d'emprunt, Colloque de la Maison René Ginouves, 8-9 juin 2006, 135-141.

QUILLIEC B., PERNOT M., 2003. Étude technique de quatre fragments de languettes d'épées du Bronze final du dépôt de Challans (Vendée), *Antiquités Nationales,* n° 34, 2002, 91-101.

ROBERTS B., OTTAWAY B.S., 2003. The use and significance of socketed axes during the Late Bronze Age, *European Journal of Archaeology,* vol.6(2), 119-140.

VERLAECKT K., 2000. Hoarding and the circulation of metalwork in Late Bronze Age in Denmark: quantification and beyond, in PARE C.F.E. (ed), 2000. *Metals make the world go round, The supply and circulation of metals in Bronze Age Europe, Proceedings of a conference held at the University of Birmingham, June 1997,* Oxbow Books, 194-208.

YORK J., 2002. The life cycle of Bronze Age Metalwork from the Thames, *Oxford Journal of Archaeology,* n°21 (1), 77-92.

Ancient texts
JULES CESAR, *La guerre de Gaule, traduction L.-A. Constans*, éditions Gallimard coll. Folio classique.

Contact

Bénédicte T. Quilliec
Post-doctorante, Fondation Fyssen
ArScAn -UMR 7041 - Protohistoire européenne
Maison de l'Archéologie et de l'Ethnologie
21 allée de l'Université
92 023 Nanterre cedex
France
benedicte.quilliec@mae.u-paris10.fr

	Traces of uses	Traces of break	Traces of damages	Uses and damages	Damges and ground context	Damages and ground hoard context	Break and ground context	Break and ground hoard context	Damages and humid context	Damages and humid hoard context	Break and humid context	Ground context	Hoard in ground context	Humid context	Hoard in all contextes	Number of studied swords
South Anglia	114	101	78	76	65	62	81	76	13	0	13	85	78	33	78	118
%	96,6	85,6	66,1	64,4	76,5	72,9	95,3	89,4	39,4	0	39,4	72,0	91,8	28,0	66,1	
East Anglia	27	27	22	22	18	17	22	21	4	4	4	22	21	5	26	27
%	100	100	81,5	81,5	81,8	77,3	100	95,5	80	80	80	81,5	95,5	18,5	96,3	
North Anglia	9	7	6	5	6	4	7	4	0	0	0	9	5	1	5	10
%	90	70	60	50	66,7	44,4	77,8	44,4	0	0	0	90	55,6	10	50	
Scotland	83	80	50	42	19	7	47	22	31	31	31	59	29	34	62	93
%	89,2	86,0	53,8	45,2	32,2	11,9	79,7	37,3	91,2	91,2	91,2	63,4	49,2	36,6	66,7	
Ulster	55	41	13	13	7	0	25	3	6	1	16	36	4	24	10	61
%	90,2	67,2	21,3	21,3	19,4	0	69,4	8,3	25	4,2	66,7	59,0	11,1	39,3	16,4	
South Ireland	113	83	46	45	30	13	50	17	16	2	33	69	18	53	20	122
%	92,6	68,0	37,7	36,9	43,5	18,8	72,5	24,6	30,2	3,8	62,3	56,6	26,1	43,4	16,4	
Armoric	131	128	119	119	119	118	127	126	0	0	0	131	130	1	130	132
%	99,2	97,0	90,2	90,2	90,8	90,1	96,9	96,2	0	0	0	99,2	99,2	0,8	98,5	
Loire	196	180	157	153	153	146	167	159	6	0	6	173	161	27	161	200
%	98	90	78,5	76,5	88,4	84,4	96,5	91,9	22,2	0	22,2	86,5	93,1	13,5	80,5	
Seine Nord	96	105	87	73	49	46	57	50	37	0	36	57	50	52	50	110
%	87,3	95,5	79,1	66,4	86,0	80,7	100	87,7	71,2	0	69,2	51,8	87,7	47,3	45,5	
South West of France	47	52	41	34	40	40	50	50	0	0	0	51	51	4	51	57
%	82,5	91,2	71,9	59,6	78,4	78,4	98,0	98,0	0	0	0	89,5	100	7,0	89,5	
Huelva Hoard	63	61	48	41	0	0	0	0	48	48	61	0	0	70	70	70
%	90	87,1	68,6	58,6	0	0	0	0	68,6	68,6	87,1	0	0	100	100	
Spain	28	26	9	9	9	1	23	10	1	0	3	24	11	4	11	28
%	100	92,9	32,1	32,1	37,5	4,2	95,8	41,7	25	0	75	85,7	45,8	14,3	39,3	
Portugal	6	6	1	1	1	1	4	1	0	0	1	4	1	1	1	6
%	100	100	16,7	16,7	25	25	100	25	0	0	25	66,7	25	16,7	16,7	
All swords	970	899	678	634	514	455	661	539	162	86	233	722	559	309	675	1036
%	93,6	86,8	65,4	61,2	71,2	63,0	91,6	74,7	52,4	27,8	75,4	69,7	77,4	29,8	65,2	

Table 1. Swords with traces in association.

DOING AWAY WITH DICHOTOMIES? COMPARATIVE USE WEAR ANALYSIS OF EARLY BRONZE AGE AXES FROM SCOTLAND

Shaun MOYLER

Abstract:
Traditional approaches to Bronze Age metalwork have very often been framed within a series of dichotomous relationships. In this contribution, the visibility of such categorisations is questioned, based on an extensive re-examination of wear, damage and states of fragmentation exhibited by a number of Early Bronze Age axes from Scotland. It is argued that the historical focus on either the production or deposition of metal has paid too little attention to what happened to objects during their often varied lifetimes.

Résumé :
Les approches traditionnelles sur le travail du métal à l'âge du Bronze ont souvent été limitées par une série de dichotomies. Au travers de cette contribution, la clarté de ces catégorisations est remise en question, sur la base d'un large réexamen de l'usure, de l'endommagement et de l'état de fragmentation d'un certain nombre de haches du Bronze ancien écossais. Historiquement, l'attention s'est en réalité porté plus sur la production ou le dépôt de métal en négligeant ce qui était arrivé aux objets eux-mêmes durant leurs vies respectives.

Moving beyond traditional approaches

The arrival of metal in the archaeological record has historically been seen as a key indicator of technical, social and economic developments in prehistoric society. However, a review of archaeological approaches to this rich body of material shows how attention has generally been centred on either production or depositional phases in an objects life. In terms of production, a focus on the manufacture, supply and movement of metal has been one of the central analytical areas, particularly in relation to the establishment and display of elite status. Such ideas are broadly conditioned by post capitalist ideas of wealth, accumulation, supply and demand. Typological methodologies have also dominated, as part of the ongoing quest for more accurate chronological frameworks (Needham 1997: 55), to map the development of increasingly efficient items over time, and to plot the spatial distributions of various object styles in a broader European setting. While these considerations have provided crucial information, they often remain at a relatively grand scale of analysis, where delineations of similar forms and styles are often taken to imply a convergence of meaning (Saunders 2000: 47). A relative lack of primary production evidence has evoked a considerable amount of experimental work, which has ascertained the fabrication sequence that lies behind the creation of the final object. In parallel, metallurgical analysis has attempted to chart both evolutionary changes in elemental composition and to question where particular ores originated, with a view to ascertaining distribution and trade patterns (Coles 1969: 54). The voluminous discussions on metalwork deposition have long debated the rationale behind such acts to the extent that the significance of metal has invariably inferred from the ways in which it was deposited (Bradley 1998: 83). What has emerged are a number of dichotomous categorisations that remain common discursive currencies today. For example assemblages have long been characterised as either single finds or hoards (or graves), and various secular or votive depositional motives have been proposed (Bradley 1990). The final state of an object has often played a key role in determining such intentions, and interpretations of hoarding practice in particular frequently recognise the fact that many of the items contained therein displayed evidence of wear, damage and fragmentation. For example, the well known typological categorisation by Evans divided assemblages by function, but also on the condition of the objects (Evans 1881: 457-470). So called 'Founder's Hoards' were identified by the presence of *worn out* items or scrap metal and seen to indicate the manufacture of metalwork. Conversely 'Merchant Hoards' were distinguishable by the presence of a number of similar items in *unused* condition, ready to be sold or exchanged. The idea that objects were deliberately damaged or broken as part of the sacrificial act of deposition has also been widely accepted. In the majority of instances, interpretations have attempted to tie such features into the past contexts from which these objects have been recovered in the present. An assumed direct link is therefore posited between an objects life in a systemic context and its ultimate location in the archaeological record (Schiffer 1987; Needham 1989: 384). On this basis, Jill York aimed to recreate the life cycles of Bronze Age metalwork recovered from the River Thames by analysing patterns of use wear and damage (York 2002). While her examination of the material reveals a range of information regarding states of wear, these findings are ultimately related to long-standing theories regarding the either the ritualised or secular deposition of material, rather than addressing how objects may have been socially perceived during their lives prior to discard.

The historical situation has served to sterilise approaches to this body of material, especially when the diverse nature of the evidence suggests a single explanation for all cases will remain ever illusive. What have often been overlooked are the complex uses and understandings of material culture by people and the endless avenues of social meaning that may be contained in the data (Cooney & Grogan 1994: 97). In this contribution, my aim is to move beyond these more familiar dichotomies and considerations to address a concern that the traditional mindset fails to adequately attend to what happens 'in between'. By this I refer to what happened to objects during their 'lives' after their 'production' and before deposition. Our common understandings have tended to homogenise the lives of objects during this part of their existence by compressing each object life time. By emphasising the depositional phase of an object life, I contend that a somewhat retrograde assessment of the evidence has been offered that starts with the perceived context of an object's discard and subsequently works backwards through a limited number of interpretive dimensions. In contrast I want to advocate a perspective from the multi dimensional view point afforded by the *a priori* position of those making, using and depositing objects (Van der Leeuw 1989). It is important to stress from the outset that my intention is not to suggest that issues of production and deposition are not salient concerns, nor to debate the idea that acts of deposition were not highly structured. Rather, I want to think about how these nominal phases of making, using and discard may be interrelated. As such, there is an essentially 'biographical' basis to my approach. Such methodologies have emerged amidst a wider concern for the role of material culture in social relations (Gosden & Marshall 1999: 169), and have become increasingly popular in the archaeological literature over recent years. Before, I continue in this vein, it is worth briefly considering the idea of an object biography, how it has been applied archaeologically, and also its potential application to metalwork.

The idea of biography

The idea of a biographic approach to material culture is aligned with the idea that as both people and objects move through time and space, they continually accumulate histories of different meaning, understandings and consequence relevant to the specific social contexts in which they have existed. The conceptual origin of this statement is to be found in an ongoing anthropological discourse that deals with the exchange and circulation of objects in social networks (e.g. Strathern 1988) and demonstrates how the boundaries between people and things are dissolved and divisible. The fact that objects could have certain qualities akin to their human counterparts was initially highlighted by Kopytoff (Kopytoff 1986), who noted that just like people, things could not be fully understood at one point in time. Rather, they should be viewed as a product of their entire life history. If objects are to be thought of in the same way as people therefore, it follows that they too must be seen in terms of their complete existence (Holtorf 2002; Jones 2002). Critically, such conceptualisations emphasise the contexts in which these lives unfold, and it is often the movement between these situations that provides the mechanism for changes in the way objects are perceived and valued through time. While the concept of an object having a life history akin to that of humans provides a suitable mechanism with which to foreground the great diversity of ways in which people and objects may be related, its archaeological application has seen it primarily used as an interpretive tool that draws on a recurrent set of ethnographic examples to cross culturally identify that material evidence *could also* have been viewed in these ways. Biographic syntheses tend to follow either a historical or metaphorical aspect. Historical biographies essentially sequence a number of events along a linear trajectory and provide an interpretive narrative to account for the changes in this progression (e.g. Hamilakis 1999). Alternatively, and particularly in relation to prehistoric evidence, a more metaphorical approach is adopted where production, use and deposition are conceived under the headings of birth, life and death. It is often deemed sufficient to merely point out that objects must have had 'rich biographies' (Whitely 2002; see also Joy 2007), and to pay lip service to the well thumbed ethnographic tomes rather than attempting to reconstruct the specific biographical trajectories of individual objects (Woodward 2002: 1040) within their intended contexts.

I contend that this state of affairs has emerged in part from a failure to examine some of the ways in which an objects history may be recognised from the physical evidence itself, let alone a consideration of how these object lives may have been connected to the personal histories of people. For metalwork, the relatively poor contextual information for any stage of an objects life has perhaps been seen as a further limit to the potency of the biographic framework. However, rather than focussing on contexts of production or deposition, an alternative stance is to consider the object itself as a context in its own right. This is something Shanks described when he stated that "the life of an artefact is accompanied by physical changes and processes (Shanks 1998: 17). An artefact wears in its use and consumption. Marks upon it attest to events it has witnessed, things that have happened to it. It can deteriorate. The artefact ages". One way in which we might begin to address this apparent lacuna therefore, is to take a closer look at states of wear damage and fragmentation. While such approaches are readily used in the analysis of lithic material (e.g. Hurcombe 1992), they have only more recently begun to feature in the assessments of metal objects (e.g. Bridgford 1997 & 2000). The potential for such analyses to reveal information has been demonstrated in a number of recent articles. Kienlin & Ottaway have identified prehistoric use wear by comparison with experimental replication and use of Alpine flanged axes (Kienlin & Ottaway 1998). Their work showed not only how signs of manufacturing, use and modern damage could be visibly distinguished from each other, but how patterns of blade damage resulting from experimental woodworking were also present on the prehistoric artefacts themselves. Allied to these findings, a second study by Roberts and Ottaway based on a similarly experimental methodology, considered patterns of use on Late Bronze Age socketed Axes from South East Scotland and East Yorkshire (Roberts & Ottaway 2003). It has shown that most of the axes in their data set had been used, a small number of which were identified as having been employed in woodworking activity. In several cases, nicks on the blade were related to possible combative activity, on account of the fact that none of their experimental axes replicated such damage from carpentry activities alone (but c.f. Darrah 2004:179 who notes blade damage from wood knots). The fragmentary condition of three axes in particular were attributed to acts of *deliberate* breakage since the degree of use displayed by each objects was deemed to have been insufficient to have broken the axes through normal usage.

Scottish Early Bronze Age axes

My intention is to build on the foundations of this previous work and to develop the scope of the object biography by exploiting the potential offered by wear analysis. It is against this background that I have begun to reconsider the evidence of wear and damage that is exhibited by many copper and bronze axes in Scotland, dating from the period c. 2,400 to c. 1,700 cal B.C. (Needham 1996). In Britain as a whole, copper and bronze axes are largely absent from grave contexts but dominate both hoard assemblages and so called single finds. They are also the sole object form whose currency extends throughout the Bronze Age (Barber 2003: 155). The typological development of these objects has been well documented elsewhere (Schmidt & Burgess 1981) and I do not wish to discuss some of the finer points of debate here. However, in very general terms the Early Bronze Age developmental sequence moves from the first copper axes, characterised by their broad thick butts and blades, to later more narrow, flat or slightly flanged examples in bronze, with lozengic profiles and narrow butts (Needham *et al.* 1985: Classes 1-4). In Scotland there are around 300 extant examples available in museum collections that pertain to this period, although new examples are now coming to light as Treasure Trove (Cowie, pers. com). In the remainder of this article, I will discuss my assessments of the 143 axes contained in the National Museum of Scotland collections, of which 35 come from hoards with the remainder being found in isolation. To avoid confusion, I will refer to these axes by their National

Museum of Scotland reference number. This work is part of an ongoing PhD research project, and represents a preliminary analysis of almost half the axes currently available for study.

Symmetry and freshness

For each axe in the collection, an assessment has been made of blade wear by measuring the amount of reduced blade symmetry. To do this, the assumption has been made that axes were symmetrical prior to being utilised, a contention supported by the regular shapes shown on known stone axe moulds (e.g. Callender 1903). A series of high resolution digital images have been taken directly above each object from which a digitised tracing has been made providing a highly accurate scaled image, showing the extant blade proportions. A second image of the blade has then been created and overlaid onto the first that replaces the assumed original symmetry of the blade. Where necessary, reference has been made to other axes of the same type in order to achieve the correct blade shape. By calculating the difference in surface areas between the assumed original outline and the extant blade edge, the percentage surface area reduction for each blade has been calculated (fig. 1).

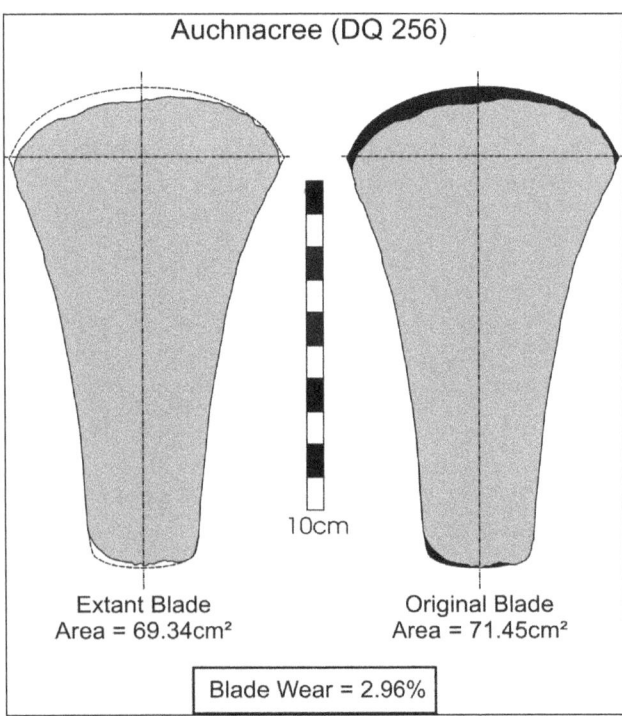

Fig. 1. Extant and proposed original outlines of one axe (DQ256) from the Auchnacree Hoard.

Larsson drew attention to the relationship between axe blade proportion and episodes of resharpening (Larsson 1986). He noted how the repeated resharpening of the blade resulted in the wearing away of the metal in certain areas resulting in asymmetry. Several other studies also note these factors (Curwen 1948: 162; Rowlands 1976; Burgess & Coombs 1979; Vankilde 1996: 32), and suggest variations in blade symmetry are related to the periods of time that an axe was in use. Such ideas have also been noted for swords (Needham 1990; Bridgford 1997; Kristiansen 1999) and daggers (Wall 1987: 115). While I am broadly in agreement with these ideas, the quantity of wear or damage to any object does not automatically infer that it was in circulation for a longer time period. There is a tension here between on the one hand the intensity of use and the duration of an object's existence (whether used or not). Due to likely variations in the intensity of use as well as disparities in resistance offered by different wood hardness, the relative percentage of axe wear according to reduced symmetry is not on its own a sufficient basis for judging the time an object may have been in circulation. In this light, a second set of assessments has been made of the relative 'freshness' of each axe at deposition. In each case, observations have been made of the relative roundness of the edges and flanges, the crispness of decoration (where present), as well as the condition of axe blade tips. These ideas build on the suggestion put forward by Coles and Taylor (Coles & Taylor 1971: 13) in relation to gold items associated with Wessex burials, where the very freshly executed ornamentation of some of the items was held to indicate a very short time in circulation after manufacture. Due cognisance has also been given to the relative freshness along damaged or broken sections of each axe. Notions of deliberate damage being synonymous with votive action imply that items were broken just prior to deposition, as part of the ritualised act of destruction. This hypothesis would suggest that breaks, strikes or cuts of the object should remain relatively fresh when they are recovered archaeologically (Jones 2002: 101). However, historical interpretations of broken objects have nearly always placed emphasis upon the most visible form of desecration. For example, the broken axes in the Collenard hoard, which are deemed to have been ritually snapped prior to deposition (Cowie 1988; Jones 2002), have been categorised on account of this fact alone. By making these judgements solely on the 'macro' nature of the damage, no visibility is given to more subtle instances of wear that they may display. While, there is clearly an inevitable subjectivity involved in assessments of freshness, I feel that the ability to cross compare axes via digital images has afforded the creation of meaningful analytical criteria.

Discussion

The results of these assessments show that nearly all the axes examined show some signs of wear. Some are almost pristine, such as the example from Darnaway (DA69), which has an excellent degree of blade symmetry, crisp edges and blade tips, and a sharp cutting edge. At the other end of the scale, the example from Fortrie of Balnoon (DA38) which has worn edges, rounded blade tips as well as reduced symmetry of 8.43%. It is interesting to note however, that either of these axes could have been recovered as a single find or as part of a hoard assemblage, since wear patterns in general do not appear to map these depositional categories. I have already noted that this division may in reality be symptomatic of our own categorisations in the present and these features add further weight to this contention. As such, there would not appear to be any definitive point in an objects functional life when they are deemed to have become 'ready' to be deposited solely on account of their physical state. My interpretation of this situation is that so called single finds were deposited by individuals whereas 'hoards' were deposited by groups (c.f. «community deposits» Needham 1988), as a medium for the creation and mediation of social liaisons. The practice of hoarding may have been the end result of community activity whereby objects that were symbolic of different social relationships were accumulated together to reinforce communal relations en masse. Different parts of society perhaps defined by age, gender, or kin association may have been subject to differing rules and regulations governing the identity of objects they were required to submit. Axe may have been defined by their specific histories and recognised by their condition. In this light, the joint internment of items physically represents the day to day social relationships. How might this be further represented in the material evidence? If we assume that the items contained within a hoard were all interred at the same time, they can provide us with snapshots of wear and degradation at their time of joint deposition. By extension, this allows comparisons to be made with the other axes within a closed assemblage. The evidence from Scotland shows that items hoarded together do indeed show varying degrees of wear, suggesting that they had each witnessed different lives. To illustrate this point further, I will focus one specific example, namely the hoard from the Hill of Finglenny, Aberdeenshire (fig. 2). Found buried under a stone, this assemblage contained seven Migdale axes and one possible armring (now lost). While three of the axes

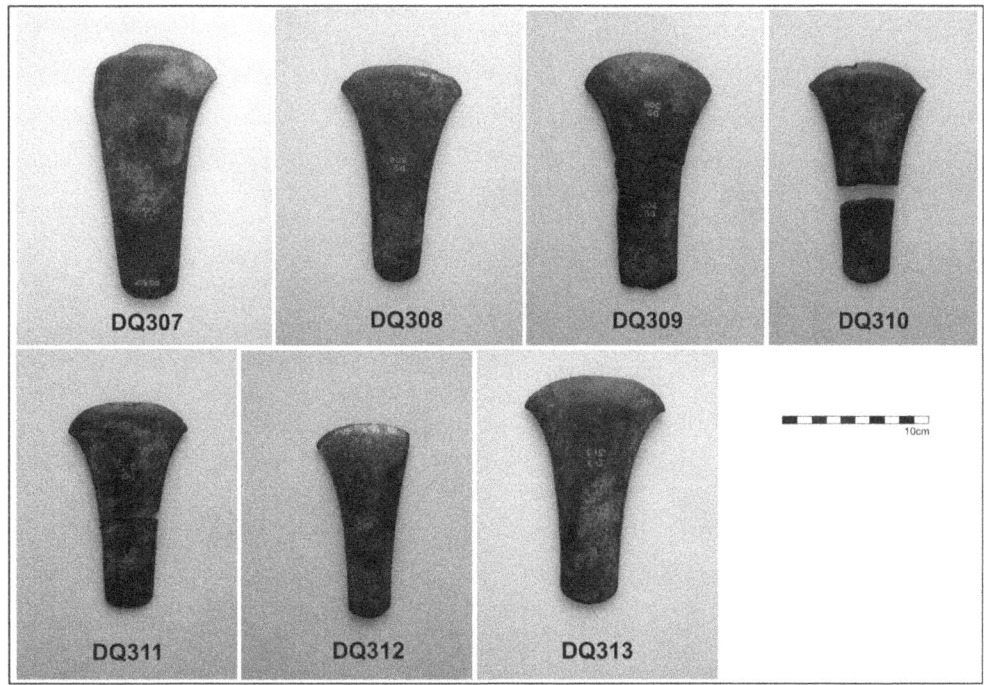

Fig. 2. Axes from the Hill of Finglenny hoard
© The Trustees of the National Museums of Scotland

Axe	Blade Condition	% Reduced Symmetry	Freshness (Edges)	Freshness (Breaks)	Striation Angle
DQ307	All Sharp	4.96	Crisp	-	30
DQ308	All Sharp	0.29	Worn	-	0
DQ309 (Blade)	All Sharp	6.06	Worn	Worn	10
DQ309 (Butt)	-	-	Worn	Sharp	-
DQ310 (Blade)	Part Sharp	6.17	Worn	Worn	12
DQ310 (Butt)		-	Worn	Sharp	-
DQ311 (Blade)	All Blunt	0.15	Worn	Sharp	28
DQ311 (Butt)		-	Worn	Sharp	-
DQ312	All Sharp	3.24	Crisp	-	5
DQ313	All Sharp	0.40	Worn	-	30

Table 1. Wear characteristics for axes in Hill of Finglenny hoard

are broken in two, all fragments were deposited together. The axes display a number of wear characteristics as set out in Table 1.

The information in the table shows that while all the axes display some form of wear, there are variations in each case. In all accept one case striations caused by use are present on the faces of the axe whose antiquity is confirmed by their position beneath the overlying surface patina (see Kienlin & Ottaway 1998 for discussion). The two axes (DQ309 & DQ310) with the highest degree of blade asymmetry maintained a cutting edge when deposited and had therefore been resharpened prior to their internment. Axe DQ311 retains nearly its original form with less than 1% deterioration and yet was completely blunt when deposited and perhaps had never been resharpened. All three show similar states of freshness along their edges. In contrast, while axe DQ307 shows around 5% reduction in symmetry, it retains a sharp blade but with crisp edges, suggesting a short period of intensive use rather than an extended period of circulation. Axe DQ308 displays very little asymmetry and no use wear striations on its face. However, on account of its rounded edges, it would appear to have been circulated for some time but little used. Similarly varied wear patterns are to be found in the hoards from Auchanacree, Collenard and Port Murray, almost as if there was some predetermined recipe of old and new or fresh and worn objects that were required to be associated together. In this regard, it is interesting that objects displaying recurring wear patterns have also been recorded in Late Bronze Age Nordic ornament hoards (Kristiansen pers. com). These features serve to highlight the point that axes lived out different existences after they had been created, and that these lives were an intrinsic part of the selection criteria for assembling groups of objects to be deposited together.

A second point of note is that two of the broken axes from Finglenny (DQ309 & DQ310) show dissimilar wear patterns across their broken sections. In both cases the broken edges on the butt fragment remains in a much fresher state than the corresponding blade section. This suggests that these individual sections of the same axes were circulated for different periods post fracture. Roberts & Ottaway have proposed that variations in wear indicate the presence of "active tools [that] became offerings to the land" (Roberts & Ottaway 2003). However, this example illustrates that fragments were also circulated in a non functional state prior to being finally reunited, in this instance at deposition. Chapman has recently considered depositional practice through the lens of fragmented objects (Chapman 2001). In considering data from the prehistoric period in Eastern Europe, he makes an important distinction between wholes and parts of objects, and how these are deliberately organised when deposited. His suggestion is that through the breakage, fragmentation, collection and exchange of wholes and parts of objects, social relations are both forged and developed. This premise seems highly applicable to the evidence presented here, especially in relation to the parts of axe which were circulated after they were broken. Fragmentation allows the multiplication of one item into more numerous pieces and the creation of a social currency that permits a greater diversity to the association and juxtaposition of other items. While Chapman's assessments are essentially drawn from depositional arrangements of items, his ideas have clear ramifications for the circulation and accumulative histories of objects in different fragmentary states, and there is an essentially biographical element to these proposals. It follows that there is a direct relationship between elements of wear over time and the life history of an object. One further observation is also worthy of mention here, namely the uniformity of edge wear along the whole length of many axes, extending beneath areas where the haft would have been attached. This strengthens Needham's (1988) suggestion that some axes may have circulated for periods of time in an unhafted non utilitarian capacity, as whole objects (Needham 1988). However, I would like to question the notion of deliberate breakage in its broadest sense, since it is very difficult to snap an axe in two without leaving some other forms of damage on the faces of the object itself. In common with the other axes in the collection, the snapped examples from Finglenny do not show any signs that they have been struck, bent or levered in any way to induce fracture. Closer examination of the broken sections in almost every case reveals the presence of a range of casting flaws, such as cracks, hollows and air bubbles (fig. 3).

The presence of such features infers that these par-

Fig. 3. Broken axe from Auchnagarron (DA85) showing casting flaw in section
© The Trustees of the National Museums of Scotland

ticular axes snapped while in use and that this breakage may in fact have been unavoidable. This does not mean to say that the breaking of these axes was not a significant event when it occurred. In some cases, cracks in the matrix of the metal are visible on the surface of the axe (Finglenny DQ308, fig. 4) and as Hoffman notes a degree of technical knowledge of an object's material properties is necessary to inform the method of breakage (Hoffman 1999). In this light, it may be that certain objects which displayed signs of poor casting were deliberately selected to be broken when in use, perhaps as part of the destructive performance.

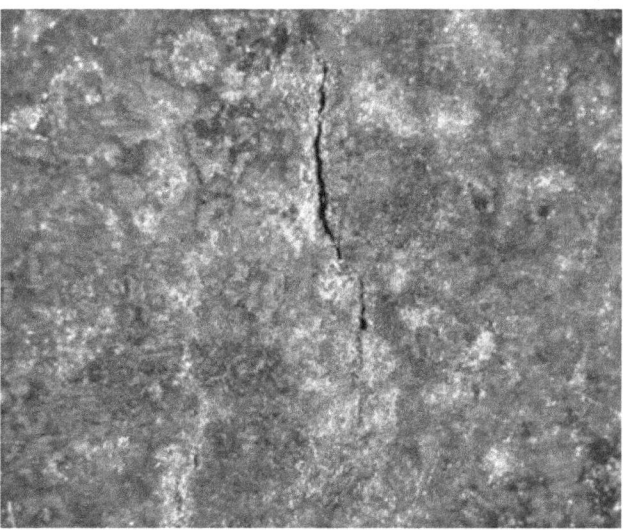

Fig. 4. Axe from Hill of Finglenny (DQ308) showing crack across face. This crack is 1mm wide.
© The Trustees of the National Museums of Scotland

The points raised so far are supported by an additional trend that is displayed in the data as a whole, namely the fact that while most axes were deposited in a functional condition, the typologically later forms display greater levels of non symmetry and more overall signs of attrition. This suggests that circulation periods increased through time. Such patterns have been noted for other metalwork types. For example, Wall describes an increased amount of wear between Wessex I and II daggers (Wall 1987) and Vankilde shows how axe blade reduction appears to become more prevalent throughout the Bronze Age in Denmark (Vankilde 1996). Increased levels of damage and fragmentation are also noted by York (York 2002), and my own analysis of material form the Irish hoard record highlights how typologically later objects were worn, damaged and fragmented with greater intensity than earlier metal objects (Moyler 2002).

Renfrew proposed that the social context of object use is perhaps not always utilitarian and that there is a move over time from a 'special' status to more 'domestic' (Renfrew 1978). Similar ideas have also been discussed in terms of pottery (Woodward 1998). These terms represent points at either end of continuum in rather the same way that issues of production and deposition underlie traditional approaches to metalwork. In contrast, I would like to argue that these recurring patterns of increased wear and attrition mirror the incorporation of metal objects into social use. Since objects are created through technological acts that are informed by the decisions and context of social actors, technology is a fundamental medium through which social relations are mediated (Dobres & Hoffman 1994: 212). It is useful to picture this relationship as a form of 'social equation' that exists in an ongoing and dynamic state of recalculation to encompass variations in its component parts facilitated by the action of people who articulate their social relationships through an engagement with the physical world. Metallurgy represents the appearance of one such variable into this formula.

In this light, the advent of a new technology arises both within this hermeneutic and must be incorporated into it through a process of adoption and modification. It follows that the way in which new technologies were received into society will have been shaped by its incorporation into the existing set of social conditions over time (Sofaer Derevenski & Sørenson 2002). The increased amount of hoards, the greater degrees of fragmentation, circulation times and wear, as well as the increased number of objects contained in Later Bronze Age assemblages may be the physical manifestation of both an increased number of liaisons as well as the increased use of metal as a medium for social exchange.

Decoration Sequence

I would like to close this chapter by discussing a number of decorated axes. Decorated axes do not appear until later in the Early Bronze Age metal axe sequence, when schemes are employed that share a set of design conventions found on a variety of objects such as beakers, grooved ware pots and lunulae (Jones 2001). Traditional approaches to decoration have essentially concerned themselves with categorising the various designs themselves and identifying possible continental connections (Megaw & Hardy 1938; Harbison 1969; Needham 1983). Only a limited amount of work has been carried out on the techniques themselves (Lowery *et al.* 1971) over and above a simplistic determination of the methods used, such as 'hammer' or 'punched' decoration. In any event, their application is normally identified as part of the production process, creating an object that has a different identity perhaps linked to the status of its owner. However, while it is not a widespread phenomenon, I would like to suggest that some decorative schemes appear to have been added after the axe has been used or certainly after it had been in existence for some time. For example, the decorative scheme on the example from Jordanshill (DA71) appears to be framed by deep gouges into one face of the axe. The fact that these gouges were present prior to the addition of ornamentation is confirmed by one of the decorative punches, which clearly overlies the damaged area (fig. 5).

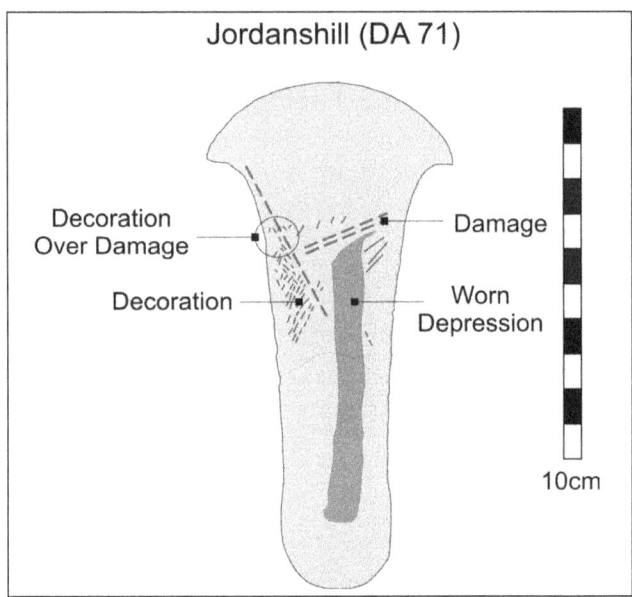

Fig. 5. Schematic drawing of the axe from Jordanshill (DA71) showing the relationship between decoration and damage

Elsewhere, the punched decoration on the Carnethy Hill axe (DA126) appears to overlay visible use wear striations at certain points. Further possible examples are the axes from Kevans (DA47) and Mainshead (DA67). On the former, the decoration appears very crisp when compared to the edges and face of the axe, which appear to be worn. In the latter, the decorative scheme has been applied or at least 'repaired' after a section of the axe face has broken away (fig. 6).

There are several implications of these findings. Firstly, unlike ceramic technology, where all incised decoration is carried out before firing, the embellishment of metal objects is not always part of the pro-

Fig. 6. Axe from Mainshead (DA67) showing a continuation of decoration over damaged area. The horizontal decoration line are 2mm wide
© The Trustees of the National Museums of Scotland

duction phase. The materiality of metal therefore allows ornamentation to be added at a later stages in an object's life, perhaps changing its identity and significance in relation to parallel transformations of its owner's social status. Moreover, it is not necessarily the maker of the axe who performs the ornamental procedure, and these techniques were perhaps subject to their own social convention and appreciation (Sofaer & Sørensen *in press*). Microscopic examination of the punch marks on nearly all the decorated examples recorded so far, shows distinct changes in morphology of the imprint, and it is tempting to suggest that some schemes were built up over time, perhaps marking events in the axe's life. The current problem with this argument is the fact that due to the cold hardening of the assumed bronze punches used to create these designs they would require periodic annealing to avoid their becoming brittle. Therefore, changes in the shape of the ornamental marks themselves may reflect both the deterioration of the punch being used as well as its revised morphology after reworking. As part of the broader research project presented here, it is hoped that ongoing experimental work may reveal further information in this regard. Nonetheless, these findings also draw attention to the question of whether the decorative schemes were ever seen to be complete, or remained in a continual state of becoming. Some of the less well documented axes in the National Museum collection add weight to this argument. Rather than displaying fully symmetrical designs, they have 'incomplete' schemes such as the one on the Jordanshill discussed previously (fig. 5). Ultimately, the fact that some metalwork may have been decorated over time rather than in just one phase has clear ramifications for the way in which that object operated and was perceived throughout its life.

Conclusion

In this chapter, I have brought together a traditional body of material, namely Bronze Age axes, with more recent theories and approaches to material culture. In so doing, the potential of wear analysis as a useful tool in the assessment of metalwork has also been developed. The arguments put forward suggest that the traditional dichotomies employed in the categorisation of such material do not seem to be represented in patterns of wear. Moreover, it has been shown that metal axes were subjected to different intensities of use in a functional sense, but were also circulated for different time periods prior to their deposition. In terms of their association with other axes in hoard deposits, I have suggested that a consideration of their individual life histories was an important criteria for their selection and juxtaposition. Their relative ages when deposited, identified by degrees of wear and attrition, may have been synonymous with both the individuals who owned and used them, as well as recounting the activities or events in which they had been involved. While the discussion presented here has involved only one class of object, the goal must now be to extend some of the key issues across the whole range of metalwork. To conclude, I hope to have shown that interpretations of structured acts of deposition must also incorporate factors relating to the life of those objects prior to their final consignment, and move to consider how these salient issues were mutually entangled.

References

BARBER, M. 2003. *Bronze and the Bronze Age*, Stroud: Tempus

BRADLEY, R. 1990. *The Passage of Arms: An archaeological analysis of prehistoric hoard and votive deposits*, Cambridge: Cambridge University Press

BRADLEY, R. 1998. *The Passage of Arms: An archaeological analysis of prehistoric hoard and votive deposits* (2nd Edition), Oxford: Oxbow

BRIDGFORD, S. 1997. Mightier than the pen? An edgewise look at Irish Bronze Age swords, In J. Carmen (ed.) *Material Harm: archaeological studies of war and violence*. Glasgow: Cruithne Press, 95-115

BRIDGFORD, S. 2000. *Weapons, warfare and society in Britain 1250-750 B.C.*. Unpublished PhD thesis. University of Sheffield

BURGESS, C. & COOMBS, D. 1979. *Bronze Age Hoards: some finds old and new*, British Archaeological Reports (British Series) 67; Oxford: British Archaeological Reports

CALLENDER, J. 1903. Notice of a stone mould for casting flat bronze axes and bars found in the parish of Insch, Aberdeenshire, *Proceedings of the Society of Antiquaries of Scotland* 38: 487-505

CHAPMAN, J. 2001. *Fragmentation in Archaeology*, Oxford: Oxbow

COLES, J. 1969. Scottish Early Bronze Age Metalwork, *Proceedings of the Society of Antiquaries of Scotland* 101: 1-110

COLES, J. & TAYLOR, J. 1971. The Wessex Culture: A minimal view, *Antiquity* 45 (177): 6-14

COONEY, G. & GROGAN, E. 1994. *Irish Prehistory: a social perspective*, Dublin: Wordwell

COWIE, T. G. 1988. *Magic Metal: Early Metalworkers in the North East*, Aberdeen: Anthropological Museum

CURWEN, E. C. 1948. A Bronze cauldron from Sompting, Sussex, *Sussex Archaeological Collection* 28: 157-63

DARRAH, R. 2004. The reconstruction experiment, In P. Clark (ed.) *The Dover Bronze Age Boat*. Swindon: English Heritage, 164-88

DOBRES, M. A. & HOFFMAN, C. 1994. Social Agency and the dynamics of prehistoric technology, *Journal of Archaeological Method and Theory* 1(3): 211-58

EVANS, J. 1881. *The Ancient Bronze Implements. Weapons and Ornaments of Great Britain and Ireland*, London: Longman Green

GOSDEN, C. & MARSHALL, Y. 1999. The cultural biography of objects, *World Archaeology* 31(2): 169-78

HAMILAKIS, Y. 1999. Stories from exile: fragments from the cultural biography of the Parthenon (or 'Elgin') marbles, *World Archaeology* 31(2): 303-20

HARBISON, P. 1969. *The Axes of the Early Bronze Age in Ireland, Prähistorische Bronzefunde*. Abteilung 4 Band 1: C.H. Beck'sche Verblagsbuchhandlung

HOFFMAN, C. 1999. Intentional damage as technological agency: breaking metals in Late Prehistoric Mallorca, Spain, In M. A. Dobres & C. Hoffman (eds), *The Social Dynamics of Technology: practice, politics and world views*. Washington D.C: Smithsonian Institution Press, 103-24

HOLTORF, C. 2002. Notes on the life history of a potsherd, *Journal of Material Culture* 7(1): 49-71

HURCOMBE, L. M. 1992. *Use wear analysis and obsidian: theory, experiments and results*, Sheffield Archaeological Monographs 4. Sheffield: J.R.Collis Publications

JONES, A. 2001. Drawn from memory: the archaeology of aesthetics and the aesthetics of archaeology in Earlier Bronze Age Britain and the present, *World Archaeology* 33(2): 334-56

JONES, A. 2002. *Archaeological Theory and Scientific Practice*, Cambridge: Cambridge University Press

JOY, J. 2007. Reflections on the Iron Age: a biography of pre-Roman Iron Age mirrors. Unpublished PhD Thesis. University of Southampton

KIENLIN, T. & OTTAWAY, B. 1998. Flanged axes of the North Alpine region: an assessment of the possibilities of use wear analysis on metal artefacts, In C. Mordant, M. Pernot & V. Rychner (eds), *L'atelier du bronzier an Europe du Xxe au VIIIe siecle avant notre ere*. Paris: CTHS (Documents prehistoriques 10), 271-86

KOPYTOFF, I. 1986. The cultural biography of things, In A. Appadurai (ed.) *The Social Life of Things: Commodities in Cultural Perspective*. Cambridge: Cambridge University Press, 64-94

KRISTIANSEN, K. 1999. Understanding Bronze Age Weapon Hoards, *A Josa András Múzeum Évkönyve XLI*: 101-7

LARSSON, T. B. 1986. *The Bronze Age metalwork in Southern Sweden. Aspects of social and spatial organisation 1800-500 B.C..*, Archaeology and Environment 6. Umea: Department of Archaeology, University of Umea.

LOWERY, P., SAVAGE, R. & WILKINS, R. 1971. Scriber, Graver, Scorper, Tracer: notes on experiments in bronzeworking technique, *Proceedings of the Prehistoric Society* 37: 167-82

MEGAW, B. R. S. & HARDY, E. M. 1938. British decorated axes and their diffusion during the earlier part of the Bronze Age, *Proceedings of the Prehistoric Society* 4: 272-307

MOYLER, S. 2002. *The making and breaking of a technology: An analysis of damage and fragmentation patterns in Irish Bronze Age hoards*. Unpublished Undergraduate thesis. University of Southampton

NEEDHAM, S. 1983. *The Axeheads of Southern Britain*. Unpublished PhD thesis. University of Cardiff

NEEDHAM, S. 1988. Selective Deposition in the British Early Bronze Age, *World Archaeology* 20(2): 229-48

NEEDHAM, S. 1989. Developments in the Early Bronze Age metallurgy of Southern Britain, *World Archaeology* 20(3): 383-402

NEEDHAM, S. 1990. T*he Petters Lane Bronze Age Metalwork. An analytical study of Thames Valley metalworking in its settlement context*, London: British Museum Occasional Paper 70

NEEDHAM, S. 1996. Chronology and periodisation in the British Bronze Age: Absolute Chronology. Archaeological Europe 2500-500 B.C., *Acta Archaeologica* (67): 121-40

NEEDHAM, S. 1997. An Independent Chronology for British Bronze Age Metalwork: The results of the Oxford Radiocarbon Accelerator Program, *Archaeological Journal* 154: 55-107

NEEDHAM, S., LAWSON, A. J. & GREEN, H. S. 1985. E*arly Bronze Age Hoards, British Bronze Age Metalwork: Associated Finds Series*. London: British Museum Publications

RENFREW, C. 1978. The anatomy of innovation, In D. Green, C. Haselgrove & M. Spriggs (eds), *Social organisation and settlement*. British Archaeological Reports (International Series) 47:Oxford: British Archaeological Reports, 89 -117

ROBERTS, B. & OTTAWAY, B. 2003. The use and significance of socketed axes during the late Bronze Age, *European Journal of Archaeology* 6(2): 119-40

ROWLANDS, M. 1976. *The production and distribution of metalwork in the Middle Bronze Age of Southern England*, British Archaeological Reports (British Series) 31:Oxford:

SAUNDERS, N. J. 2000. Bodies of metal, shells of metal, *Journal of Material Culture* 5(1): 43-67

SCHIFFER, M. 1987. *Formation processes of the archaeological record*. Albuquerque: University of New Mexico Press

SCHMIDT, P. K. & BURGESS, C. B. 1981. The axes of Scotland and Northern England, *Prähistorische Bronzefunde. Abteilung 9 Band 7*. Munchen: C.H. Beck'sche Verblagsbuchhandlung

SHANKS, M. 1998. The Life of an Artefact, *Fennoscandia Archaeologica* 15: 15-42

SOFAER DEREVENSKI, J. & SØRENSON, M. L. S. 2002. Becoming Cultural: society and the incorporating of bronze, In B. Ottaway & E. C. Wager (eds), *Metals and Society. Papers from a session held at the European Association of Archaeologists Sixth Annual Meeting in Lisbon*. British Archaeological Reports (British Series) 1061. Oxford: BAR Publishing, 117-21

SOFAER, J. & SØRENSEN, M. L. S. *in press*. Technological change as social change: the introduction of metal in Europe, In M. Bartelheim & V. Heyd (eds), *Continuity- Discontinuity: Transition Periods in Eu-ropean Prehistory*. Rahden/Westf.: Marie Leidorf

STRATHERN, M. 1988. *The Gender of the Gift*, Berkeley: University of California

VAN DER LEEUW, S. 1989. Risk, perception and innovation, In S. Van der Leeuw & R. Torrence (eds), *What's new? A closer look at the process of innova-tion*. London: Unwin Hyman, 300-29

VANKILDE, H. 1996. *From stone to bronze: the me-talwork of the late Neolithic and earliest Bronze Age in Denmark*, Aarhus: Jutland Archaeological Society

WALL, J. 1987. The role of daggers in Early Bronze Age Britain: the evidence of wear analysis, Oxford *Journal of Archaeology* 6(1): 115-8

WHITELY, J. 2002. Objects with attitude: biographical facts and fallacies in the study of Late Bronze Age and Early Iron Age warrior graves. Cambridge Archaeological Journal 12(2): 217-32

WOODWARD, A. 1998. When did pots become domestic? Special pots and everyday pots in British prehistory, *Medieval Ceramics* 22-23: 3-10

YORK, J. 2002. The life cycle of Bronze Age metalwork from the Thames, *Oxford Journal of Archaeology* 21(1): 77-92

Acknowledgements

I would like to offer my appreciation to the following people for their continued inspiration and assistance: Tim Champion, Jo Sofaer, Neil Burridge, Trevor Cowie, Jim Wilson, Jody Joy, and as ever, Alison Stephens. Thanks also to Caroline and Benedicte for inviting me to speak at the EAA conference in Cork and to publish my paper here.

Contact

Shaun Moyler
18 Richmond Road
Swanage
BH19 2PZ
England
shaun.moyler@gmail.com

HOARDS AND FLINT BLADES IN WESTERN FRANCE AT THE END OF THE NEOLITHIC

Ewen IHUEL

Abstract:
Using the Pressigniens hoard blades technical analysis allows us to presume that it is possible to distinguish various categories of deposits at the end of the Neolithic period even though the deposit phenomena is observed since the Palaeolithic. This is during the Neolithic that this activity starts to be more frequently encountered. From then on the notion of deposit represents various realities which can be exemplified via the Pressignien craft with 3 major types of deposits: blades deposit, knives deposit as well as diverse and isolated deposits in humid environments. The interpretation of these deposits allows us to discuss the distance from production areas as well as the economic and social signification of the objects deposited. In addition, based on technological observations it is possible to discuss the final or temporal character of these deposits as well as their signification such as storage, religious offerings, thesaurization, etc.

Résumé :
A partir de l'exemple des poignards pressigniens, nous avançons qu'il est possible de distinguer plusieurs catégories de dépôts à la fin du Néolithique grâce à l'analyse technologique. Le phénomène de dépôt est attesté depuis le paléolithique mais c'est durant le Néolithique que cette pratique se rencontre fréquemment. Dès lors la notion de dépôt recouvre des réalités fort différentes. L'exemple de l'artisanat pressignien nous offrent trois grands types de dépôts, dépôts de lames brutes, dépôts de poignards et dépôts isolés en milieu humide. L'interprétation de ces dépôts s'intègre dans une discussion sur la valeur accordée à la fois à la distance aux centres de production et aussi à la signification économique et sociale des objets déposés. A partir des observations technologiques, il est possible de discuter le caractère définitif ou provisoire des dépôts et leur signification comme stock, offrande, thésaurisation etc.

Introduction

We cannot consider Hoards as a superficial phenomenon of the Metal ages. On the contrary, they reflect some timeless preoccupation of human groups to anticipate the future in a material or spiritual way. In fact, flint hoards were already known during the Palaeolithic period but quite rare. The first hoard attested in Prehistory was the Palughetto hoard (Italia) and consisted of six core preformed deposit. It was discovered in a pit located in a humid environment. This small accumulation of raw material had been interpreted as an attempt for storage (Bertola *et al.* 1997). Knowledge on hoards has improved with the Magdalenian culture for which several examples of small concentration of pieces, almost blade like, were found in Polish excavations of Swidry Wielke I, Grzybowa Gora or Swidry Mate (Bertola *et al.* 1997). A handful of examples with preformed core were also found in the magdalenian layers of the Montgaudier cave (Charente, France). In France, Gérard Cordier counts less than 20 hoards that could be date back to the Palaeolithic (Cordier 1973). In fact, most of the hoard manifestations involving hunter-gathered communities are rare and far in between. They seem only to be based on economic strategies of raw material supplying. Other prehistoric preoccupations, religious or social, escape from our understanding of the hoard phenomenon.

We have to allow for new discoveries about the Neolithic period in order to progress in our understanding of hoards. Examples increase with mass production, which is characteristic of agro-pastoral societies. The difficulty in the research lies in the fact that the production of hoards represents only a side activity of the Neolithic economy, especially when it comes to instruments such as axes and blades.

Chronology

The raising number of blades came with the adoption of copper usage which can be dated around the last centuries of the fourth millennium in the South of France. Many hoards appear precisely after the adoption of a new tool in the western part of France: the flint dagger, obtained from a long retouched blade. The way this new object arrived in Europe is still obscure. This typological aspect seems strongly linked to metallic models, which are much older than their flint homologue. Around the Adriatic, the first evidences of copper dagger can be dated back to 4,000-3,500 B.C. cal in Mondsee, Rinaldone or still Bodrogkeresztur cultur (Vaquer *et al.* 2006). In the Middle-East, the dagger might have appeared more than five millenniums ago.

In this study we are interested by the products of one of the most important complex of long blade workshops of the Late Neolithic of Western Europe: the Grand-Pressigny region. The chronological sequence of flint dagger production has mainly been constructed by data collected in humid contexts. Dendrochronology precision is a decisive help for dating different kinds of lithic productions consumed by Late Neolithic groups settled on the lake shores of France and Switzerland.
Two main phases of long blades production are distinguished, corresponding to both kinds of production methods:

- 3,040 B.C, a few long blades from the Grand-Pressigny ,750 km from The Jura

The first long blades to appear were located in the Grand-Pressigny and appeared first around 3,040 B.C. cal. at Chalain 4 (Jura, France). They differ from the short and broad blades found between the 31th/28th centuries B.C., again in The Jura, on both Switzerland and France territories. These long blades were retouched but not transformed in dagger. It is at Clairvaux "la Motte-aux-Magnins", , that one of the first flint dagger known has been discovered in the layers ABC (Jura, France) in 2,890 B.C. cal. (Pétrequin & Pétrequin 1977; Pelegrin *forthcoming*). A 22 cm long blade had been obtained from a core with specific geometry; two lateral ridges flanked the superior plan of flaking and the arrangement of the blade's removal was mainly bipolar.

- 28th /24th centuries B.C., long and narrow blades: The Jura, Switzerland and France.

Charavines on the Paladru Lake's shore (Jura, France) and "Terrain des sports" at Delley-Portalban (Switzerland) give us first attestation of blades around 2,850-2,800 B.C. cal. (Mallet 1992). Very long blades, more than 30 cm long, have been obtained from cores. This method is known for a long time by archeologists, one of the first production has been recognized in the middle of the 19th century by Evans and better understood during the 20th century (Evans 1878; Kelterborn 1980; Pelegrin 2002).

- The Grand-Pressigny's workshops (Indre et Loire, France)

The major part of the daggers and blades discovered in western France came from the Grand-Pressigny region. Flint resources are abundant along the large valleys of the Claise and Creuse rivers and belong to the Paris Basin, which formation dates back to the Secondary Era. Big blocks of the Cretaceous Turonien have been especially employed for long blades production.

We have very little knowledge of the first phase of the blades production, as there is no evidence of use of any blades of this complexity in any hoard. The second phase, on the contrary, is very well known and concerns the hoard phenomena. Several characteristics distinguish the Grand-Pressigny workshops from the domestic production of blades. The former was more efficient and emphases the high value given to the specialization of production which required a long apprenticeship of at least a year, if not more. The know-how was very sophisticated for the shaping of the core, and required different techniques such as hard and indirect percussion (Pelegrin, 2002). The preparation by "pecking" of the flaking operation appears to be specific of Neolithic's procedure. The technical processes of blade flaking could reveal a native concept that would have been invented in situ to improve the blade lengths.
This very developed know-how required resulted in improvement in quality. Domestic blades in Late Neolithic contexts never reached 15 cm long and had an irregular shape. Grand-Pressigny's livre de beurre blades are never less than 22-24 cm long and their thickness as well as width was very regular for all the previous removals (Pelegrin & Ihuel 2005).

Recent calculations of the quantities produced reveals amazing results. We estimated that the number of blades produced during a period of 4 to 5 centuries could have excess several millions (Villes 2004). Even if considering this number inflated, it is still very impressive.

Workshops were concentrated around the resource areas, either at the bottom of valleys or higher, on the

Turonien layers, but the distribution of the products could cover 400 square kilometres. Some products could even be found from several hundreds kilometres to 1.500 km to the East.

Economic aspect of the blades and daggers

Blades are seldom used without retouch. Actually most were transformed into end scraper, then, most of them retouched in unilateral dagger.
Flint daggers didn't have a trivial signification during the late Neolithic, on the contrary, they wore a very high social value.
When these products were found in a domestic context, blades could be accompanied with scarce Grand-Pressigny flint flakes, although most of the blades found are broken. The interesting thing is that even broken blades were always recycled in various commonly used smaller tools, like scraper, scourer, burins. We find evidences of a high rate of broken pieces being recycled, which is the main character of the Grand-Pressigny flint blades in all Neolithic settlements. It reveals a preoccupation, sometimes non pragmatic, to extend the objects' life.
In burials, the situation was quite different: blades were a major component of the Late Neolithic funeral attributes and were found in most of megalithic tombs, although obviously, not everybody was buried with its own dagger. In Chenon, 13 dagger per 45 adults were found in dolmen B1 T (Charente, France) and only one dagger for 76 adults in layer III of Bury passage grave (Oise, France; Chambon et al. 2004: 79). But despite a few exceptions, deposits consist of only a few daggers, one to three objects maximum for a collective grave.

Therefore, we wonder if the circulation of long blades was really based on economic preoccupations, such as cereal harvesting, or if it was an answer to social expectations. Let us have a look at the hoards phenomenon in order to explain part of its economical significance as well as clarify a little more the fundamental reasons for the circulation of long blades.

The flint blade in hoards: first characteristics

Flint material cannot be recycled. Thus, the theory of storing for recasting or retraining high value objects is excluded for flint. This makes a big difference with one of the main interpretation for metallic hoard, which were used as blacksmiths reserves of raw material. In fact, the flint objects were deliberately withdrawn of the economic traffic and always consisted in finished or semi-finished products with no evidence of wasted materials.

The deposit of flint blades. A reality with several aspects (fig. 1)

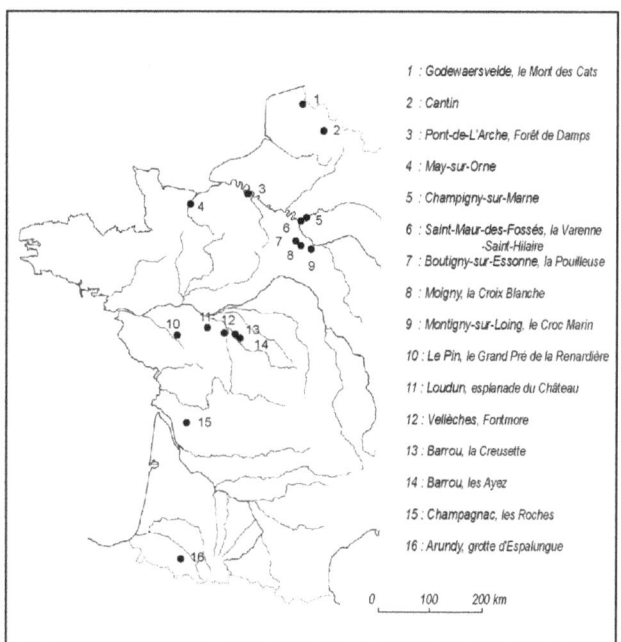

Fig. 1. Map of Neolithic hoards with long blades (from Cordier 1986).

Even with a limited inventory, the documentation gathered in 1986 per G. Cordier is still current (Cordier 1986). No more excavation or discovery has implicated hoard since the 1970's at La Creusette (Indre-et-Loire, France, see Geslin & Geslin 1970). On the other hand, new specific studies, technology based, on hoards material, like J. Pelegrin research at La Creusette, have provided observations that have changed our comprehension of the phenomenon (Pelegrin 1997). They add quality observations and inform us on the constitution processes for these deposits.

- *La Creusette à Barrou, Indre-et Loire* (fig. 2)

La Creusette hoard has been discovered in November 1970 by the Geslin's family while ploughing deeper than usual in their farm property (Geslin & Geslin 1970). The field is located on the east side of the Creuse Valley, at 800 meters from the river. In fact, it is located at the core of ancient workshops area. The first 36 blades were pulled out when the ploughing was stopped. Then, after a detailed exca-

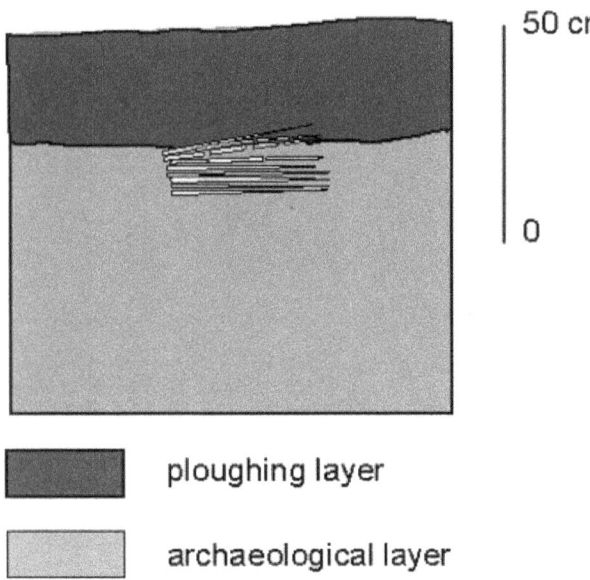

Fig. 2. La Creusette, Barrou (Indre-et-Loire) schematical cross section of La Creusette hoard (from Geslin, *et al.*, 1975)

vation in laboratory, 133 blades were identified in the structure (see Geslin *et al.* 1975). The hoard had not been moved nor even barely altered by prior ploughings before this discovery. Blades were found in small pits of about 50 cm wide. They were arranged with their cutting edge on the ground, in only one or two superposed lines, and all had their tips oriented in the northern direction.

All the blades were made in a local, homogeneous flint material from the dissolved Turonien layers, found a dozen meters deep in the Creuse Valley. Jacques Pelegrin's study was based on technological observations to reach a particular goal: he was looking for new information on the livre de beurre production methods. His work adds important information on the cutting processes and on the economic meaning of these archaeological arctifacts. He evidences considerable refitting, and proves that all the blades came from a single session of craftsmanship, including around 50 to 80 flakes. La Creusette hoard does not contain all the blades of this single session but seems to only represent less than one eighth (Pelegrin, 1997, p. 33). It is true that many of the first blades are missing. Nevertheless, the material buried can not be easily qualified as second choice. Many of blades are more than 33 cm long with only 9 blades under 27 cm. The smallest blade is 25 cm long (Pelegrin 1997: table 6). All the blades are not retouched and there is no trace of shaping operations in the remains.

- *Les Ayez à Barrou, Indre-et-Loire* (fig. 4)

The discovery of Les Ayez is older than La Creusette. Both hoards are located in the same commune, Barrou, at the heart of the workshops area, and are only separated by about 2.5 kilometres. Circumstances of the discovery are related by many people (Chasteignier 1983; Chauveau 1951; Cordier 1986). G. Cordier, who had tried to compile the most complete documentation he could, proposes the best critical description of the facts. In 1883, the ploughings showed evidences of a flint blades hiding place which led Mr. Chauveau, an elementary school teacher at Barrou, to

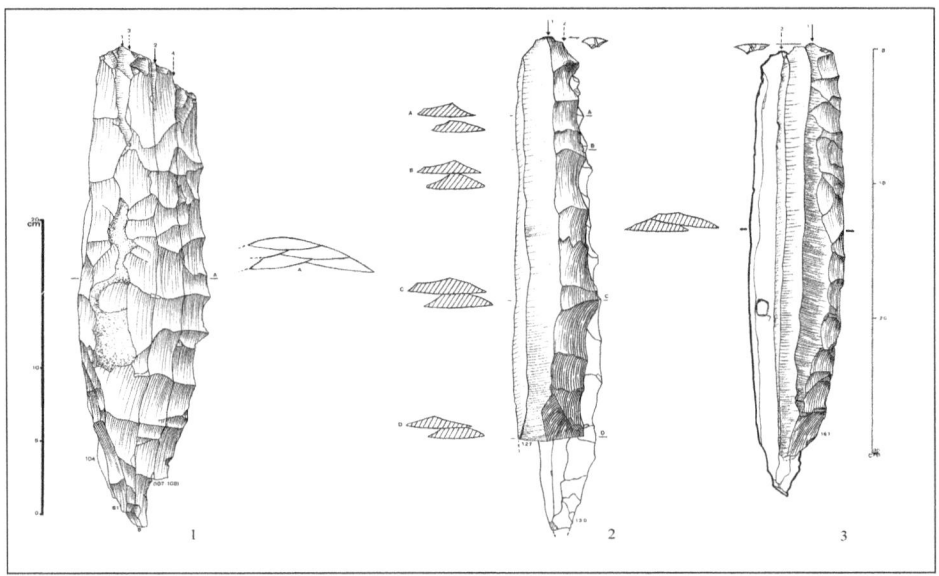

Fig. 3. La Creusette, Barrou (Indre-et-Loire), three examples of flint refitting. Drawings are made by G. Bastien (from Geslin, *et al.*, 1975)

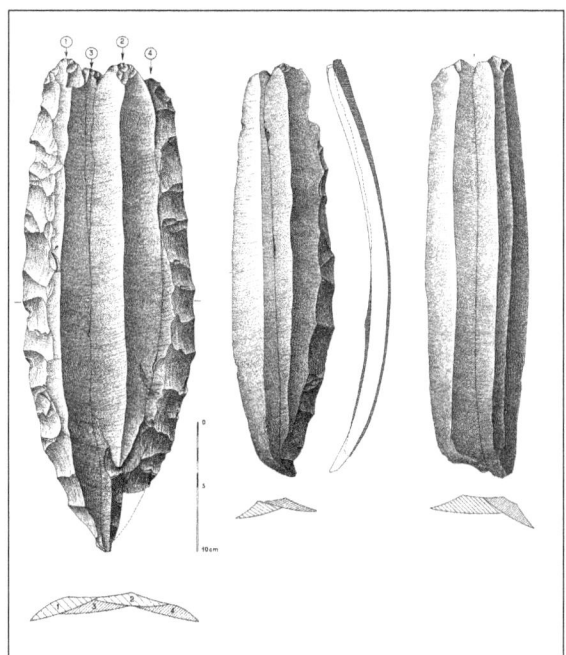

Fig. 4. Les Ayez, Barrou (Indre-et-Loire), two examples of flint refittings. Drawings are made by G. Cordier (from Cordier, 1986).

excavate there with his school boys. At the end of the day, the teacher came back to the school with a full wheelbarrow of Neolithic blades! Since then blades have been distributed around the country.

G. Cordier estimates the total amount of pieces found to about 122 blades, which seems to be the best estimate. Actually, a little under 100 blades are still conserved in several museums in France, such as Bordeaux (39 pieces), Tours (2), Chinon (1) Saint-Germain-en-Laye (4) and Grand-Pressigny (31). All the flint we can observe has a homogeneous characteristic: it is local and seems to come from Abilly, near the Claise valley, less than 5 km away.

Because of the collection spread, no recent technological observations have been realised on the totality of the blades, especially for global refitting methods, which appear very different for each collection (Cordier 1986).

The quality of the blades is as good as the one from La Creusette hoard. Some of the blades are the longest we know for livre de beurre production, approaching 38 cm, the shorter blade being 22 cm long. In this context, again, it is hard to consider these blades as "second choice" even if some examples, for instance one Saint-Germain blade, show a technical error with a major hinged removal located in the middle of the blank. But then, the remedial operation done to correct this mistake required a very high know-how of the craftsman, who produced a 31 cm long blade instead. As for La Creusette none of the products are retouched and there is no trace of shaping operation.

- *La forêt de Damps, Ponts-sur-l'Arche, Eure et Loire* (fig. 5)

G. Morel and A. Blondel have described for the first time in 1903 the discovery of four daggers in La forêt de Damps. The study material is now lost, nevertheless this hoard has been commented by G. Cordier, then further by J.-P. Watté (Watté 1995). La Forêt de Damps is 200 km away from the workshops of the Grand-Pressigny complex which is the reason why the nature of the collection is very different from the two previous cases studied. It was composed of only four daggers which blanks were created from a long blade from livre de beurre.

The four daggers are made of yellow/honey Grand-

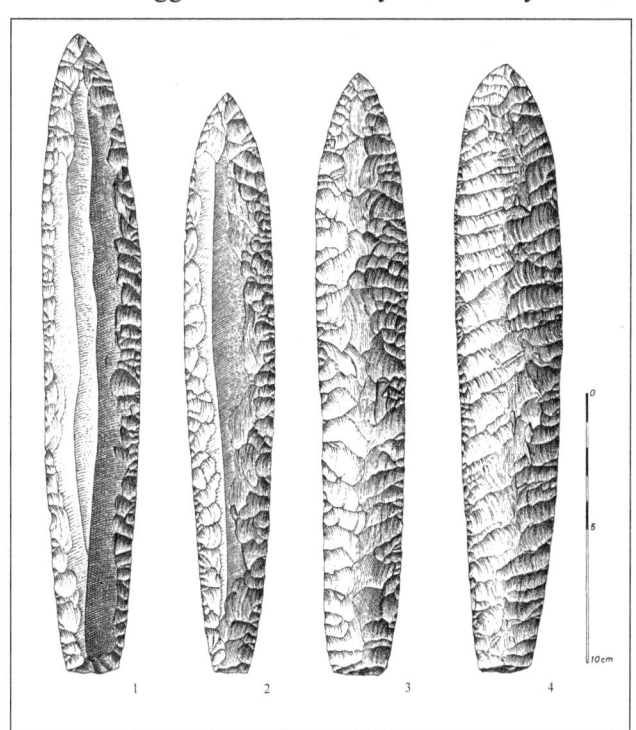

Fig. 5. Pont-de-L'Arche, forêt de Damps (Eure), the four daggers of the hoards. Drawings are made by G. Cordier (from Cordier, 1986)

Pressigny flint and, according to the different authors and photos, the raw material seems homogeneous. It could be a good argument to support the idea of the constitution of the hoard in a short time, and may be even in one single session (Morel, Blondel, 1903, Cordier, 1986, Watté, 1995). The blanks are livre de beurre blades. They are 24, 22, 23 and 23 cm long. No refitting is mentioned. The dagger can be considered as finished but for some reasons seem unused, or at least only slightly worn.

The Typological characteristics of the Late Neolithic dagger are as follow: long blade, unilateral retouch, rectilinear basis and much frayed point. Morphology is quite identical for the four daggers. Retouch seem to have been done with a very meticulous direct percussion; it is aimed in two cases while covering in one case. Only one dagger has the advantage of a secondary treatment that consists in a covering retouch operated by pressure. This very regular retouch could not have been obtained without a major phase of polishing on the superior face of the dagger. It is a delicate procedure that could have required several hours and was not strictly necessary as the blade was used for the cutting of vegetal materials.

- *Moigny, La Croix blanche, Essonne* (fig. 6)

Moigny is also part of earlier discoveries (1890). The original number of blades may have been between 15 and 20 (Mallet *et al.* 1994). Material is partially conserved at the Etampes museum, excepted for one lost piece. This collection, including at least 12 blades, has been studied a few years ago by J. Pelegrin who has delivered very precious and precise descriptions (ibid). The hoard location is over 200 km away from the workshops priory mentioned.

J. Pelegrin and N. Mallet's observations show a large variety of flints even if they all come from the Grand-Pressigny region. Variety could be explained by several supply phases over a long period of time. That reason could explain why J. Pelegrin did not see any refitting among the blanks. Two distinctive characteristics can be observed, as in Damps, between used daggers (Mallet *et al.* 1994, n°3 fig.3), and unused daggers.

This hoard is composed of various typological elements, including different daggers types but also three unused end-scrappers. Among the daggers we can distinguish very long daggers, 32 cm for the longest, which is quite remarkable as the longest flint dagger ever known is 34 cm long (also found in Essonne, at Boutigny). They generally have a rectilinear basis, exactly like in Damps hoard, with a few exceptions where the basis is not reformatted.

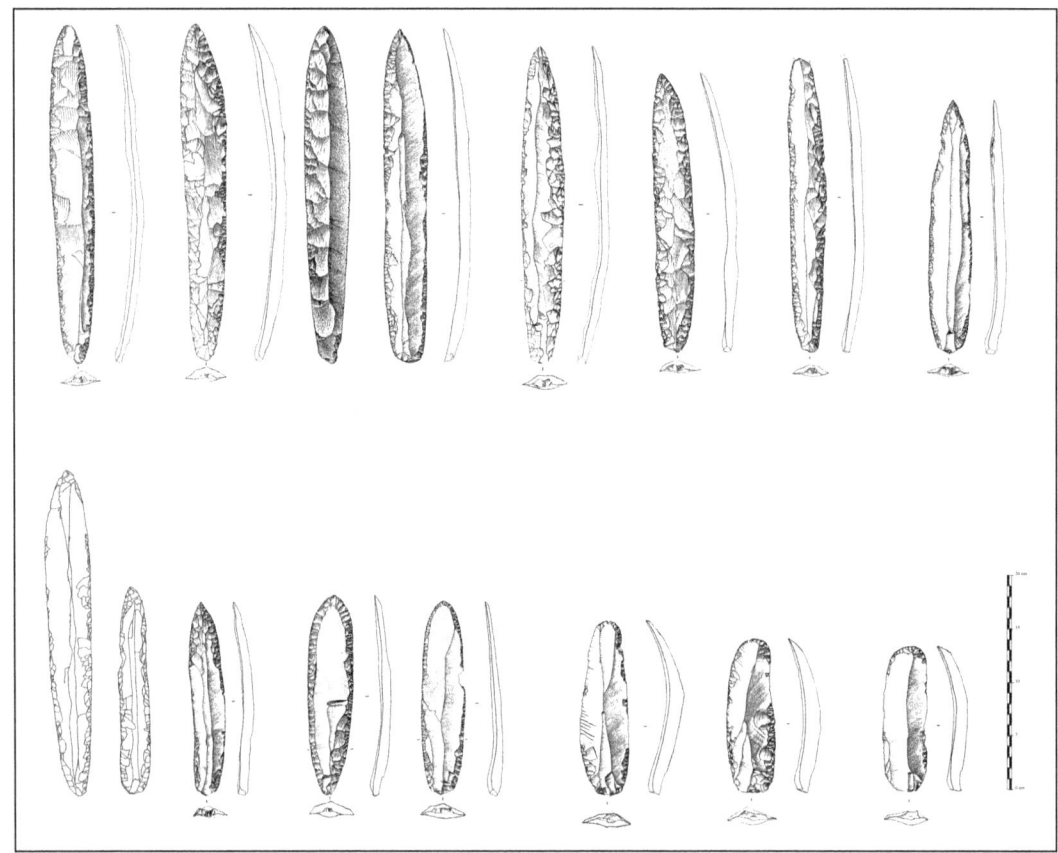

Fig. 6. Moigny, la Croix-Blanche (Essonne).
Drawings are made by M. Reduron-Ballinger (from Mallet, *et al.*, 1994)

We observe the same typological dichotomy among the small daggers group with two kinds of blade blanks depending whether they were made during the first or second phases of blade's production (see supra). The only exception is for two blades which show dihedral butt unpicked associated with big cortical surface, a technique characteristic of the first phases (Mallet *et al.* 1994, fig. 5 p. 31) although the fabrication technique of the butt could be indicative of an advanced procedure and most certainly can be dated to the end of this first phase (Pelegrin, pers. comm.). It is crucial to note that this is one of the few sites which evidence the transition between the two production techniques.

Rivers discoveries (fig. 7)

We can't finish this presentation without the mention of isolated discoveries often made in river beds or in humid contexts. We can distinguish two types of usage made for the material found:
- Part of the discoveries belongs with no doubt to Late Neolithic settlements along rivers. This is the case for Ouroux-sur-Saône (Thevenot 1973) and may be for the Penhouet Basin located at the end of the Loire River (Ihuel 2004). The Material found in these contexts is typical of river settlements, with used and recycled single daggers, both long and short. The research conducted on all major French rivers, on about twenty archaeological sites, further evidences this theory. One of the most impressive pieces comes from the Saône River and is conserved in Saint-Germain Museum (Mallet 1992; Ihuel 2002).
- The other part of the discoveries presents valuable examples with a suspected totally different usage and comes from both the Aisne River in Jaulzy (Oise) and from the Seine River, right in the heart of Paris under both the Iena and Austerlitz bridges (Ihuel 2002). Given the busy location of the later it is astonishing that very long daggers, on livre de beurre blank, were found unused and so miraculously preserved, only slightly eroded by water. The reason that can be advanced for this great stage of conservancy is that these single daggers from ancient settlements did not seem to have been used for day to day activities as none of these objects are broken, nor show any trace of voluntary destruction. Similarly to other Bronze Age swords left in humid soils (Quilliec, 2003), we could wonder if these single daggers with their unusual stage of freshness had not been used in rituals linked to water.

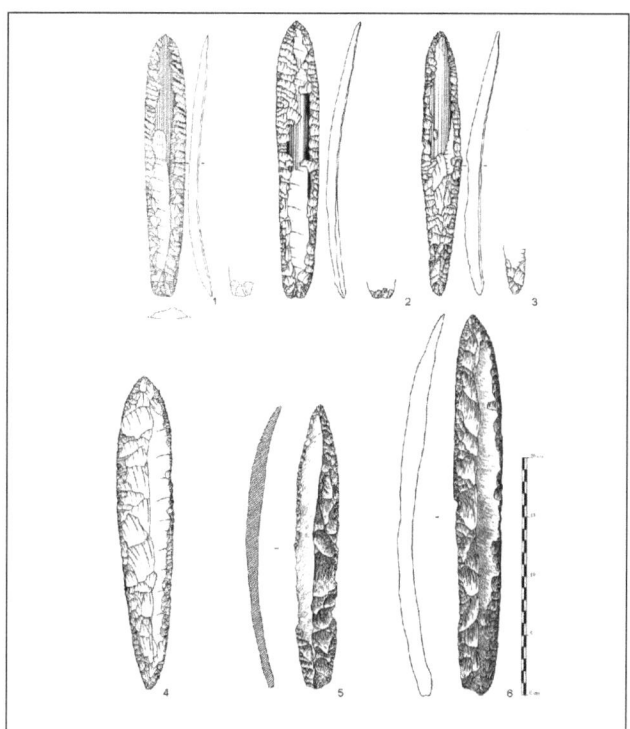

Fig. 7. Daggers found by river drags.
1. Marolles on the Seine river (Seine-et-Marne) ;
2. Paris on the Seine river near Iena bridge ;
3. Paris on the Seine river between Alma bridge and Austerlitz bridge ;
4. Chalon-sur-Saône on the Saône river (Saône-et-Loire) ;
5. Near Blois on the Loire river (Loire-et-Cher) ;
6. Jaulzy on the Oise river (Oise).
Drawings : 1-4 : E. Ihuel, 5 : J. Despriée, 6: G. Bastien. 5 and 6 from Mallet, et al. 1994.

Synthesis

Although the eighteen blade hoard inventory seems limited in comparison with the 87 examples of axes inventoried by G. Cordier (Cordier & Bocquet 1973), the various technical states observed on the material give us new information and allows us to date the evolution as follow:

Blades hoards were still rare in the Late Neolithic and even still so at Bronze Age dawn. The first daggers or long blades found in hoard seem to have appeared around 2800 B.C. cal, and correspond to an increase of this specialised production (Mallet 1992). But, among the eighteen cases gathered by Cordier, only Moigny seems to be partially concerned by the first phase of long blade production. Typological data indicates that the major phase would be between 2800 and 2400 B.C. especially for the well-known livre de beurre blades (Mallet *et al., forthcoming*).

factors for the interpretation of the economical and social impact of the hoard production.

We mainly distinguish two types of deposits for the Pressignian phenomena.

The first type of hoard deposit is composed of raw blades. It is located in the production area and gathers part of single cutting sessions. Observations of J. Pelegrin show that the blades have been a bit manipulated before being buried. The constitution of the deposit was not only based on a clear quality choice between first and second rank products, even if we can notice that there are a few first blades missing and no blanks smaller than 25 cm long. Also, we presume that the choices seem to have been made at each cutting stage rather than at the end of the full session although it is impossible to be fully certain of this. J. Pelegrin has interpreted La Creusette material as a surplus which couldn't be moved. The most acceptable hypothesis in his opinion is that it was a hidden place for itinerant craftsmen who distributed their products on their own and needed a set storage place in between travel periods (Pelegrin 1997: 33). The number of blades found in Les Ayez and La Creusette is very similar (122 and 133 blades). It is hard to consider this fact as a fortuitous coincidence of an equivalent excess of unused production. Unfortunately, there is no data that could help us understand this convergence. Proportions and quantities of the material found could suggest that this type of hoard was created by somebody or some Neolithic institution using a predetermined portion of the production based on blade proportion criteria, but why and what for? As symbolic clues are inexistent at either site and no other object had been added to the 'hideout', the hypothesis of protection against Socio-economic interests of other Neolithic groups or individuals may be more acceptable. The hidden nature of the hoards could have been a protection against those with an indirect role in the production such as extraction workers, owners of raw material, people involved in the transportation, chiefs or castes with socio-economic control ambitions, etc. This said, we agree with J. Pelegrin by considering that this is an intriguing strategy to hide the goods you want to exchange to maintain socio-economic relations or activities. Another explanation could come from the fact that extraction and flaking activities could be more seasonal than the retouch phase which could be practised indoors during the whole year. This hypothesis could explain the necessity to store blanks, close to the workshop or to the living place of the craftsman.

In any case, we present these hypotheses as propositions to explain the structure that constitutes the organisation of the daggers production.

The second type of deposit is composed of hoards located far away from workshops and is not easier to understand. Even though it is true that these deposits only concern finished products, some details show significant differences in time for constituting the blade assemblage and the final objects per se. Damp hoards may evidence a rapid fabrication. On the other hand daggers reveal different kinds of aesthetic treatment and know-how for a single deposit and therefore must have required more time to produce. In some cases it seems that a secondary treatment of the dagger is not so clearly associated with a single person, which could bear the mark of a link between social rank and craftsmen skills.

At Moigny, the constitution of the hoard seems to have been carried out for a long time as it is suggested by some changes in the dagger techno-typology. It could be interpreted as a family treasure, whose transformation involved several generations. Diversity of flint material and typology reflect the history of the hoard modified on many occasions. The set of three end-scrappers could be interpreted as one of this instance. It can not be excluded that this hoard could be representative of a group effort, maybe the dagger collection of some group, caste or family.

Extreme typological specialisation of the French hoards is really impressive for both types of hoards. Moreover, neither axes, nor any other Neolithic objects, have ever been found along with long blades in any hoard located within the French territory (Cordier 1973). Then, this observation could appear minor if limited to the large complex of workshops in the Grand-Pressigny region, but it is quite more surprising regarding discoveries made far away from any workshop, in remote private fields. How can we explain this absence of hoard mingling with other precious objects with high social value or ritual meaning? The only example noticed is the one where three fresh end-scrappers were found among daggers at Moigny, but, even in this case, both kinds of tools are made based on long bladed blank. This is quite remarkable as Neolithic family's treasures were composed of plenty of objects of different natures and diverse materials, like jewels, axes, daggers, arrows. This leads us to believe that, in these instances, where verse materials, like jewels, axes, daggers, arrows. This leads us to believe that, in these instances, where socially highly valued objects were found, other than blades and daggers, the major meaning of this kind of hoard excludes a functional aspect.

Given above facts and observations we can deduct that the Neolithic society had created two types of hoards, both hidden places, but with different goals. One type composed of precious objects of high social values or ritual signification, sort of hideouts for individuals or family treasures. And a second type, of a functional and economic nature, composed of blades and daggers.

Conclusion

Late Neolithic society is characterised by the increase of specialised handicrafts that include the cutitng of very long blades, blank for shaping unilateral flint dagger. The development of specialized handcrafts has often been linked with the establishment of societies getting increasingly socially ranked or hierarchical, with stable long distance exchanges.

The first type of hoards participates to the elaboration of this theory by stigmatizing an appropriation by the social elite of objects with high social value (Pétrequin & Pétrequin 2000). The long distance exchange concept is only working for the second kind of hoard, located far from craftsmen usual habitat. We can observe it at Moigny where two fabrication processes are favoured, individual or collective: the abundance of different types of flint material means necessarily several imports of similar material spaced out in times or a preset redistributing point for material extracted at various locations. Both hypotheses infer an established network of communication (Renfrew 1977).

Damps example of the four similar daggers or the three end-scrappers of Moigny may evidence the quantity that a single individual was able to keep at a single point of time. It could illustrate a key of the exchange system, with a limitation on who had the ability to redistribute the material. This being true or false, we are never the less astonished by the very restrictive partitioning observed in hoards utilized by functional groups, like axes and daggers, in other words, tools that could be used as weapons if required. During the Neolithic, no mixed hoards exist. By that we mean hoards containing axes, arrows, daggers or others objects, all at once.

This represents a complete opposite behaviour compared to the one observed in funeral deposit, such as in the Rupestrian representations in Mont Bego (France) or statue-menhir of Mediterranean borders. In these cases, high social value seems to increase with the juxtaposition of diverse kinds of symbolic and remote objects, often jewels or weapons (Bailloud 1974; Guilaine & Zammit 1998; Saulieu 2004).

Still, the meaning of hoards is hard to understand, especially when it comes to ritual preoccupations, with hypothesis based on individual or family found treasures but not so much on broader groups, which does not always allows for conspicuous conclusions. By inserting this ritual concept in the redistributive system part of the phenomena could be explained but may be reducing it to a more economic than social signification.

The third kind of hoard, based on single objects deposited in river or humid contexts, gives us real evidences of non economic preoccupations. This specific type of hoard, can be interpreted as a territorial boundary or symbolic limit between earth and water (Bradley 1990), and could have been the theatre of social challenges or religious practices which start to take place more often in the Metal ages. In that specific aspect, this type of deposit could be the first premises of Bronze age practices (ibid., Quilliec, 2003).

All the data collected so far does not necessarily give us a full understanding of Neolithic society, but, we can imagine that future research will widen the knowledge in this field.

References

BAILLOUD G. 1974. Le Néolithique du Bassin parisien. 2e éd. Paris: éditions du CNRS. 433 pp.

BERTOLA S., DI ANASTASIO G., PERESANI M. 1997. Hoarding unworked flints within humid microenvironments. New evidence from the mesolithic of the southern alps. Préhistoire européenne 10: 173-185

BRADLEY R. 1990. The passage of arms. An archaelogical analys of hoards and votive deposit. Oxford : Oxbow books. 234 pp.

CHAMBON P., PARIAT J.-G., THEVENET C. 2004. Les inhumés. In Salanova L. éd. Allée couverte de

Sainte-Claude à Bury (Oise), SRA PIcardie, Amiens : 38-81.

CHASTEIGNIER A. (de) 1883. Présentation des couteaux découverts à Barrou. Bulletin de la Société des Antiquaires de l'Ouest. 1883: 183.

CHAUVEAU P. 1951. Découverte des lames des Ayez à Barrou., Bulletin des Amis du Musée du Grand-Pressigny, 1951: 25-57.

CORDIER G. 1986. Les dépôts de lames de silex en France. études préhistoriques 17: 33-48.

CORDIER G. & BOCQUET A. 1973. Le dépôt de la Begude-de-Mazenc (Drome) et les dépôts de haches néolithiques en France. Etudes préhistoriques 1973: 1-17.

EVANS J. 1878. Les Âges de la Pierre Paris.

GAURON G. & MASSAUD J. 1983. La Nécropole de Chenon (Charente). supplément à Gallia-Préhistoire, vol. XVIII. Paris : éditions du CNRS. 195 pp.

GESLIN J.-P. & GESLIN M. 1970. Découverte d'un nouveau dépôt de lame à Barrou (Indre-et-Loire). Bulletin des Amis du Musée du Grand-Pressigny 21: 98-100.

GESLIN M., BASTIEN G., MALLET N. 1975. Le dépôt de grandes lames de la Creusette, Barrou. Gallia Préhistoire 18 : 401-422.

GUILAINE J. & ZAMMIT J. 1998. Le sentier de la guerre. Visages de la violence préhistorique. Seuil ed. Paris. 372 pp.

IHUEL E. 2004. La diffusion du silex du Grand-Pressigny dans le Massif armoricain au Néolithique. CTHS n°18/AMGP suppl. n°2. 180 pp.

IHUEL E., avec la collaboration de MALLET N. & LOUBOUTIN C. 2002. Les collections pressigniennes du Musée des Antiquités Nationales de Saint-Germain-en-Laye. Antiquités Nationales 2002: 29-76.

KELTERBORN P. 1980. Zur Frage des Livre de beurre. Annuaire de la société Suisse de Préhistoire et d'Archéologie vol. 63: 7-19.

MALLET N. 1992. Le Grand-Pressigny, ses relations avec la Civilisation Saône-Rhône. AMGP, suppl. n°1.

MALLET N., PELEGRIN J., REDURON-BALLINGER M., 1994. Sur deux dépôts de lames pressigniennes : Moigny et Boutigny (Essonne). Bulletin des Amis du Musée du Grand-Pressigny 45: 25-37.

MALLET N., IHUEL E., VERJUX C., *forthcoming*. La diffusion du silex du Grand-Pressigny au sein des groupes culturels des IVe et IIIe millénaire. In Les industries taillées des IVe et IIIe millénaires en Europe occidentale. Toulouse, 7-9 avril 2005.

MOREL, A. & BLONDEL G., 1903. communication relative à quatre lames néolithiques trouvées dans la forêt de Pont-de-l'Arche. Bulletin de la société des amis des Sciences Naturelles de Rouen : 161-174.

PELEGRIN J. 1997. Nouvelles observations sur le dépôt de la Creusette (Barrou, Indre-et-Loire). Bulletin des Amis du Musée du Grand-Pressigny 48: 19-34.

PELEGRIN J. 2002. La production des grandes lames de silex du Grand-Pressigny. In Guilaine, J.éd., Matériaux, productions, circulations du Néolithique à l'Âge du Bronze. Paris : édition Errance : 131-148.

PELEGRIN J. *forthcoming*. Notes technologiques sur les pièces en silex du Grand-Pressigny de Chalain-Clairvaux rapportées à la fin du 4e millénaire et au tout début du 3e millénaire. In P. PETREQUIN & A.-M. PETREQUIN ed. Les sites littoraux néolithique de Clairvaux et Chalain (Jura). T IV : du Ferrières au groupe de Clairvaux (31e et 30e siècle av. J.-C.), éd. Maison des sciences de l'Homme, Paris, coll. «Archéologie et culture matérielle».

PELEGRIN J. & IHUEL E. 2005. Les 306 nucléus de la ruine de La Claisière. Bulletin des Amis du Musée du Grand-Pressigny 56 : 45-65.

PETREQUIN P. & PETREQUIN A.-M. 2000. Ecologie d'un outil : la hache de pierre taillée en Irian Jaya (Indonésie). éditions du CNRS ed. Paris. 461 pp.

QUILLIEC B. 2003. L'Épée atlantique : échanges et prestige au Bronze final. Paris: Université de Paris I, thèse de doctorat, 3 vol., 893 p.

RENFREW C. 1977. Alternative models for exchange and spacial distribution. In Earrle T.-K., Ericson J.-E. éds, exchange system in Prehistory, New-York : New-York Academic Press, 71-90.

SAULIEU G. (de) 2004. Art rupestre et statue-menhirs dans les Alpes. Des pierres et des pouvoirs 3000-2000 av. J.-C. éditions errance ed. Paris. 191 pp.

THEVENOT J.-P. 1973 - Le village préhistorique d'Ouroux-sur-Saône, n°1, Macon : Travaux du centre de recherche de Solutré. 174 pp.

VAQUER J., REMICOURT M. & VERGELY H. 2006. Les poignards métalliques et lithiques du Chalcolithique pré-campaniforme des petits et grands causses dans le midi de la France, in:, Gasco, J., Leyge, F. and Gruat, P. éd., Hommes et passé des Causses. Hommage à Georges Constantini, Actes du colloque de Millau, 16-18 juin 2005, Editions des Archives d'Ecologie Préhistorique : 155-179.

VILLES A. 2004. Fouille de sauvetage sur l'Atelier de taille pressignien «La Claisière» à Abilly (Indre-et-Loire). In Internéo 5 – 2004: 115-123.

WATTE J.-P. 1995 - Le néolithique en Seine-Maritime d'après les découvertes de la basse Seine et de l'ouest du Pays de Caux, Revue Archéologique de l'Ouest, suppl. 7: 103-120.

Acknowledgements

I am very glad and thankful to Benedicte Quilliec and Caroline Hamon for inviting me to participate to this research. It was a very interesting experience. I am grateful to J. Pelegrin who provided me with precious advice and documentation on long blades technology. Special thanks to Hannah Deboffe.

Contact

Ewen Ihuel,
doctorant,
UMR 7055, Préhistoire et Technologie
MAE, 21, allée de l'université,
F-92023 cedex Nanterre
France
ewen_ihuel@yahoo.fr

OTHER THAN BRONZE: SUBSTANCES AND INCORPORATION IN DANISH BRONZE AGE HOARDS

Steven MATTHEWS

Abstract:
Recent archaeological perspectives on the subject of personhood have suggested worlds of confused categories of people, animals and artefacts that subvert our modern understandings of these things as distinct, individual and physically bounded entities. Such studies suggest a significantly different approach from which to interpret prehistoric hoards. For example, just as a hoard may represent a composition of particular artefacts, each artefact also represents a composition of different substances, with both being bound-up in systems of worldly and symbolic knowledge that affect the choices that were made in their formation. The processes of 'technological choices' in the formation of Bronze Age hoards from Denmark is explored in terms of the relational contexts of certain associated substances, materials and practices, with a particular emphasis upon animal remains, in burials and agricultural practices, and concludes with a speculative discussion of ways in which these practices may have been organised so as to represent how people in the past may have valued various compositions of artefacts and substances.

Résumé :
Les perspectives archéologiques récentes sur le thème de l'individu ont engendré toute un panoplie de catégories confuses de personnes, animaux et artefacts qui ont bouleversé notre appréciation moderne de ces entités perçues comme distinctes, uniques et physiquement indivisibles. De telles études suggèrent une interprétation significativement différente des dépôts préhistoriques. Ainsi, tout comme un dépôt peut être constitué de certains artefacts particuliers, chaque artefact est également composé de plusieurs substances, liées entre elles par un système de connaissances internationales et symboliques qui traduisent les choix présidant à leur formation. Les choix techniques à l'origine de la formation des dépôt de l'âge du Bronze au Danemark sont explorés à travers les relations entretenues entre certaines substances, matériaux et pratiques, et en particulier à travers les restes animaux en contexte funéraire ou agricole. La manière dont ces pratiques ont pu être organisées peuvent refléter l'appréciation qu'ont pu avoir les hommes préhistoriques des associations variées d'objets et de substances.

«*Such composition of glorious natures doth put life into busines*»
Francis Bacon, *Essayes* (1612: 464)

Introduction

Artefacts are often compositions of both substances and other composite artefacts (fig. 1). However, the analysis of these material artefacts, and assemblages of such artefacts, such as in the study of prehistoric hoards, is more commonly based upon archaeological typologies founded upon a totalised modern aesthetic of completeness or wholeness: of an artefact as a singular bounded entity or form. As an alternative to this reification of the central role of 'the object' is the suggestion that meaningfully constituted and existent artefacts, places and animals also contribute significantly to processes of identity and event formation. This destabilising of the passivity of material culture, established as a consequence of perspectives relating to notions of material artefacts as human co-specifics (Fowler 2004: 59-64) or as having 'personalities' (Thomas 1996: 153) has significant consequences for the study of material assemblages from prehistoric depositions such as hoards.

The study of the hoards of the European Bronze Age has traditionally been based upon an assumed differentiation between certain types of artefacts and their circumstantial occurrence (Bradley 1998: 6-14), including:

- Between that of single and multiple finds
- Between tools, weapons and ornaments
- Between wet and dry locations
- And between the ritual and the non-ritual

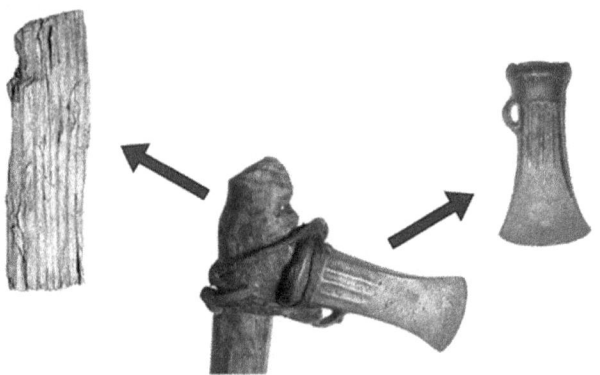

Fig. 1. A 'complete' artefact, in this case a Bronze Age socketed axe which has been hafted, represents a composition of different substances including bronze (also a composite substance), wood and plant material (photo: *Museum of London, London*).

These reductive categories produce simplified archetypes of what were of course complex practices that may also have been, to a lesser or greater degree, individually negotiated performances, a dialogue, rather than rigidly adhered to cultural practices. These traditional approaches have produced a wealth of interesting patterns regarding the practice of hoard deposition, and within these already established frameworks we might now begin to construct observations on the more idiosyncratic technological choices and performances which may have related to the social and cultural perception of value, meaning and cosmology during this period. As well as studying the typological nature of artefact occurrence that may have constituted particular hoards, we also need to begin to question what may have constituted such things as these individual artefact types to begin with and how people in the past may have valued those substances and materials that went into their manufacture and depositional context.

Therefore, in this paper, I want to develop a compositional approach to the hoards of the European Bronze Age, in this case to the analysis of artefact production and depositional practice, that speculates on a complimentary means of interpretation. The relationship of different types of substances to the artefactual and contextual constitution of hoards can be presented as a two-step process: the composition of the individual artefact, and the relationship of artefacts to the deposition of other materials in hoards (for a similar discussion concerning Bronze Age swords see Matthews 2005).

These two aspects of composition can be summarised as:

- First, the way in which the production of material culture would have been an intimate act of incorporation, a symbiosis of varying and meaningful substances (things), technological knowledge and choice (skills), and corporeal performance (technical gestures)

- Secondly, how practices of incorporation were inherent in how people and groups thought about and dwelt within their world: for example, the social and cosmological frameworks within which substances were used in the construction of varying forms of material culture

Substances and the materiality of the Bronze Age

The introduction and development of bronze in prehistoric Europe represents an apparently significant technological innovation. Discussing the relative nature of bronze in relation to its social character, Sofaer Derevenski and Sørensen (2002: 118) argue that:

«*With regard to the first regular use of copper and bronze, one can suggest that the potentially destabilising effect of this new resource was quite severe and that it posed a significant threat to existing social relations.*»

However, with regards to the introduction of these first metals into northern Europe this appears not to be the case, and instead of representing any significant change the earliest copper, bronze and gold artefacts were in fact both sporadic in occurrence and were subsumed into contexts similar to that of Neolithic artefacts (Barber 2003: 11). The 'destabilising effect' of metal is suggested to refer to changes in social practice 'in which some people shifted away from local productive activities to become involved with metal prospecting and the production and exchange of bronze and bronze objects' (Sofaer Derevenski and Sørensen 2002: 119). Such networks of specialisation, however, were also already at work during the Neolithic, with studies of stone and flint sources and their products, as well as other classes of artefact, demonstrating the existence long before metal of extensive local and regional networks of contact, trade and exchange throughout Europe (Whittle 1996).

Whilst there is little doubt that the development of metal eventually did have a significant impact upon societies in Europe, the transformation from Neolithic to Bronze Age traditions may have instead been a relatively inclusive and understated affair, representing the exploitation of already familiar materials, processes and places (Sherratt 1976). The significance of the introduction of bronze perhaps lay less in its impact as a new material for the production of artefacts types (though this was indeed to prove significant in the long-term) and instead as a new mechanism by which to perceive the world, a medium both literal and symbolic, for prehistoric societies to explore new ways of thinking about and interacting with those familiar materials, processes and places.

As a meaningfully constituted substance bronze is likely to have embodied a number of divergent qualities. By this, I refer to its compositional nature as an alloy. A number of scientific studies have highlighted the significance of the compositional structure of bronze, analysing the constitutive elements of artefacts in relation to such things as the location and type of source material, differential compositional structure (quantity of lead, arsenic, nickel, etc.), and the affiliation of bronzes to each other and to possible production centres or 'workshops' (e.g. Brown 1982; Tylecote 1986 & 1987; Northover 1982; Rohl & Needham 1998; for an overview of such studies and their results see Harding 2000: Chapter 6; for a study of early Danish bronzes see Liversage & Liversage 1989). Such studies have established that bronze alloys are significantly diverse and that we should be cautious in assigning a single social character to it.

The social and cultural meaning of bronze as a compositional material, and as a consequence of qualitative technological choices, remains, however, largely unexplored (see, however, Quilliec this volume; for an alternative perspective see Budd 1993). The substances or ores that were utilised to produce bronze artefacts are generally viewed in terms of 'raw' materials (e.g. Harding 1999, 2000: 206-217), entities that show up as having only a utilitarian value and therefore lacking any symbolic or socially meaningful value, with this latter quality instead relating only to the finished category of 'bronze' or bronze artefacts. This symbiosis of different substances, that would themselves have held specific cultural values and qualities, may have significantly affected the nature of how various artefacts made of bronze would have been perceived and used. As a compositional substance it may therefore require a far more complex system of categorisation than just that of 'bronze'. The materials that composed it were meaningful entities or substances in their own right and therefore warrant considerable interpretative as well as empirical attention (cf. Boivin & Owec 2004). For example, in a study of Early Bronze Age metalwork from northern Italy, Pearce (1998) has suggested that different compositions of copper may have been intentionally used in the production of different artefact types, and that 'composition reflects a deliberate choice by the ancient metalworker' (Ibid: 58) with arsenical copper being used for halberds and daggers and purer copper used for flat axes. Pearce suggests that these technological choices related to the final artefacts social and symbolic value, and therein establishing a meaningful and intentional relationship between primary substances and final forms.

In the context of hoard depositions the nature of bronze composition will prove to be, in this author's opinion, not only significant in terms of the study of bronzes but also in reflecting purposeful technological choices made by persons in the past. This line of argument obviously requires further development. However, it is instead to the contextual composition of such materials found in hoards that we will now direct this discussion.

Detailed excavation reports and summaries for hoard contexts are rare. This is a consequence of hoards being either a product of early antiquarian excavation (lacking the kind of detail we now consider normal in an archaeological excavation) with their emphasis being primarily the recovery of bronzes, or as a by-product of early industrial activity or agricultural practices, and the fact that even today such finds are still predominantly chance recoveries. For example, in a review of a substantial sample of the original source material used by Eogan (1983) in his The Bronze Age Hoards of Ireland, I was able to recover little in the way of any description of environmental circumstance and no description whatsoever of any other materials than those of bronze. Nonetheless, the study of composition can still compliment the more traditional studies of the differentiation of hoard types by relating the way that objects, and the substances involved in their composition, may have been valued socially and symbolically by society and the persons involved in the deposition of hoards by utilising a cross-contextual or relational comparison (for a discussion of a 'intercontextual' approach see Kristiansen 2004). Moreover, the few contexts where materials other than bronze have been recovered suggest that there was indeed far more to hoards than mere metal. Those hoards that have been subjected to modern excavation procedures often contain quantities of organic materials such as wood, textiles, human and animal bones, pottery, and demonstrate instances of burning. These objects suggest that the relationship between different objects and different hoard types is much more complex than simply between the occurrence and circumstance of particular types of bronze artefacts.

This differential use of such materials and substances can be related to alternating spheres of social interaction, in similar ways to that of bronze artefacts such as ornaments and weapons (e.g. Kristiansen 1978; Sørensen 1997), and therefore to different social categories, such as gender, age and class. For example, the type of knowledge related to the production of different objects and depositional contexts, such as particular settlements, houses, burials, or hoards, may have been produced by different people with differential access to artefacts and substances (things), technological knowledge and choice (skills), and forms of corporeal performance (gestures and techniques) (e.g. Matthews 2004; Quilliec 2004). To illustrate this point, the compositional structure of hoards from Bronze Age Denmark will be explored in terms of these relational contexts, with reference to such phenomenon as social values, symbolic capital, esoteric meanings and cosmological structures.

The Danish Bronze Age was part of the northern European Nordic Bronze Age tradition. Its chronology was, of course, established entirely upon the study of bronze artefacts (Montelius 1917) and is divided between an Early and Late Bronze Age:

Early Bronze Age:
    Period I   1800 – 1550 B.C.
    Period II   1550 – 1300 B.C.
    Period III   1300 – 1100 B.C.

Late Bronze Age:
    Period IV   1100 – 950 B.C.
    Period V   950 – 750 B.C.
    Period VI   750 – 600 B.C.

The depositional circumstance of these bronzes, however, changes significantly during this time as a consequence of the fluctuating occurrence of burials and hoards, which is argued to have operated as an inter-related phenomenon functioning as part of a single structure of deposition (Kristiansen 1998: 178). This fluctuation can be characterised as a shift from the relatively short depositional emphasis upon predominantly male-associated artefacts (such as swords and other weapons) in burial contexts, to a much longer emphasis upon predominantly female-associated artefacts (such as ornaments) in hoards (Kristiansen 1984: 86-91), and thereby establishing a relation between males and burials in the earlier part of the period and females and hoards in the later part.

Other than bronze : animal remains from Danish Bronze Age hoards

Fig. 2. The Budesene hoard from Møn, southeast of Zealand. This Late bronze Age hoards contained numerous bronze ornaments, as well as a variety of organic materials including wood, stones, and domesticated animal remains (photograph from Levy 1982).

As has already been suggested, the depositional practices relating to hoards may have consisted of far more meaningful acts than just the laying down of bronzes. A particularly significant example is that of the Budsene hoard (fig. 2) from Zealand (Levy 1982: 17; fig.3), which consisted of numerous ornamental bronze artefacts. The artefacts from this deposit had been placed at the bottom of a hollowed trunk of Alder that had been sunk into a water-bearing stratum, forming a well. Situated about 1 meter below the surface, the trunk had been packed around by hand-sized stones, and inside the bronze ornaments had been surrounded by the bones of domesticated pig, horse, cattle, sheep and dogs. The Budsene hoard therefore consisted of a composition of numerous different substances, primary among them being organic materials: wood, stone, water and animal remains.

The inclusion of animal bones may have been highly significant, and whilst Levy described this hoard as a 'ritual' deposit, distinguishing it from other more mundane or utilitarian hoards, these remains should not be considered more important or meaningful than those remains deposited in other contexts, such as pits and settlements (Levy 1982: 17). Furthermore, this distinction between spheres of 'ritual' and 'non-ritual' practice has been shown to be highly questionable (Bradley 1998: xviii; 2005: Chapter 5). Animals are far more than mere commodities, with the intentional exploitation of secondary animal products and materials (Sherratt 1981, 1983), and the practice of divergent subsistence strategies in agriculture, animal husbandry and pastoralism during the Bronze Age (Harding 2000: 133-143), creating a situation whereby animals were a constant and intimate aspect of the life and events of Bronze Age communities. The important and meaningful role of animals is attested to by the numerous examples of models and depictions of animals on various media from through

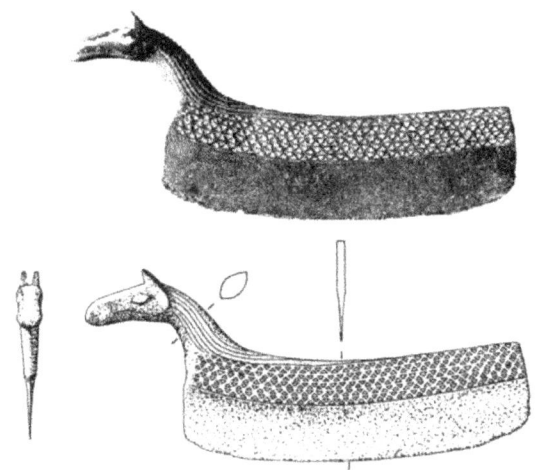

Fig. 3. Bronze razor from a burial in northern Zealand with horses head handle
(after Brøndsted 1966 and Kaul 1998).

out Bronze Age Europe, including their frequent depiction upon various types of bronzes and rock carvings, and as figurines (fig. 3). The deposition of animal bones and animal-derived artefacts, whilst by no means common, occurred with sufficient frequency in burials and settlements as to suggest that it was a consistent and significant event in the routines of these communities (Harding 2000: 335), and the deposition of animal remains in hoards is no exception (Bradley 1998: 111).

Using Levy's (1982) description of the hoards from Bronze Age Denmark we can establish a list of those deposits, and their locations (fig. 4), associated with animal remains (numbers in brackets refer to the catalogue numbers assigned by Levy):

Period III:
1. *Taarup, Zealand* (#64): One spear-point, chisel, four sickles, one hammer, two ankle rings, fragments of sheet bronze. Found in a bog.

Period V:
2. *Gjerlev, Zealand* (#208): Set of 445 round rings of approximately 2 cm in diameter and 37 'clapper' belt ornaments. Found in dry location.

3. *Budsene, Zealand* (#214): Two hanging vessels, one belt ornament, three spiral armrings. Found in a well surrounded by animal bones.

4. *Rørmosen, Zealand* (#223): Two neck-rings with ornamented endplates. Found in a bog.

5. *Trørod, Zealand* (#225): Two twisted neck-rings with ornamented endplates. Found in a bog.

6. *Hasmark, Zealand* (#228): Three neckrings with ornamented endplates, one spearpoint and a sheath attachment. Found in a field.

7. *Langtved, Funen* (#236): Gold armband, double wire spiral armband of gold, one fibula. Found in a field in a hole containing ashes and stones.

8. *Bellinge, Funen* (#249): Two neckrings, two spiral armrings, toggle pin, sickle, dagger blade. Found in gravel, apparently wrapped in an animal skin.

9. *Glerup, Jutland* (#264): Two hanging vessels, one belt ornament, two twisted neckrings with oval end-

plates, two fibuli, two armbands, two spiral armrings, one armring overlain with gold. Animal bones were spread around the hoard. Found in a bog.

Period VI:
10. *Antvorskov, Zealand* (#306): Two neckrings with reversing twist, four neckrings with quadrilateral cross-section, one kidney-shaped armring, two celts, one pin with curled head, one large and one small ring with eye. Found in remains of an ancient spring covered with charcoal, animal bones, and pottery.

11. *Kirke Søby, Funen* (#318): Two fragments of sword, one oversized spearpoint, one unique oversized chisel. Found next to a bog and associated with a well containing animal bones, pottery and stones.

Using some of the basic characteristics (i.e. types of objects and location) established by Levy (1982: 26-42, fig. 6.2) to analyse these hoards, Table 1 summarises the different nature of those hoards that contained animal bones.
In her study of these hoards Levy (1982: 81) associated this occurrence of animal bones, and similarly sickles and pottery, with food and feasting practices. Whilst animal products, pottery and often certain types of artefacts are indeed a necessary practical aspect of eating, such elements also constitute significant symbolic and mnemonic mediums in relation to the social and corporeal practice of consumption (Hamilakis 2002). However, Table 1 shows that the occurrence of animal bones, sickles and pottery are few. Rather, the most common association that can be made between these remains of domesticated animals is with ornaments and wet locations and less frequently with weapons and dry locations. Having established this basic set of associations within the immediate context of these depositions, using traditional approaches of occurrence and frequency, we can now begin to explore the relational contexts of animals and animal remains recovered from other circumstances in the Danish Bronze Age before returning to the hoards themselves.

Animals and Bronze Age society: symbols and domesticates

As has already been mentioned, parallel to this deposition of particular materials in hoards, was the practice of artefact deposition in burials. Of note are the series of oak coffin and stone cist burials of Periods II and III for they contained animal remains, parts of animals and transformed animal materials deposited alongside the various types of bronzes (e.g. Glob 1974).

For example, the burial at Hvidegård (Ibid. 1974: 114, 116), dating to the early part of Period III (Kaul 1998: 16), consisted of a stone cist scattered with small flints, on the top of which lay an Ox hide, and laid out as if worn were a cape and a cloak, a bronze sword in its scabbard, a belt, a bronze brooch, and finally beneath these lay the cremated bones of an adult male. The burial also contained a leather purse which held a remarkable collection of objects (fig. 5): a piece of amber, one whole and one broken conch shell, a small cube of wood, a flint flake, a number of dried roots, a piece of bark, a grass-snakes tail, the claw of a falcon, bronze tweezers, a knife in a leather case, a razor with a horses head handle wrapped with a thin leather thong, a flint strike-a-light knife stitched into a bladder or other internal organ, the lower jaw of a squirrel inside a small leather case, and a number of small stones (Glob 1974; Kaul 1998: 116).

Similar purses are known from almost 30 graves from Period II and III, but often survive only as a

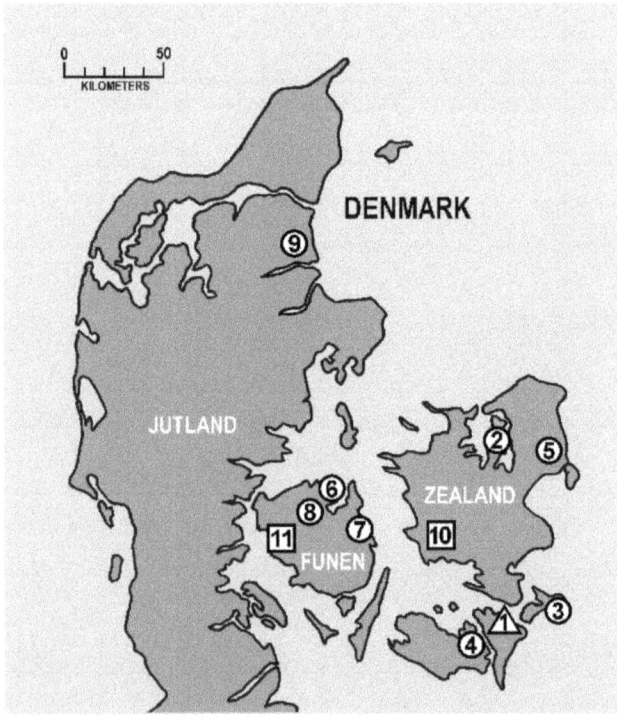

Fig. 4. Distribution of hoards containing animal bones in Denmark: Triangle) Period III; Circle) Period V; Square) Period VI. Numbers relate to hoards listed in text (information from Levy 1982).

	Wet	Dry	Ornaments	Weapons	Sickles	Pottery	Number of ornaments in each set
Period III:							
1. Taarup, Zealand	X		X	X	X	X	1
Period V:							
2. Gjerlev, Zealand		X	X				0
3. Budsene, Zealand	X		X				2/3
4. Rørmosen, Zealand	X		X				1
5. Trørod, Zealand	X		X				1
6. Hasmark, Zealand		X	X	X			1
7. Langtved, Funen		X	X				2
8. Bellinge, Funen		X	X	X	X		2
9. Glerup, Jutland	X		X		X		4/5
Period VI:							
10. Antvorskov, Zealand	X		X			X	4
11. Kirke Søby, Funen	X		X	X		X	0

Table 1. Summary of the different types of locations and classes of artefacts associated with hoards containing animal bones in the Danish Bronze Age (information from Levy 1982).

dark colouring in the soil (Kaul 1998: 18). Where these purses have survived, their contents appear quite uniform, such as that recovered from the Løfthoj barrow, also from north Zealand. At 35 m across and 7 m high, Løfthoj is one of the biggest barrows in Denmark, and contained one of the few oak coffin burials from Zealand. This male inhumation contained a bronze flange-hilted sword, a gold armlet, and what remained of a leather purse containing a small bronze knife, a broken razor, tweezers, a piece of wood wrapped in strips of skin, two leather cases tied with string, and a flint strike-a-light wrapped in leather (Glob 1974: 114).

One of the later of these burials from northern Zealand is the Maglehøj burial (Glob 1974: 162), containing a female cremation dated to the end of Period III (Kaul 1998: 16). Again a stone cist, although this time much smaller, contained numerous bronze objects, including a belt-box, a double-headed fastener, a knife and a fibula atop the cremated bones wrapped in a piece of woollen clothing. Within the belt-box had been placed two horses teeth, the bones of a weasel or marten, a wild cats claw, the bones of perhaps a young lamb or fawn, part of a birds windpipe, vertebrae from a snake, fragments of burnt bone, fragments of wood, pebbles of quartz, pieces of clay and pyrites, a sheet of bronze and a piece of bronze wire (Glob 1974: 162; Coles & Harding 1999: 521).

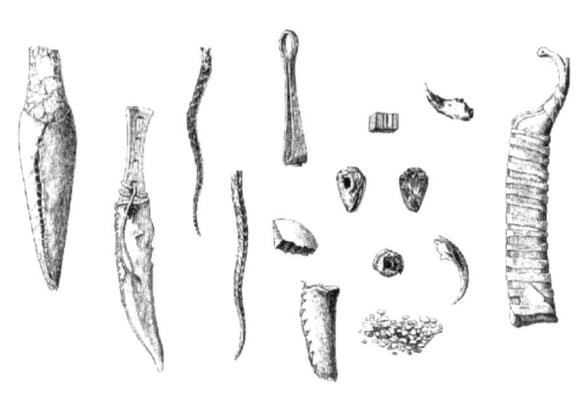

Fig. 5. Animal remains and animal-derived artefacts, organic materials substances, and bronzes recovered from the Hvidegård burial in northern Zealand
(after Glob 1974)

The presence of animal remains and other organic materials have led some to suggest that these materials had an esoteric or magical purpose (Kaul 1998: 16) and that the dead buried in these barrows were extra-special in some way, perhaps 'shamans' (Glob 1974: 114). However, as Harding has pointed out (Harding 2000: 96), there is no reason to believe them to have been exceptional at the time they were deposited, with the barrows being much like any other, and similarly the tree-trunk coffins (e.g. Ibid. 2000: 103-109) and stone cists. Rather, it is the degree of archaeological preservation that is exceptional.

From these examples from Zealand, it appears that these burial deposits represent an oppositional emphasis to hoard depositions. Although several generations earlier than those hoards described above, which consisted of primarily domesticated animals, these burial deposits appear to emphasis the wild or non-domesticated. The cattle hides that the inhumations and cremations were laid down upon were most likely to have been procured from domesticated animals, and similarly the leather to make the purses, but the contents appear to represent species of animal unrelated to the processes and practices of agriculture and domestication.

Despite these exceptional deposits, and similar in many ways to the basic component substances of bronze, animals are commonly attributed the status of 'raw material' and ascribed merely the role of a material mediator in human relationships, portrayed as passive objects rather than meaningful subjects in their own right (Noske 1993). As integral elements in human economic formations from prehistory onwards, animals constitute merely consumable resources, prestige commodities and a means of production. Such views represent a common perception of the privileged position of agricultural practices as one of domination (Ingold 1994). However, this domination does not necessarily mean that animals were devoid of social and cultural meaning, on the contrary, as a central element of Bronze Age economies animals enjoyed a privileged and significant position in society. It has already been suggested that any differentiation between 'ritual' and 'non-ritual' practice is highly problematic (Bradley 2005), and therefore distinguishing between the involvement of animals in symbolic practices, such as in hoards and burials, and the exploitation of animals involved in subsistence practices is not tenable.

The environmental evidence for such practices from Bronze Age Denmark indicates an extensive landscape of predominantly pasture and heathland, reflecting a pastoral economy dependant on cattle and sheep, with possibly some 30 to 40% of the land being settled according to the distribution of graves (Kristiansen 1978), with many of these settled areas being heavily deforested (Kristiansen 1984: 92). Although cattle was, in most regions, the major meat supplier, significant changes took place in the relative balance of animals in several regions during the middle Bronze Age (1100-700 B.C.), and compared with earlier times, sheep/goat and pig became more common, but regional variations are considerable (Ibid. 1998: 107). Ecological changes are reflected in dry open land becoming more common, and shifts in exploitative strategies, with sheep for example now being producers of wool rather than just meat and milk (Ibid. 1998: 109). These variations are most evident from settlements, such as Voldtofte, Funen, one of the largest settlements in Denmark (Thrane 1984; Berglund 1982; Kristiansen 1998: 175-180). At Voldtofte 80 per cent of all animal bones were cattle, representing a new economic division between chiefly settlements dominated by cattle, and normal settlements dominated by sheep/goat and pig, with the latter settlements perhaps supplying wool for the chiefly settlement, along with other products (Kristiansen 1998: 109). Moreover, the analysis of the animal assemblages from Voldtofte also revealed an almost total absence of wild or non-domesticated species of animal (Berglund 1982: 62).

Animals and hoards: summation

Varying patterns of practice in relation to different types of animals are clearly evident from the hoards, burials and settlements described above. The animal assemblages from Early Bronze Age burials contained entirely wild or non-domesticated species, whereas the Later Bronze Age hoards appear instead to have contained primarily domesticated species, such as sheep and pig and particularly cattle. This significant internal differentiation within what is normally considered a single totalising sphere of practice demonstrates that a more pervasive cosmological perspective was operating during the Bronze Age than traditional differentiations between ritual and non-ritual spheres can accommodate for.

The nature of agricultural practices and settlement organisation clearly constituted a potent source of symbolic capital for communities, not only in terms of human-animal economic relationships structured around a position of human dominance, but also in representing how people structured themselves in terms of the places and relationships that they chose to share, or not to share, with particular types of animals. In comparing burials with settlement evidence we can suggest similar but not identical sets of associations and oppositions as between hoards and burials, notably the almost total absence of wild animals from large centralised or chiefly settlements and the similar absence of domesticated species from the animal remains recovered from burials.

This relationship between certain types of settlements and domesticated animals, between burials and wild or non-domesticated animals, and finally between hoards and domesticated animals suggests that human-animal relationships in the Danish Bronze Age break down into associations based around a much wider system of attracting and opposing dualisms (Tilley 2004: 200), which can be briefly summarised thus (based upon Kristiansen 1984, 1998, 2001, 2004; Levy 1982; Sørensen 1987, 1997; Kristiansen & Larsson 2005):

Nature	Culture
Gods	Humans
Wild	Domesticated
Female (foreign)	Female (local)
Male	Female
Male (warrior chief)	Male (priestly chief)
Male (twins)	Male (twins)
Burials	Hoards
Burials	Settlements
Settlements (chiefly)	Settlements (non-elite)
Elite	Non-elite
Weapons	Ornaments
Wet locations	Dry locations

The extent of complexity that existed within these apparently simple categories, however, can be clearly demonstrated by the social, material and depositional circumstances related to horses: an animal and animal motif of some significance throughout the time of the Danish Bronze Age (Kaul 1998: 200). The material technology of horse riding occurs frequently amongst Later Bronze Age hoards in the form of bit and bridle equipment, and often in association with both ornaments and wet locations, extending the affinity of females and hoards to include horses and horse-riding. Despite these associations, the horse, as either an individual mount or in relation to the use of chariots, is usually described as a male preserve associated with the 'warrior' persona (Kristiansen 1999; Treherne 1995) of the Late Bronze Age (a role that has been erroneously extended to the Early Bronze Age) and with other male-orientated sumptuary goods such as swords and axes (Levy 1982: 83). This relationship between males and horses in Denmark is materialised in the depiction of equines upon male-associated bronze artefacts such as razors (Kaul 1998: 199-215), which are predominantly recovered from Later Bronze Age burials, consolidating this affinity between males and horses. Perhaps the differing gender associations relates to the maintenance and husbandry of horses, most likely within settlements, such as at Voldtofte where horse remains have been found (Coles & Harding 1979: 496), as a female dominated domain, and the riding and use of horses as a primarily male sphere of practice. It is, of course, reasonable to argue that there was in fact no exclusive association of the horse with any particular social or gendered practice. However, the distinction between domesticated and wild that has been established between hoards and settlements on the one hand, and burials on the other, could also be attributed to horses. Females were perhaps associated in some manner with the domesticated character of horses, exemplified in artefacts such as the bridle-gear found in a number of hoards, and males with the wild or pre-domesticated aspect of a horses character. This latter relationship may have been signified by artefacts such as the bronze razors recovered from burials, many of which were cast with handles shaped like horses heads (fig. 3) and had stylised depictions upon them of seemingly un-mounted, running or raising-up hoses (Kaul 1998: fig. 131). The horse was likely to have been a particularly significant animal and potent symbol, constituting a form of boundary entity between hoards and burials, females and males, domesticated and wild, and between certain organic substances (such as cheek pieces carved from bone) and bronzes.

The suggestion that animals and natural substances played a significant role in Bronze Age worldviews has been suggested by Kaul (Kaul 1998), whose reconstruction of a Nordic Bronze Age cosmology from various bronze materials, particularly razors, and their associated iconography, has strong animalistic connotations, whereby the daily passage of the sun across the sky is heralded by a ship and at different stages in this daily cycle it is assisted by a horse and a snake, and finally the passage of the sun during the night being associated with a fish. Moreover, many of the horse depictions upon these bronze razors appear to show these 'wild' horses, or what Kaul (1998: 202) refers to as 'sun-horses', towing a depiction of a sun or sun-disc, similar to that of the Trundholm Sun Chariot – a material representation of this belief that the sun was drawn across the sky by a horse (Ibid. 1998: 200; Kristiansen 2004).

The patterns established by such dualisms as male/wild and female/domesticated can also be argued to relate to other gendered spheres of social practice and institutions (for a discussion of the problems surrounding sex and gender roles in Bronze Age Scandinavia see Sørensen 1992). Examples of such social structures have been suggested by Randsborg (1985: 150) in his analysis of the sexual division of Early Bronze Age roles and of the association between females and the household, and also by Gibbs (1987: 85), who draws similar conclusions for the Later Bronze Age. I strongly disagree, however, with the suggestion that associations such as that between females and the household should somehow reduce or create a restricted sphere of female influence amongst Bronze Age communities (Randsborg 1985: 152). On the contrary, the role of the house and the household during the Bronze Age is likely to have been central to the organisation of society (cf. Fokkens 2002), and may in fact have acted as a primary platform in establishing a significant degree of independent political power amongst females, despite the assertion by Levy (1982: 79) that female status was entrely dependant on an associated male, such as a father or husband. It is interesting to note that the construction or initial phases of Bronze Age houses in northern Europe are associated with practices concerning the deposition of the remains of domesticated animals (Bradley 2003: 19, fig.10). Furthermore, Kristiansen (1984: 94) has emphasised the development of the role that females may have played in stabilising the animal-wealth economy of the Later Bronze Age in Denmark and in maintaining the flow of bronze into the region from Central Europe.

The changing nature of these gender roles in the Later Bronze Age is evident from the increasing number and complexity of bronze ornaments found in hoards, and of the greater number and emphasis upon ornaments in sets (Levy 1982: 69-74; Kristiansen 1974), and of their association with other materials such as the inclusion of domesticated animal remains from the end of Period III onwards. The associations of these sets and their organisation appear to relate to a structured system of intra-gender ranking of females relating most likely to age and class (Sørensen 1987). Table 1 shows the number of these sets in relation to those hoards containing animal remains, as well as other materials, and its type of location.

Analysing Table 1 using traditional associations of the number and complexity of ornaments types and sets, and the presence and absence of weapons, the hoards from Period V clearly divide between finds from wet and dry locations. Those from wet locations contain the greatest representation of ornament types and sets and the greatest number of ornaments overall, and contain no weapons. The hoards found in dry locations during this period contain the most weapons, and although these are still greatly under-represented compared to the number of overall ornaments from this period, these hoards do contain the least number of ornaments in comparison to hoards from wet locations. The study of use-wear upon these ornaments from Period V by Kristiansen (1978) demonstrates that on Zealand, which has the highest concentration of hoards from wet locations containing animal remains from our sample, the number of ornaments with evidence of moderate or no wear at all increased in comparison to the preceding period, whilst ornaments with evidence of heavy wear decreases. This is in contrast to the area of Funen, for example, which has the largest number of hoards from dry locations from our sample, wherein we find the opposite pattern, with the number of ornaments with evidence of moderate or no wear at all decreases and the number of ornaments with evidence of heavy wear increases. Following Kristiansen's line of argument, this pattern suggests that a small (but increasing) number of ornaments were staying in circulation longer in this area, where as on Zealand an ever growing number of ornaments were kept in circulation for only a limited time, and therefore represent a greater number of ornaments being deposited during this period in the region of Zealand than of Funen, as is illustrated in Table 1 and fig. 4.

Although Period VI is represented by only 2 hoards from a total of 44 for this period (Levy 1982: Appendix 1, 153-149), both are significant for being located not just in wet locations but in or close to sources of water: a well and a spring. Both hoards, unlike in Period V, are also associated with pottery. The relationship between ornament/wet and weapon/dry is here subverted with only one containing just ornaments and the other containing both weapons and ornaments. It is interesting to note that the hoard containing only ornaments is associated with the natural spring, whilst the hoard containing both weapons and ornaments is associated with a well, a constructed source of fresh water, maintaining the social and technological division between nature and culture. This latter association is also found in a hoard from Period V that was deposited with a well and which was also the only hoard from a wet location that contained weapons of any sort. The female connotations associated with hoards and wet locations therefore is mirrored by a symmetrical association of water and males, for example, in the relationship established between the burial cairns, coastal regions and rock-carved ships that we find so closely related further to the east in Sweden (Bradley 1997).

Particular types and associations of ornaments have been suggested to relate to the construction and maintenance of certain forms of identity and social roles (cf. Sørensen 1997; Matthews 2004), the kind of identities that apparently required a degree of materialisation and fixity. If such identities were closely related to particular lifestages, rites of passage or social position (Fontijn 2002: 244), then whilst hoard assemblages cannot be directly associated with the physical death of a person they might instead be argued to represent the death of a particular identity or of a particular stage or position in a persons life. Hoards therefore may represent themes of death and of transformation in relation to female practices and roles, themes that might be argued to share strong connotations with the deposition of animal remains, a particular type of social being and material culture that frequently undergoes a series of human witnessed or human-related transformations, such as in animal husbandry, as well as slaughter, cooking and consumption, and the production of varying forms of material culture such as bone items and clothes. Just as the taking up and laying down of bronze ornaments during various stages of a females life represents a distancing from who they may have been before and who they were to perhaps become, so to these transformations of animal remains represent degrees of distancing from what a particular species may once have been and what parts of it may have been transformed in to. Moreover, with regard to the changing roles and statuses of females during the course of their life, this distancing may have taken on a very real dimension during the course of the Early Bronze Age with Danish 'wives' finding their way into the communities of central Europe, as evident from the appearance of ornaments some distance from their normal extent of distribution (Sørensen 1997), representing the central role that females may have played in the politics of intra-regional alliances – social compositions of different communities and persons – perhaps in an attempt by elite sections of society to control and maintain the importation of bronze into the region during a period of declining supply (Kristiansen 1984: 94).

Composition and distancing : material intersections

A major problem in studying such substances and materials as qualitative phenomenon is that their significance and value is historically and culturally contingent. Our own understanding of 'natural' materials and substances is as a result of a particular mode of thought unique to 'modernity' (Thomas 2004: 216-222) as a consequence of the development of Western industrialisation and the rise to pre-eminence of 'the economy' over all else (Marx 1970), resulting in a mode of dwelling that neglects or forgets the compositional nature of material reality, and the meaningful way in which we intersect and perceive the different substances and qualities of things (Merleau-Ponty 2004: 59).

How then are we to study substances and processes of composition without simply reconstituting another wholly modern understanding of these practices? The various social characteristics of different types of substances described above has attempted to demonstrate that a reductive approach to materials and material production is inadequate. These social characteristics represent an ordering of the 'nature of things' pertaining to both transformed and untransformed materials, and the process of transformation itself, and is evident throughout prehistory, representing an important aspect of the human comprehension of the social worlds in which they dwell (e.g. Bradley 2000; Fowler & Cummings 2003; Thomas 1999; Tilley 2004: Chapter 4). This ordering of things transcends modern rationally ordered classificatory systems and is instead more cosmological and socially negotiated in nature, with these social categories being clearly intimately interwoven and interconnected. The creation of ordered constellations of knowledge regarding the production, use and understanding of material culture by a society is central to its organisation (Gosden 1994: 82-84), wherein humans share an evolutionary and socially symbiotic relationship with material culture (Leroi-Gourhan 1993: 106, 239-242). As well as being the means by which humans make sense of the world in the broader sense, it is also that by which human compositions – societies – are able to organise and define themselves, literally and symbolically, through the unavoidable necessity of material acquisition, manufacture, distribution, and utilisation. The choice of compositional objects and substances for their symbolic value would therefore have been as important as choosing materials and substances for their possible functional capacity.

The way in which things-in-the-world could be fragmented and broken down, distributed, accumulated, and deposited through the enacting of social relationships has been argued to have been a significant aspect of early prehistoric relationships throughout Europe (e.g. Chapman 2000; Chapman & Gaydarska 2007; Fowler 2004). However, the processes, both social and technological, by which substances and particles of substances were brought together to create wholes, both new and hybrid, formed from both worked and un-worked materials, were those practices that provided a basis which allowed events of fragmentation to occur in the first place. These practices of composition and incorporation facilitated processes by which new conceptual and material 'wholes' could be constituted from these significantly fragmented social and material realities, both literally, in the material sense, and metaphorical with regards to the way people ordered the world in which they lived and their corporeal selves in both life and death.

The ceremonial axe of the Sabarl of Papua New Guinea (Battaglia 1983: fig 2) is a good example of how different natural materials, varied social and kin relations and the human body can all act as powerful metaphors for the parts and elements of 'whole' material things, with each element having individual meanings and associations (fig. 6).

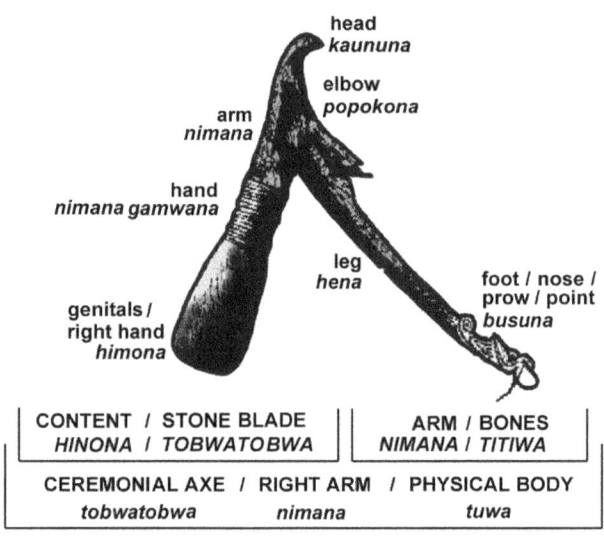

Fig. 6. The ceremonial axe of the Sabarl of Papua New Guinea, showing the relationship between different parts of the axe (and different substances) and their metaphorical social associations (redrawn from Battaglia 1983)

Similarly, the architecture and artefacts of the European Bronze Age were sites of material and symbolic composition, created from particles and substances that could be literally drawn up from the earth (e.g. Brittain 2005). Despite the various typologies that have sought to define particular architectural traditions and material typologies, an enormous diversity of form exists within each tradition: evidence of a shared cosmology perhaps uniquely performed in each particular case. Like each unique human body brought into the world, formed and constituted as a particular shared form of person, containing within it familiar material substances.

Unlike modern industrial and agricultural practices, whereby society seeks to obscure the means by which natural elements of the world are incorporated into material, social and consumptive practices, the processes of material transformation and 'distancing' from natural elements are far more complex in prehistory. Instead, the sourcing of such materials – pottery fabrics, stone, ores and minerals – have been suggested to represent an important relationship between place and substance in the production and exchange of material artefacts (e.g. Bradley & Edmonds 1993), suggesting that incorporating practices were a meaningful element of prehistoric social life and material production.

Two distinct procedures can be recognised with regards to this 'material distancing' in the state of natural materials through transformative and compositional practices:
1. 'Appropriation', where transformation of a substance or material is negligible
2. 'Alteration', where the natural materials are rendered virtually unrecognisable through this process of transformation and incorporation

Rather than there being a structured dichotomy within 'appropriation/alteration' it is more appropriate to think in terms of a sliding scale between various states of the two with 'appropriation' and alteration' being the most extreme. For example, figure 7 demonstrates the placing of bone points, pottery and metallurgy upon a scale of this material distancing.

The oak coffin and stone cist burials of the Danish Bronze Age (Glob 1974) that we have already described are good examples of this. The majority of the grave structure and grave goods are made up of organic materials derived from the environment, including animal bones, leather bags, wood coffins, and of course the earthen mound of the burial itself. This is contrasted with the primary medium, or at least archaeologically, of material culture during the Bronze Age: bronze. The primary distinction between the two is that the organic materials have undergone far less modification than the bronze artefacts. This process of 'material distancing', whereby an objects original form or association is obscured, is more severe in bronze artefacts than amongst organic materials such as wood, stone or animal materials. This observation however, does not necessarily represent a consistent or observed distinction between the two classes of material, but is rather a practice of varying degrees observed in particular contexts.

Here in figure 8 we see that the scale and extent or the 'volume' of different materials involved in the composition of an artefact is also important with regards to the degree of alteration and appropriation of materials.

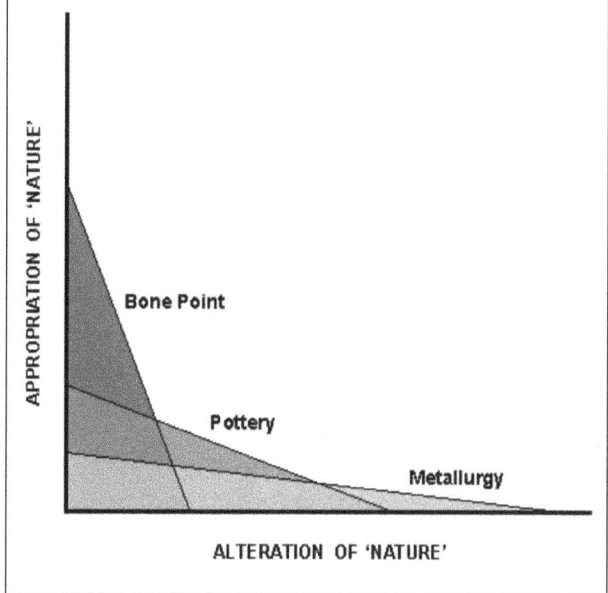

Fig. 7. Scale of 'material distancing' to which materials are transformed during the production of artefacts

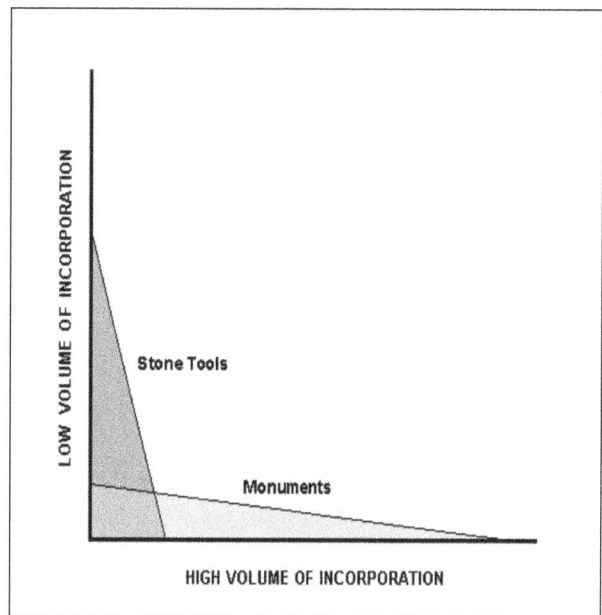

Fig. 8. The volume of 'natural materials' involved in the production of artefacts.

The relationship of the extent of transformation (i.e. appropriation and alteration) and the volume of materials used appears not to be exclusive, and is therefore variable according to circumstance. For example, a hafted, socketed bronze axe (fig. 1) represents a number of different incorporated materials (stone, wood, possibly plant material, etc.) but certain aspects of this artefact, such as the handle, only demonstrates a low degree of alteration, compared to the bronze axe itself. Therefore, a more contextual and performative analysis is required. Moreover, objects involved in the manufacturing process, as well as human/human and human/artefact relationships, must also be taken into consideration, such as technical gestures (Matthews 2004 & 2005), even if they are not apparent in the final form of the object.

A good example of this process is suggested by Sørensen (1997) in her discussion of articles of female clothing recovered from the oak coffin and stone cist burials similar to those discussed above. Sørensen (Ibid: fig. 2) differentiates between cloth, clothing and costume, demonstrating the way in which the same substance, in this case wool, can be transformed and differentiated depending on different states of materiality and the value that these would have held for certain sections of the population and the contexts in which they were procured, produced and used. For example, the articles of clothing described by Sørensen have been recovered from burials located in barrows, a formal method of disposal during this period that was not available to the majority of society (Harding 2000: 96). Moreover, the settlement evidence already discussed above suggests that wool would have had to have been procured from outside of the chiefly settlements, due to their alternative emphasis upon cattle instead of sheep, compared to smaller settlements (Kristiansen 1998: 109).

The final aspect of compositional practices and relational materials that I wish to draw attention to is the practice of absence: or in other words, those things that have either been purposefully left out or removed. The notion of the exclusion of various object types or materials is pertinent in any discussion of hoards or depositional practices, and whilst the absence of particular bronze forms has often been used to differentiate various types of hoards, the exclusion of particular substances from hoards has generated, to my knowledge, little or no interest. Under good find and excavation circumstances, human and animal bones and organic materials can also be conspicuously absent and under these circumstances the lack of such materials cannot be accounted for as a consequence of going unrecorded or having been overlooked. The choice to leave something out is as important as the choice to include something: it is a meaningful act. The breaking of bronzes and the separation of bronze from other materials, such as wood, is therefore very significant and suggests that the relationship between bronze and other substances was an important one.

The choice of particular materials and the nature of their deposition and presentation are significant: their liminal location, objects being often damaged and fragmented, and rendered unusable in very particular and specific ways. For example, axes are often devoid of their wooden hafts, and spears separated from their shafts, representing not only a 'distancing' in the production and composition of artefacts but also their use. This distancing relates not only to organic materials, such as earth, plant materials and stone, but also involved once living mediums represented by animal and human remains, and of course, the still living themselves.

This process of occurrence and absence is an important factor in the location of hoards, and in general the deposition of bronzes, within the landscape appears to be a significant factor in their constitution (Bradley 2000: 59). The classification by Levy (1982: 24) of the hoards of the Danish Bronze Age relied heavily upon the presence or absence of place, notably the differentiation between dry and wet locations. In southern Scandinavia, Larsson (1986: 139-58; after Bradley 2000: 59) has observed that the main groups of rock carvings are found towards the edges of regions with metal finds, and suggests that some of these images may have been regarded as another form of 'deposit'. For example, excavations in the parish of Bohuslän (Hallström 1917; after Yates 1993: 62-63) revealed little in the way of any bronze artefacts within the vicinity of the rock carvings. Similarly, Fontijn (2002: fig.14.2) has also argued for a pattern of distancing and exclusion for certain types of bronzes in the southern Netherlands during the Late Bronze Age, where we see a depositional pattern related to the spatial meaning of particular artefacts, with local forms being deposited close to or in association with settlements and foreign or 'alien' artefacts being buried in liminal locations away from settlement areas.

Conclusion

In conclusion then, the choice of particular substances does not necessarily relate to the availability of resources or a substances functional capacity but can be a matter of technological choice: i.e. what substance may matter in terms of systems of meanings or symbolism. In other words, the various components that constitute particular objects or depositional circumstances have a social and emotive context. Material culture is primary in the construction of varying social roles and identities in the world. The ability to recognise ones Self as being in some way distinct is based upon the recognition of the Other as being in some way dissimilar. This processes of material symbiosis or composition has significant consequences for identity politics in the construction of varying identities in prehistory, for it suggests that the perception of what may have constituted notions of Self and Other were not only complex but that the fractal and syncretic nature of prehistoric personhood was spread widely between relations of people, places, artefacts and animals.

Empirical approaches and scientific studies concerned with the compositional nature of bronzes are significant and demonstrate that typological studies alone of bronzes are insufficient, and we need to remember the social and symbolic qualities of such materials that constituted artefacts. In doing so, it is necessary therefore to look beyond the immediate context of any particular object of study to its relational context, not just so as to frame that object within an appropriate social environment, but in order to explore the webs of cultural significance and meaning that would have structured the nature of such objects. Circumstantial evidence, as well as material from other contexts such as burials, suggests there existed a strong and intimate relationship between animal and human remains and the deposition of bronze materials during the Bronze Age, and a similarly direct relationship between bones and hoards in the circumstances of the few well excavated contexts that we have available to us.

References

BARBER M. 2003. *Bronze and the Bronze Age: Metalwork and Society in Britain c 2500 – 800 B.C.*, Stroud: Tempus.

BATTAGLIA D. 1983. Projecting personhood in Melanesia: The dialectics of artefact symbolism on Sabarl Island, *Man* 18. 2: 289-304.

BERGLUND J. 1982. Kirkebjerget – a Late Bronze Age settlement at Voldtofte, south-west Funen, *Journal of Danish Archaeology* 1, 51-63.

BRADLEY R. & EDMONDS, M. 1993. *Interpreting the Axe Trade: Production and Exchange in Neolithic Britain*, Cambridge: Cambridge University Press.

BRADLEY R. 1997. Death by water: boats and footprints in the rock carvings of western Sweden, *Oxford Journal of Archaeology* 16.3: 315-324.

BRADLEY R. 1998. *The Passage of Arms: An Archaeological Analysis of Prehistoric Hoard and Votive Deposits* 2nd Ed, Oxford: Oxbow.

BRADLEY R. 2000. *An Archaeology of Natural Places*, London: Routledge.

BRADLEY R. 2003. A life less ordinary: the ritualization of the domestic sphere in later Prehistoric Europe, *Cambridge Archaeological Journal* 13.1: 5-23.

BRADLEY R. 2005. *Ritual and Domestic Life in Prehistoric Europe*, Abingdon: Routledge.

BRITTAIN M. 2005. Layers of life and death: aspects of monumentality in the Early Bronze Age of Wales, In V. Cummings and C. Fowler (eds), *The Neolithic of the Irish Sea: Materiality and Traditions of Practice*, Oxford: Oxbow Books, 224-232.

BRØNDSTED J. 1966. *Danmarks Oldtid: II. Bronzealderen*, Copenhagen: Gyldendal.

BROWN M. A. 1982. Swords and sequence in the British Bronze Age, *Archaeologia* 107: 1-42.

CHAPMAN J. 2000. *Fragmentation in Archaeology: People, Places and Broken Objects in the Prehistory of South-eastern Europe*, London: Routledge.

COLES J. M & HARDING A. F. 1979. *The Bronze Age in Europe: An Introduction to the Prehistory of Europe c. 2000-700 B.C.*, London: Methuen & co Ltd.

EOGAN G. 1983. *The Hoards of the Irish Later Bronze Age*, Dublin: University College Dublin.

FOKKENS H. 2002. Vee en voorouders, centrale elementen uit het dagelijks leven in de Bronstijd, In H. Fokkens & R. Jansen (red), *2000 jaar bewoningsdynamiek, Brons-en ijzertijdbewoning in het Maas-Demer-Scheldegebied*, Leiden, 125-148.

FONTIJN D. R. 2002. Sacrificial Landscapes: Cultural Biographies of Things, Objects and 'Natural Places' in the Bronze Age of the Southern Netherlands, C. 2300-600 B.C., Leiden: University of Leiden/ *Analecta Praehistorica Leidensia* 33/34.

FOWLER C. 2004. *The Archaeology of Personhood: An Anthropological Approach*, London: Routledge.

GIBBS L. 1987. Identifying gender representation in the archaeological record: a contextual study, In Hodder, I (ed), *The Archaeology of Contextual Meaning*, Cambridge: Cambridge University Press, 79-89.

GLOB P. V. 1974. *The Mound People: Danish Bronze Age man Preserved*, London: Faber and Faber.

GOSDEN C. 1994. *Social Being and Time*, Oxford: Blackwell.

HALLSTRÖM G. 1917. Bohusläns fasta fornlämningar från hednatiden: 7. Tanums härads bronsåldersgravar, *Göteborgs och Bohusläns Fornminnesforenbings Tidskrift*, 1-78.

HAMILAKIS Y. 2002. The past as oral history: towards an archaeology of the senses, In Y. Hamilakis, M, Pluciennik and S. Tarlow (eds), *Thinking through the Body: Archaeologies of Corporeality*, New York: Kluwer/Plenum, 121–36.

HARDING A. F. 1999. North-south exchanges of raw materials, In K. Demakopoulou, C. Eluère, J. Jensen, A. Jockenhövel and J-P. Mohen (eds), *Gods and Heroes of the European Bronze Age*, London: Thames and Hudson, 38-42.

HARDING A. F. 2000. *European Societies in the Bronze Age*, Cambridge: Cambridge University Press.

INGOLD T. 1994. *From trust to domination: An alternative history of human-animal relations*, In A. Manning & J. Serpell (eds), Animals and Human Society: Changing Perspectives, London: Routledge, 1-22.

KAUL F. 1998. *Ships on Bronzes: A Study in Bronze Age Religion and Iconography*, Copenhagen: National Museum of Denmark.

KRISTIANSEN K. 1974. Glerupfundet. Et depotfund med kvindesmykker fra bronzealderens femte periode, *Hikuin* 1: 7-38.

KRISTIANSEN K. 1978. The consumption of wealth in Bronze Age Denmark: A study in the dynamics of economic processes in tribal societies, In K. Kristiansen and C. Paludan-Müller (eds), *New Directions in Scandinavian Archaeology*, Copenhagen: National Museum of Denmark, 158-90.

KRISTIANSEN K. 1984. Ideology and material culture: an archaeological perspective, In Spriggs, M (ed), *Marxist Perspectives in Archaeology*, Cambridge: Cambridge University Press, 72-100.

KRISTIANSEN K. 1998. *Europe Before History*, Cambridge: Cambridge University Press.

KRISTIANSEN K. 1999. The emergence of warrior aristocracies in Later European prehistory and their long-term history, In J. Carmen and A. Harding (eds), *Ancient Warfare: Archaeological Perspectives*, Stroud: Sutton, 175-189.

KRISTIANSEN K. 2001. Rulers and warriors: symbolic transmission and social transformation in Bronze Age Europe, In J. Haas (ed), *From Leaders to Rulers*, New York: Kluwer/Plenum, 85-104.

KRISTIANSEN K. 2004. Institutiosn and material culture: towards an intercontextual archaeology, In E. Demarrias, C. Gosden & C. Renfrew (eds), *Rethinking Materiality: The Engagement of Mind with the Material World*, Cambridge: McDonald Institute Monographs, 179-193.

KRISTIANSEN K & LARSSON T. 2005. *The Rise of Bronze Age Society: Travels, Transmissions and Transformations*, Cambridge: Cambridge University Press.

LARSSON T. B. 1986. *The Bronze Age metalwork in southern Sweden: Aspects of social and spatial organisation 1800-500 B.C*, Umeå: University of Umeå.

LEROI-GOURHAN A. 1993. *Gesture and Speech*, Cambridge, Mass.: MIT Press.

LEVY J. E. 1982. S*ocial and Religious Organization in Bronze Age Denmark: An Analysis of Ritual Hoard Finds*, Oxford: BAR International Series 124.

LIVERSAGE D & LIVERSAGE M. 1989. A method for the study of the composition of early copper and bronze artefacts: an example from Denmark, *Helinium* 28.1: 42-76.

MARX, K. 1970. *Capital*, Vol. 1, London: Lawrence and Wishart.

MATTHEWS S. G. 2004. Gesture, gender, ethnicity: The instantiated communities of Bronze Age Europe. In S. E. Hakenbeck & S. G. Matthews (eds), Reconsidering Ethnicity: Material Culture and Identity in the Past. Cambridge: Archaeological Review from Cambridge, 19.2: 56-72.

MATTHEWS S. 2005. *The materiality of gesture: Intimacy, emotion and technique in the archaeological study of bodily communication*. Paper presented to 'The Archaeology of Gesture: Reconstructing Prehistoric Technical and Symbolic Behaviour' session at the 11th Annual Meeting of the European Association of Archaeologists, 5-11 September 2005, Cork, Ireland. Available from: http://www.semioticon.com/virtuals/archaeology/materiality.pdf

MERLEAU-PONTY M. 1962. *The Phenomenology of Perception*, London: Routledge (reed. 2002).

MONTELIUS O. 1917. *Minnen fraan vaar Forntid*, Stockholm: P. A. Norstedt & Söners Förlag.

NORTHOVER J. P. 1982. The exploration of the long-distance movement of bronze in Bronze and Early Iron Age Europe, *Bulletin of the Institute of Archaeology London* 19: 45-72.

NOSKE B. 1993. The Animal Question in Anthropology: A Commentary, *Society and Animals* 1.2: 185-190.

PEARCE M. 1998. Reconstructing prehistoric metallurgical knowledge: the northern Italian Copper and Bronze Ages. *European Journal of Archaeology* 1.1: 51-70.

QUILLIEC B. 2004. *Atlantic swords: a technological approach for Late Bronze Age societies*. Paper presented to the Bronze Age Forum, University of Southampton, Southampton, 13th – 14th November 2004.

RANDSBORG K. 1985. Women in prehistory. *Acta Archaeologica* 55: 142-154.

ROHL B & NEEDHAM S. 1998. *The Circulation of Metal in the British Bronze Age: The Application of Lead Isotope Analysis*, London: British Museum.

SHERRATT A. G. 1976. Resources, technology and trade: an essay in early European copper metallurgy, In G. Sieveking (ed), *Problems in Economic and Social Archaeology*, London: Duckworth, 557-581.

SHERRATT A. G. 1981. Plough and pastoralism: aspects of the Secondary Products Revolution, In I. Hodder, G. Isaac and N. Hammond (eds), *Pattern of the Past: Studies in Honour of David Clark*, Cambridge: Cambridge University Press, 261-305.

SHERRATT, A. G. 1983. The secondary exploitation of animals in the Old World, *World Archaeology* 15: 90-104.

SOFAER DEREVENSKI, J. AND SØRENSEN, M. L. S. 2002. Becoming cultural: society and the incorporation of bronze, In B. S. Ottaway and E. C. Wager (eds), *Metals and Society: Papers from a session held at the European Association of Archaeologists Sixth Annual Meeting in Lisbon 2000*, Oxford: BAR, International Series 1061, 117-21.

SØRENSEN M. L. S. 1987. Material order and cultural classification: the role of bronze objects in the transition from Bronze Age to Iron Age in Scandinavia, In I. Hodder (ed), *The Archaeology of Contextual Meaning,* Cambridge: Cambridge University Press, 90-102.

SØRENSEN M. L. S. 1992. Gender archaeology and Scandinavian Bronze Age studies, *Norwegian Archaeological Review* 25.1: 31-49.

SØRENSEN M. L. S. 1997. Reading dress: the construction of social categories and identities in Bronze Age Europe, *Journal of European Archaeology*, 5.1: 93-114.

THOMAS J. 1996. *Time, Culture and Identity: An Interpretative Archaeology*, London: Routledge.

THOMAS J. 1999. An economy of substances in earlier Neolithic Britain. In J. Robb (ed), *Material Symbols: Culture and Economy in Prehistory*, Carbondale: Southern Illinois University Press, 70-89.

THOMAS J. 2004. *Archaeology and Modernity*, London: Routledge.

THRANE H. 1984. Lusehøj and Voldtofte: en sydvestfynsk storhøj fra yngre Broncealder, Odense: Fynske Studier XIII.

TILLEY C. 2004. *The Materiality of Stone: Explorations in Landscape Phenomenology*, Oxford: Berg.

TREHERNE P. 1995. The warrior's beauty: the masculine body and self-identity in Bronze Age Europe, *Journal of European Archaeology* 3.1: 105-44.

TYLECOTE R. F. 1986. *The Prehistory of Metallurgy in the British Isles*, London: Institute of Metals.

TYLECOTE R. F. 1987. *The Early History of Metallurgy in Europe*. London: Longman.

WHITTLE A. 1996. *Europe in the Neolithic: The Creation of New Worlds*, Cambridge: Cambridge University Press.

YATES T. 1993. Frameworks for an archaeology of the body, In C. Tilley (ed), *Interpretative Archaeology*, Oxford: Berg, 31-72.

Acknowledgements

I would like to thank both Caroline and Benedicte for kindly inviting me to speak in their session at the European Association of Archaeologists 2005 annual meeting, and for allowing me to participate in this subsequent publication. Between that paper and this I have benefited from the helpful discussion and insight of Kristin Oma. Thanks must also go to Kristian Kristiansen for the interest he has demonstrated in my research on Bronze Age society. Due to the fortuitous delay in the publication of this paper I have more recently benefited from (but sadly unable to act upon) the kind comments of Sue Hamilton and Daan Raemaekers with regards to this paper. I would also like to thank Inger Woltinge for her help with translating the abstract at short notice.

Contact

Steven Matthews
Groningen Institute of Archaeology,
University of Groningen
Poststraat 6
9712 ER Groningen
The Netherlands
s.g.matthews@rug.nl

www.ingramcontent.com/pod-product-compliance
Lightning Source LLC
Chambersburg PA
CBHW041705290426
44108CB00027B/2862